KT-473-830

WITHDRAWN FROM
THE LIBRARY

UNIVERSITY OF
WINCHESTER

# A CENTURY OF TRAVELS IN CHINA

Hong Kong University Press thanks ...... Press ...... ...... Nord
Calligraphy for the covers of its books ...... ...... ...... published

KA 0346666 3

# A CENTURY OF TRAVELS IN CHINA

## Critical Essays on Travel Writing
## from the 1840s to the 1940s

**Edited by Douglas Kerr and Julia Kuehn**

UNIVERSITY OF WINCHESTER
LIBRARY

香港大學出版社
HONG KONG UNIVERSITY PRESS

Hong Kong University Press
14/F Hing Wai Centre
7 Tin Wan Praya Road
Aberdeen
Hong Kong

© Hong Kong University Press 2007

ISBN 978-962-209-845-9 (Hardback)
ISBN 978-962-209-846-6 (Paperback)

All rights reserved. No portion of this publication may be reproduced or transmitted in any form
or by any means, electronic or mechanical, including photocopy, recording, or any information
storage or retrieval system, without permission in writing from the publisher.

Secure On-line Ordering
http://www.hkupress.org


British Library Cataloguing-in-Publication Data
A catalogue copy for this book is available from the British Library


Printed and bound by Liang Yu Printing Factory Co. Ltd. in Hong Kong, China

UNIVERSITY OF WINCHESTER

03466663 | 809.933
KER

Hong Kong University Press is honoured that Xu Bing, whose art explores the
complex themes of language across cultures, has written the Press's name in his
Square Word Calligraphy. This signals our commitment to cross-cultural thinking
and the distinctive nature of our English-language books published in China.

"At first glance, Square Word Calligraphy appears to be nothing more unusual
than Chinese characters, but in fact it is a new way of rendering English words
in the format of a square so they resemble Chinese characters. Chinese viewers
expect to be able to read Square Word Calligraphy but cannot. Western viewers,
however are surprised to find they can read it. Delight erupts when meaning is
unexpectedly revealed."

— Britta Erickson, *The Art of Xu Bing*

# Contents

# Illustrations

*(Following page 74)*

# Acknowledgements

The editors are very grateful to Marina Ma for expert editorial assistance, and to the Hong Kong University Committee for Research and Conference Grants for help that enabled us to bring this project to fruition.

# Notes on Contributors

**Elizabeth Chang**, an Assistant Professor of British literature at the University of Missouri-Columbia, focuses in her research on nineteenth-century British visual culture and the British empire. She is currently at work on a book-length project detailing the British conception of a Chinese way of seeing that, in its reception, circulation, and revision, shaped the development of a modern British visual consciousness. A portion of this work, entitled " 'Eyes of the Proper Almond Shape': Blue-and-White China in the British Imaginary, 1823–1883" appeared in *19th-Century Studies,* Vol. 18 (2005).

**Nicholas Clifford**, Emeritus Professor of History and former Provost at Middlebury College, holds his B.A. from Princeton University, and his Ph.D. from Harvard University. Among his works are *Spoilt Children of Empire: Westerners in Shanghai and the Chinese Revolution of the Nineteen Twenties* (1991); *A Truthful Impression of the Country: British and American Travel Writing in China, 1880–1949* (2001); and a novel, *The House of Memory* (1994).

**Ross G. Forman** is Visiting Assistant Professor in the Department of English at Skidmore College in New York. He holds a Ph.D. in Comparative Literature from Stanford University. A specialist in nineteenth-century imperialism, he is currently completing a book entitled *Empires Entwined: Britain and the Representation of China, 1840–1911*. His work has appeared in various journals, including *Criticism*, *Victorian Studies*, and *Victorian Literature and Culture*. He is also the author of the chapter on "Empire" in the forthcoming *Cambridge Companion to the Fin de Siècle*.

**Hugh Haughton** teaches English at the University of York. He has recently completed *Derek Mahon and Modern Irish Poetry* (2008). He is the editor of *The Chatto Book* *of Nonsense Poetry* (1985); Rudyard Kipling, *Wee Willie Winkie* (1988); *John Clare in Context: Bi-Centenary Essays* with Adam Phillips (1994); *Alice in Wonderland and Through the Looking-Glass* (1998); Elizabeth Bowen, *To the North* (1999); Sigmund Freud, *The Uncanny* (2003); and *Second World War Poems* (2004). He is currently co-editing (with Valerie Eliot) the *Letters of T.S. Eliot*.

**Elaine Yee Lin Ho** is Associate Professor in the School of English at the University of Hong Kong. Her recent publications include two monograph studies of *Timothy Mo* (*Contemporary World Writers Series*, 2000) and *Anita Desai* (*Writers and Their Work Series*, 2005). She has published articles on Hong Kong anglophone literature as minority literature, women and gender in the films of the Hong Kong filmmaker, Ann Hui, and Indo-English fiction. She is currently researching and writing on imperial globalization and vernacular cosmopolitanism in anglophone Hong Kong literature.

**Douglas Kerr** is Professor in the School of English at the University of Hong Kong, and has been visiting scholar at Oxford and London universities. His published work includes *Wilfred Owen's Voices* (1993) and *George Orwell* (2003), and essays and articles in *Essays in Criticism*, *Textual Practice*, *Modern Language Review*, *The Journal of Commonwealth Literature,* etc. His current work is concerned with the history of representations of Eastern people and places in English writing, from the time of Kipling to the postcolonial period. He is on the editorial board of *Critical Zone: A Forum of Chinese and Western Knowledge*.

**Julia Kuehn** is Assistant Professor of English at the University of Hong Kong. Her research interests lie in nineteenth and early twentieth-century literature and culture, with particular focus on popular writing. She is the author of *Glorious Vulgarity: Marie Corelli's Feminine Sublime in a Popular Context* (2004), and has published in *Women's Writing* and *The Journal of Popular Culture*. Her current work is on exoticism in novels set in North Africa, the Middle East and India, between 1880 and 1920. She is also co-editor of a collection of critical essays on recent developments in travel writing studies, and of a collection of critical essays entitled *China Abroad: Travels, Spaces, Subjects*.

**Susan Morgan**, Distinguished Professor of English and Faculty Affiliate of Women's Studies at Miami University of Ohio, is the author of *In the Meantime: Character and Perception in Jane Austen's Fiction*; *Sisters in Time: Gender in Nineteenth-Century British Fiction,* and *Place Matters: Gendered Geography in Victorian Women's Travel Writings about Southeast Asia*. She has published critical editions of Anna Leonowens' *Romance of the Harem* (1872); Marianne North's *Recollections of a Happy Life* (1894); and Ada Pryer's *A Decade in Borneo* (1893). Her present area of interest is Victorian women's travel writings, particularly about South, Southeast, and East Asia. She has just completed a cultural biography of Anna Leonowens.

**Thomas Prasch** is Associate Professor and Chair of the Department of History at Washburn University, Topeka, KS. He received his Ph.D. in modern British history from Indiana University in 1995, writing a dissertation on photographic representations of working-class subjects in Victorian Britain. He has research interests in Victorian British and imperial photography, exhibitions, and museums.

**Susan Schoenbauer Thurin**, Professor Emeritus, Department of English and Philosophy at the University of Wisconsin-Stout, is the author of *Victorian Travelers and the Opening of China, 1842–1907*, and editor of *The Far East*, Vol. IV of *Nineteenth-Century Travels, Explorations and Empires, 1835–1910*, and she has published widely on Victorian novelists and travelers. Her interest in travel writing was forged by years teaching in Liberia, England, China, and Sweden. She is currently at work on *Retiring Minds*, a collection of writings about retirement by academic retirees, and a biography of Constance Gordon Cumming.

**Q. S. Tong** is Associate Professor of English at the University of Hong Kong. He has been at work on issues and problems of critical significance in cross-cultural studies, with special attention to the historical interactions between China and Britain on different levels, political, cultural, and intellectual. He is an editorial member of several international journals including *boundary 2: an international journal of literature and culture* and co-editor of *Critical Zone: A Forum of Chinese and Western Knowledge*, a series devoted to cross-cultural studies.

**Tamara S. Wagner** obtained her Ph.D. from the University of Cambridge in 2002 and is currently Assistant Professor of English Literature at the School of Humanities and Social Sciences at Nanyang Technical University in Singapore. She is the author of *Longing: Narratives of Nostalgia in the British Novel, 1740–1890* (2004) and *Occidentalism in Novels of Malaysia and Singapore, 1819–2004: Colonial and Postcolonial "Financial Straits"* (2005). Her previous publications include articles on the cultural discourses of nostalgia, occidentalism, and the functions of commerce in fiction. Wagner's latest project is a book-length study of financial speculation in Victorian literature. She is also editing a collection of essays on nineteenth-century consumer culture.

# Introduction

*Douglas Kerr and Julia Kuehn*

China to the Western traveler has always been characterized by excess. There is too much of China to travel to, to experience, to comprehend, to describe, and certainly too much of it to subdue or convert. To Archibald Little, traveling through "the illimitable western mountains" of China towards Tibet at the end of the nineteenth century, the apparently endless prospect of mountains beyond mountains was both sublime and disheartening; it was a landscape which seemed to have no beginning and no end.[1] The title he gave to the account of his travels, *Mount Omi and Beyond*, moves from a specific location into a helpless — and romantic — gesture of what we might call ulteriority. How could the individual relate to something so huge, especially the individual who was a stranger? Christopher Isherwood, re-reading his own account of his travels in China in the 1930s, felt that he cut a rather ludicrous figure — "Little Me in China."[2] Peter Fleming, more suavely, turned his own inadequacy into a gambit in the "Warning to the Reader" that prefaces his *One's Company: A Journey to China*.

> The recorded history of Chinese civilization covers a period of four thousand years. The population of China is estimated at 450 millions. China is larger than Europe.
>
> The author of this book is twenty-six years old. He has spent, altogether, about seven months in China. He does not speak Chinese.[3]

Everything about China was immense: its area, its population, its variety, the problems and opportunities it seemed to contain. Even its degradations were outsize. And the magnificent recession of Chinese history stretched back through the millennia in a way that made Europeans, and Americans, seem mere newcomers, encouraging them — and this becomes an important theme in Western travel writing — to think of themselves by contrast as specialists in modernity. Meanwhile if China was hard to grasp in the scope of its geography and history, the intricacy of its culture and language, there was also an inner dimension to Chinese ulteriority, the secret life of the mind and feelings of Chinese people, so often baffling, unfathomable, or simply closed to the outside observer. "People *may* describe with success the soul of a people," wrote Elizabeth Kemp, "provided it is sufficiently near the surface, but the foreigner who has known and loved China for a lifetime would be the first to repudiate the possibility of doing this in the case of China."[4]

For the foreigner there was always more of China than could be traveled, sketched, subjugated, dealt or traded with, inventoried, lectured or marveled at; China was a *mise-en-abîme*. And in the 1840s, though it was on the point of coming for the first time at least partially under the protocols of Western control, the country was also in the process of becoming more confusing. Chinese history is punctuated by periods of fragmentation and turmoil whose significant form emerges only in retrospect, if at all. The hundred years covered by this volume, from the time of the first Opium War to the foundation of the People's Republic in 1949, were a period in which profound and painful changes overtook China in every sphere of life, and Western foreigners traveling the country were witness to these changes as well as, in some cases, playing a part in them. The Chinese Empire collapsed in 1911. Whether the People's Republic has inaugurated a permanent change in the pattern of Chinese history, it is (as Zhou Enlai is reported to have said of the effects of the French Revolution) too soon to say.

But if China represented a daunting challenge, for the Western traveler and still more for the travel writer, there was no shortage of men and women eager to take it up, and the century that followed the 1840s was not only the high period of European imperialism, but also of a cultural self-confidence that characterizes most of the travelers whose journeyings are discussed here. The spread across the globe of the influence, control and rule of Western nations seemed proof of the success of their cultures as well as of their armed forces and economic practices. The West was richer and more powerful than China, its progress more advanced, and to many it was in possession of a religious truth which had not yet been vouchsafed to the benighted Chinese. Even when it is accompanied by disclaimers of expertise, this confidence is a feature of most Western travelers in this period, though we can watch it becoming unsettled in some of the twentieth-century writers discussed here.

Bertrand Russell, for example, writing in the aftermath of the disastrous Great War in Europe, found in China "a way of life which, if it could be adopted by all the world, would make all the world happy."[5] But though he was anxious to dissociate himself from Western assumptions of superiority, he had no hesitation in describing what he saw in China, and his own reactions to what he saw, and proceeding inductively from these observations — as in this description of the contrast between the Chinese part of town and the foreign quarters in the Treaty Ports.

> Often one passes through a gate, suddenly, from one to the other; after the
> cheerful disordered beauty of the old town, Europe's ugly cleanliness and
> Sunday-go-to-meeting decency make a strange complex impression, half-

love and half-hate. In the European town one finds safety, spaciousness and hygiene; in the Chinese town, romance, overcrowding and disease. In spite of my affection for China, these transitions always made me realize that I am a European; for me, the Chinese manner of life would not mean happiness. But after making all necessary deductions for the poverty and the disease, I am inclined to think that Chinese life brings more happiness to the Chinese than English life does to us. At any rate this seemed to me to be true for the men; for the women I do not think it would be true.[6]

This short passage is "travel writing" of a high order, and though it is not typical it does display a number of the tropes, the rhetorical moves, which we will find in many other observers of China — the moralized landscape; the binary opposition of East and West, here inscribed in the topography of the treaty port, but also in the contrast between European modernity and Chinese "romance;" a reflection on the writer's own cultural identity and loyalties, his enjoyment of the Chinese scene accompanied by a poignant sense of his permanent foreignness; the move to ethnographic and historical generalization; a modest uncertainty about his interpretation of what he sees; finally (and this is something almost all our travelers remark on) attention to the gender politics of Chinese life.

## Perceptions of China

Western perceptions of China change as China changes, but they are also refashioned, of course, according to the West's needs, preoccupations, and sense of itself.[7] Intellectuals of the Enlightenment era had found much to admire in China, which they knew as an ancient and dignified civilization, even though a despotic one. The Jesuits, before their withdrawal from the country in the 1770s, had reported the richness of Chinese intellectual and aesthetic life. Chinese gardens, tea, porcelain, and design, were to play a major role in the shaping of European taste, and the Chinese language was exciting to linguists and philosophers. To a Europe emerging from a period of debilitating wars of religion, the secularism of Chinese society was something to be envied. The delicacy of Chinese artifacts, a Confucian emphasis on tradition and the family, and the apparent stability of the Chinese state, also recommended themselves. But as the eighteenth century ended, Europeans were taking a more practical interest in the country, an interest that most frequently expressed itself in a trope of "opening." The Chinese empire might think of itself as self-sufficient (the Qing state had no Ministry of Foreign Affairs),[8] and there were many restraints and prohibitions limiting foreigners' movements and activities, but it was clear to many in the West that China needed to open itself, or be opened, to the manifest benefits of international "free trade" and of Christian missionary activity.

Lord Macartney observed the Chinese carefully in the course of his unsuccessful embassy to the Qianlong emperor in 1793. Macartney, who had been sent by the East India Company acting in agreement with the government of George III, admired the "wonderful ability and unparalleled success" of the government of the Chinese empire, but he expected it to collapse in his lifetime.[9] Pressures from outside were building. European merchants in Macao and Guangzhou chafed under restrictions on their activities. The English demand for tea from China was being paid for by the supply of opium from India, by the East India Company and other European and American traders, and aggressive trafficking in opium led to conflict with the Qing state. Our period begins with the first Opium War, which led to the establishment of the colony of Hong Kong on Chinese territory, and in the next hundred years other conflicts in the interest of the "China trade" would leave the map of China dotted with extraterritorial treaty ports, on coasts and rivers, open for foreign residence and mercantile activities. As the Qing government weakened further, the Western powers and Japan established and managed spheres of influence and interest in China, a process reaching a kind of culmination in the wholesale invasion of the Japanese in the 1930s.[10]

If China was to be opened to trade with the foreigners, it also received the attentions of their religion. Robert Morrison, the first British Protestant missionary, arrived in Guangzhou in 1807, and there were more than thirty Protestant missionary groupings in China by 1865. Missionary work, as well as trading and diplomatic activity, was one of the major reasons for Western travelers to come to China, and to recount their journeys, before the advent of the professional travel writer. Many of the leading sinologists were missionaries, who left some of the most sympathetic and sensitive accounts of the country and its people; but missionaries could also be arrogant, racist and bigoted.

As the foreigners constructed an image of China — ancient, traditional, beautiful, ingenious, disciplined, spiritual and full of wisdom, or old-fashioned, hidebound, quaint, devious, cruel, superstitious and lacking in energy — the Chinese and their government had to get used to a foreign presence within their borders and beyond their absolute control, at a time of increasing domestic instability and unrest. Foreigners were perceived, correctly, as one of the most destabilizing and dangerous factors in the situation. But at the same time, while China tried spasmodically to reform and modernize itself, foreigners were also seen as the bearers of the technology and ideas that might be adapted to bring a saving modernity to China itself. These are the conditions in which Victorian travelers visited China and reported on it. With the collapse of the Qing and the emergence of the Republic, twentieth-century China began to be seen as a participant, however awkward, in a global modernity, its turmoils and hopes being played out in the grip of the same forces that were shaping the destinies of Russia, Spain and India.

Land and customs are the staples of the travel writer's account. Here we have the topography of China, from the bustling coastal cities to the mountains of the West. Male travelers are supposed to pay more attention to political and economic factors, female travelers to social and domestic life, but if this is a rule we will meet plenty of exceptions to it. Further, in observing how the Chinese live, these travelers are drawn to report what is distinctive and different. Canals were arguably a far more vital feature of Chinese life than foot-binding, but travel writers show much more interest in foot-binding than in Chinese canals. A canal was just a canal, whether in Suzhou or Solihull. But foot-binding was unknown in Western societies: exotic and grotesque, it was a practice which seemed to say something important about the Chinese, and about familiar themes of China travel writing such as cruelty, tradition, sexuality, and the position of women.

Much criticism of recent decades has been concerned to trace the inextricability of the more disinterested Western academic or literary writing about the Orient, including travel writing, from discourse that more manifestly served Western political and economic interests. When China or Chinese life is represented as insufficient, backward, misguided, in need of correction or improvement, one way to see this is as a justification — whether deliberate or unconscious, before or after the fact — for Western interference in China. There are plenty of examples of this in the writers discussed here. But there are also many instances of admiration and wonder and learning, enjoyment of Chinese places and ways and things. These must be seen in the context of history, but should not be vulgarly dismissed as merely an inventory for Western seizure of Chinese assets. Nor should all criticism of China be discounted as denigratory and serving a hegemonic agenda. As Nicholas Clifford points out in his essay here, foreign travelers' criticisms of aspects of Chinese life were often the same as those leveled by Chinese reformers themselves.

"Upon arriving in a new place," says Michel Butor, "I will need to begin learning to read once more. The gestures will not be the same: other manners, other laws, other traffic rules."[11] Travel is a kind of research. But all travel is also a form of self-discovery, a mode of perceiving the self. Even a tourist in the most insulated resort has left behind the familiar world, to experience things for a while in a different modality, while the traveler with open eyes and ears can see and hear other places and people, and can experience being seen and heard, in ways that can both clarify and alter subjectivity. All travel writers about China, in recording an impression of the country, have also portrayed themselves, whether as the briefest sketch or in a full-blown self-portrait for which China is simply the background. We can only become aware of ourselves in relation to others beyond ourselves, and for these writers this is the other meaning of China's ulteriority.

## Theoretical Approaches and Areas of Interest

The second half of the nineteenth century was an age of Western imperial expansion — in China, largely a non-colonial imperialism — and of the development of tourism, and by the end of the century guidebook-clutching globetrotters were beginning to share the roads and waterways with the missionaries and traders, and with professional travel writers. An increased consciousness of cultural heterogeneity, which was itself partly a consequence of the experience of travel, led, it has been argued, to a greater self-consciousness and introspection in twentieth-century travel writing.[12] By the mid-century, with which this volume ends, Evelyn Waugh was complaining that, in the wake of the Second World War and "in a world of displaced persons," travel itself had become impossible.[13] Certainly both the experience of journeying, and writing about journeys, had changed profoundly in nature over a century of travels.

Travel writing received a new academic attention in the 1980s, as a mode of writing that foregrounds attempts to find the terms for or come to terms with different cultures

UNIVERSITY OF WINCHESTER
LIBRARY

and natures.[14] The study of travel literature developed its own vocabulary, often adapted from other disciplines. Attracting mostly scholars from literary and cultural studies, history (including art history and the history of science), anthropology, geography, sociology, and area studies, studies in travel writing have become a fruitful site for cross-disciplinary interaction and approaches.

Its hybrid, "androgynous" qualities,[15] which place travel writing between the literary and the factual, also account for the variety of critical approaches used over the last two decades. Mary Campbell sees the beginning of the critical discourse of travel writing in Edward Said's *Orientalism*, and the epistemological shift it initiated in studies of culture(s). Borrowing Michel Foucault's concept of "discourse" for an understanding of the problem of Western imperial domination over the East, Said's questioning of "what we know and how we know it" and "who 'we' are" introduced a new epistemological paradigm into all disciplines.[16] His application of sophisticated hermeneutic tools (hitherto used to approach high literary texts) to non-poetic and non-fictional texts — and indeed his refusal to separate off literary and academic from diplomatic and political discourse and action — not only opened up the field of literary studies to a seemingly infinite supply of new and socially relevant texts, but also gave rise to a methodology that still informs the study of travel writing today.

One field of interest asks "literary" questions about form, genre and tradition, (narrative) voice and modality, and fictionality. Formal matters here include the enquiry into the nature and function of stereotyping, the question of etymologies, aesthetics, authorship and subjectivity, autobiography, the truth value in narrative writing, the rhetorical nature of "fact," the issue of "identification in the reading process, inter-cultural 'translation,' " and the use and function of metaphor and other figures.[17]

Another field of enquiry focuses on the "factual" and discursive side of the travel text. Influenced by history, women's studies, colonial discourse analysis and postcolonial theory, modes of enquiry have included issues of nationalism and imperialism and the male and female traveler's stance towards them, the (fe)male gaze, imperial eyes, contact zones, transculturation, and questions of sex and gender in the travel text. Ethnographers and anthropologists have illuminated particular lines of argument or suggested particular methodologies for the study of travel writing, as have, more recently, psychoanalytical models of alterity, which have in turn been taken up by postcolonial social and cultural theorists.[18]

Another recent move has been the development of postmodern theories of space and mobility which are now replacing what Campbell calls "the polemics and models produced by an academic collectivity concerned mostly with locatable cultures, bounded nations, and the imperial past."[19] In the postmodern age, questions put to travel writing are likely to be framed in terms of concepts such as exile, displacement, nomadism, globalization, diaspora, inexpressibility, elusiveness, and otherness.

No doubt the study of travel writing will continue to be a site for multi-disciplinary and inter-disciplinary methodologies, which illuminate and learn from one another.

## Issues of Representation

The essays in this volume find a common interest in matters of representation. There are basic questions which any reader of the travel text must ask — about the material selected by the traveler for description, her point of view and ideological assumptions, and the degree of realism, detail, and credibility the travelogue offers. Beyond these questions, a larger and more theoretical field of enquiries opens up. At this more abstract level, we might consider the ways the world of China in the nineteenth and early twentieth century is re-imagined through various representations, how journeys from familiarity to otherness can be described, and the connection between travel and writing explored. In their collection of essays, James Duncan and Derek Gregory speak of the multiple sites at which travel writing takes place, and they point to the spatial nature of representation.[20] Notebooks, diaries, journals, letters, and logs are just a few of the textual manifestations which are combined, revised and edited for publication, thus turning the final travel text into a series of different spatialities entering into its own construction.

If the pen is constantly in motion, as is the author, in producing various mental and physical versions of what will later become his travelogue, the various media with which the traveler records his impressions are also important, as Duncan and Gregory suggest. Interdisciplinary studies have long moved beyond a neat distribution of media into compartments, and the scholar of travel writing may make use not only of journals, letters and published writings (formerly assigned to literary scholars and historians), but also of sketches and paintings (the art historian's domain), postcards, photographs, and films (previously reserved for historians of photography and the moving image), maps and geographical charts (geography's domain), and various non-fictional descriptions of peoples and cultures (the ethnographer's field). Attending to what Duncan and Gregory call the "physicality of representation" implies reading the travel text across different forms and analyzing their different valences and silences.[21]

Another point related to representation is the act of translation. Travel writing moves in a liminal space between knowledge of the self and the encounter with and understanding of the other. Translation, literally meaning being transported from one place to another, entails both losses and gains, but most importantly it is never value-neutral or innocent. In fact, travel writing is, as Michael Hanne argues, "always concerned in one way or another, with the *construction* of an Other."[22] Travel accounts often adopt an extreme method of translation by either, in an imperialist gesture, domesticating and thus reducing the foreign to fit into a framework that reproduces that of the self, or, in an opposite anti-imperialist gesture, exoticizing the Other so as to make it distant and simply alien from the observing self. We expect from travel writing a truthfulness that we do not expect from, for example, the novel, but the lines between fact and fiction, embellishment and reality, and the nature of rhetoric, are constantly negotiated in the travelogue.[23] The more time we spend in the space-in-between of the travel text, the more authorities, approaches and assumptions are questioned rather than confirmed.

## Introduction to the Essays

If China is too big a subject for traveler or writer to cover, the same is true of travel writing about China from the 1840s to the 1940s. This is not an encyclopedia, but a collection of essays on a selection of topics and writers; gaps and omissions are inevitable, but so is a lively diversity of subjects and approaches. The essays here discuss a variety of sites or genres within the travel account; they introduce different media and analyze how unfamiliar experience takes form in writing and images. While this collection discusses a representative variety of travel texts about China, it also introduces many of the historical traveler types Mary Campbell lists: "colonial masters, pilgrims, explorers, ambassadors, ambivalent wives, roving soldiers, ecstatic cross-dressers, conquistadores, missionaries, merchants, escaped slaves, idle students of the gentry and aristocracy, 'adventurers,' and alienated modern artists."[24]

With John Francis Davis — sinologist, an East India Company employee in Canton, and later a member of Lord Amherst's failed diplomatic mission to Peking in 1816 — we encounter a traveler who moves between his fascination with the country and his British loyalties. Tamara Wagner's essay discusses Davis's book *Sketches in China* (1841) in light of its paradoxical struggle on the one hand to fabricate the self-portrait of a curious post-Romantic traveler mesmerized by China's otherness, and, on the other, to embed this idealistic celebration of the foreign country's "lost" civilization within an intrinsically imperialist discourse of superiority, which is visible in shrewd observations about the country's military and commercial values. Travel writing as a genre becomes not only appropriated, but defined differently through such ruptures in the representation, and further through a deliberate distancing from earlier, Romantic, accounts.

Elizabeth Chang's essay discusses another important type of China traveler, the missionary. Her essay suggests, like Wagner's, that the Western intercourse with China depended on presuppositions about the inextricability of Chinese economic and political practice from more aesthetic concerns. While it shows how the Reverend Walter Medhurst's travel narrative, *A Glance at the Interior of China: Obtained through a Journey in the Silk and Green Tea Districts* (1850), engages with the commercial possibilities of two significant import products, Chang's essay also reads his text in the context of a larger general process of visual conversion that was progressively opening China to Victorian eyes. With the successes of the First Opium War, British travelers and writers were increasingly able to penetrate and revise the closed visual system that had defined British notions of a Chinese way of seeing. Medhurst's narrative, in its printed text as well as its engraved illustrations, offers both a duplication of this alternative Chinese visual aesthetic and an intimation of its eventual undoing.

"Imperialism," argues Q. S. Tong, "is by definition necessarily 'traveling,'" given its innate desires to extend its domains of control and to expand its spheres of influence, primarily, though not exclusively, for economic interest and trading privileges." His example of James Bruce, the Eighth Earl of Elgin, who traveled to China twice in the 1850s, suggests that diplomatic missions to China are metonymic of a collective imperial movement, driven and defined by the need to materialize the British Empire's vision of itself — a project Elgin was not completely at ease with. Tong demonstrates how Elgin's accounts of his missions to China are characterized by the only seemingly paradoxical co-existence of liberal ideas and imperialist duties, a mixture of motives characteristic of England itself in much of the nineteenth century.

A central concern in this collection — the question of representation — recurs in Tom Prasch's essay on John Thomson's China photography. While the Scottish photographer Thomson expresses, in his notes and commentaries, a fundamental faith in the straightforward representational character of photography as a medium, his practices belie such simple realism. Prasch suggests that Thomson brings into the field his own Victorian conceptions about race, class and civilization, which, in turn, affect the pictures he takes, from the choices he makes in picking "characteristic scenes and types" to the compositional strategies he employs in posing his chosen subject. Social-scientific preconceptions and artistic conventions come together to create images of the Chinese people as Thomson, and his Victorian audience, expected them to be.

The focus of Ross Forman's essay is not on a particular journey or group, but on one of the great themes of all travel. He discovers in Chinese food, and in the way it has been consumed, enjoyed and appreciated, refused and vilified, compared, misunderstood, and imitated by foreigners (and sometimes adapted to their taste), a whole history of cultural interaction with its own language, oral, visceral, and ritualistic. All travelers' tales are about food. In travel writing the strangeness of its food was a code for China's alterity, but a Chinese banquet also proved often a test for the visitor, the most inward of all encounters with China's material culture.

Julia Kuehn combines the enquiry into recent critical approaches to the travel genre — including the feminist and the (post-)colonial paradigms — with consideration of the process of approaching, describing and understanding otherness. Focusing on the Chinese travel accounts of a number of female travelers at the turn of the century, which include the British travelers Isabella Bird, Constance Cumming, and Alicia Little, and the Australian novelist Mary Gaunt, this essay understands the Westerner's encounter with Chinese institutions, city and landscapes as a potential site for an active hermeneutical process which results in a "fusion of horizons," in which the observer and observed ideally meet in an inter-subjective space where subject and object positions are eradicated in favor of dialogue.

Alicia Little (Mrs. Archibald Little) is one of the best-known of the China travelers. Arriving in China with her husband in 1886, she was to produce three novels and five travel books about the country. She was also a social activist, robustly determined to alleviate the suffering she saw about her in China, and she played a leading role in the early phases of the anti-footbinding movement. Susan Schoenbauer Thurin's essay considers in particular this aspect of Little's travels and writing. Alert as we have become to the "othering" process of the traveler, as well as to the pitfalls of sentimentalism, cultural superiority, and condescension, both Chinese and Western readers seem unsure how to respond to the humanitarianism of Little's activities and her representation of China's poor and disadvantaged. Thurin's essay sets itself the historical task of recovering the contemporary meaning of Little's altruism, which seems to fascinate and embarrass us in equal measure.

If Thurin's essay is structured by Little's ideological framework centering on charity, Susan Morgan's discussion of Isabella Bird Bishop uses another common rhetorical and ideological frame for the discussion of China at the time: the magical notion of the "China trade." Bird is the other famous female traveler in China, and Morgan shows how her travelogue *The Yangtze Valley and Beyond* (1899) employs a rhetoric that clearly invokes the book's informational agenda. The opening of China to the West put a premium on knowledge about the vast country. Bird's travelogue and her collection of images, *Chinese Pictures: Notes on Photographs Made in China* (1900), suggested to the British public that China was not unfathomable, but, indeed, manageable; "a quality," writes Morgan, "which speaks both to its economic promise for British merchants and investors and to its appropriate international position as dependent 'on the statesmanship and influence of Great Britain.' "

With the twentieth century, and the increased momentum of those political changes that revolutionized Chinese lives, the themes of Victorian travel assume new shapes. In the new century — an age in which, as Thomas Mann remarked, the destiny of man presented its meanings in political terms — travelers often seemed disposed to view China as a political problem, or puzzle, or cause. Elaine Ho's essay concentrates on the Pearl River as an axis between colonial Hong Kong and a mainland fermenting momentous change. Governor Lugard of Hong Kong, the scholarly orientalist Charles Eliot, and those globetrotting Fabian observers Beatrice and Sidney Webb, all created different kinds of knowledge of Chinese people and their lives in the early years of the new century. Each brought with them a professional agenda that equipped them to see China in a particular way, but Ho's essay also shows what they were not able to see, the China which these travelers' imperialist and orientalist optic rendered invisible.

Nicholas Clifford writes about the American traveler Harry Franck, whose books about China belong to the 1920s. Franck was not a missionary, sinologist, diplomat, political analyst, or practitioner of beautiful writing, but he turned his remarkably independent-minded gaze on everyday life, and offered what he claimed was an account of the authentic China, a "truthful impression" animated by a vivid sense of place. His work raises for Clifford the question of the truth of any traveler's report; Franck's travel books are entirely truthful, Clifford concludes, but we need to consider just what they are truthful about.

By the end of the 1930s we are in what Paul Fussell called "the decadent stage" of the "between-the-wars travel book."[25] China under Japanese attack elicits a war book, and W. H. Auden and Christopher Isherwood's *Journey to a War*, discussed here by Hugh Haughton, is a highly self-conscious, internally dialogic document. Haughton shows how it picks its way past the wandering rocks of propaganda on the one hand and romantic Orientalism on the other, to try to make out, in wartorn China, the truth of the present ("And maps can really point to places/ Where life is evil now") and the shape of the future. The wars of aggression and ideology that were convulsing China would soon break again over Europe; for Auden and Isherwood, and for the poet and teacher William

Empson, one reason for travel was the need to see one's own culture and predicament more clearly.

Meanwhile, the challenge of foreign experience was always also a challenge for the writer. The American journalist and political activist Agnes Smedley, whose path crossed briefly with that of Auden and Isherwood in 1938, was a fierce partisan of the Chinese revolution, and felt that her own background in poverty and struggle enabled her to identify strongly with the soldiers of the Red Army. In the last essay here, Douglas Kerr examines the tension, even contradiction, between the often declared motive of Smedley's China reporting, which was to tell the unvarnished truth about the Chinese people and what they were undergoing, and the carefully crafted rhetorical and narrative tropes she employed to tell their story.

The themes of the Victorian travelers to China — aesthetic, missionary, political, ethnographic, critical, comparative — frequently emerge again in the twentieth-century accounts, in a different idiom; so do many of the questions they raise. And in a similar way, the reader of these essays will encounter topics, approaches, and ideas that lead back, or point forward, to the work of other writers in this volume. Travel and reading are strangely analogous activities. If the traveler needs, as Butor says, to begin learning to read once more, the reader too may hope to learn new understandings of travel, from others who have passed along the way. Reading, like traveling, has its own ulteriority, but neither need be a solitary experience.

# 1

## Sketching China and the Self-Portrait of a Post-Romantic Traveler:
### John Francis Davis's Rewriting of China in the 1840s

*Tamara S. Wagner*

When John Francis Davis published his *Sketches of China* in the early 1840s, he capitalized on a significant increase in China's appeal to the imagination, yet even more importantly, his work spanned crucial shifts in Britain's political, commercial, and cultural attitudes to China over the course of the nineteenth century. A contradictory as well as complex text, the book encapsuled most effectively changing responses to China that were propelled by Romantic literary legacies, on the one hand, and early Victorian imperialist commercialism, on the other. As such, it indeed remarkably bridged two different sets of attitudes to the Celestial Empire. The 1840s significantly saw a strikingly ambiguous fascination with a country with which the British Empire was at war, and which yet also promised new commercial resources and a source for new literary imaginaries. Davis's revision of his *Sketches of China* is therefore of peculiar interest for his retrospective reworking of the China of his youth and, at the same time, for self-consciously registering the need to update his descriptions to reflect the ongoing shifts in popular perceptions. In thus revamping the impressions of the past, doubly filtered through Romantic aesthetics and commercial interests, *Sketches* does, in fact, more than simply testify to marked revisions in the conceptualization of China or anticipate its changing "semi-colonial" status. Instead, it often engages, I seek to show, very critically with prevailing discourses on "the East" and the way it was imagined in nineteenth-century British literature and culture. In order to bring out the double lens of this vision of China, I shall therefore also align Davis's reconsideration of his own responses with that of other nineteenth-century writers, both Romantic and Victorian. I shall then in particular highlight the implications of Davis's awareness of discourses of superiority, both occidentalist and orientalist.

Born in 1795, Davis was a sinologist who had been appointed writer in the East India Company's factory at Guangzhou (Canton) in 1813. It was primarily because of his linguistic abilities that he was chosen to accompany Lord Amherst on a diplomatic mission to what was at the time considered fascinating *terra incognita*. Davis was then twenty-one, barely of age, and had only lived in Guangzhou for three years. His residence in China was ultimately to last for over two decades. In 1834 he was appointed joint commissioner with Lord Napier and later became chief superintendent of trade, second governor and commander-in-chief of Hong Kong until he left in 1848. When he died in 1890, he had seen both opium wars and their repercussions. As an administrator, he proved extremely unpopular, but he significantly contributed to the textual "re-presentation" of China in nineteenth-century Britain. His *oeuvre*, in fact, consisted of a bulk of travel writing, commentaries on China's foreign politics and history, "miscellaneous" essays on various parts of Asia, from Western Tartary to British India, as well as translations of Chinese classical literature and a detailed study of Chinese poetry: *Poeseos Sinensis Commentarii: On the Poetry of the Chinese* was published in Macao in 1834 and continued to be reprinted regularly until the 1960s.

Most importantly, however, when Davis drew on earlier diplomatic missions for his *Sketches*, the "opening" of China may have seemed still remote, yet speculation on commercial advantages was already part and parcel of his detailing of information he deemed useful for military strategies. It is this reconstruction of the commercially viable as well as the strategically useful that makes especially the works he published during or towards the end of the First Opium War (1839–42) striking points-of-entry into far-reaching shifts that irrevocably changed foreign travel in and travel writing on China. He indeed considered his knowledge of China of particular importance because of the war, and that regardless of the fact that his material referred to a China of nearly three decades ago. Commerce had of course been a powerful incentive to exploration from the beginning of British-Chinese relations. During the war, however, the circumstances that had led to it needed to be revaluated, and that perhaps particularly because opium had become an icon as much of British Far Eastern trade as of colonial dependency, of a twofold imperialist addiction that permeated society abroad as well as at home. Partly in response to this demand, partly to come to terms with a disturbing sense that his initial, primarily aesthetic, reaction to the Far East had come to seem outmoded in comparison with the new thrust towards commercial penetration, Davis continuously rewrote or added to his material.

In updating his account of extensive travels from Guangzhou to Beijing and back, Davis moreover sought to cater for a mid-Victorian readership. So even if his travel writing never achieved the popularity of the progressively proliferating books on China by Archibald and Alicia Little or Isabella Bird Bishop later in the century, or even of Davis's own work on Chinese literature, his project of "re-presenting" an early nineteenth-century diplomatic mission casts a particularly revealing light on changing ideas on China at the time. If he was to appeal to more than narrowly specialist target groups at the mid-century, he had to bridge a marked distance in popular perceptions of "the Orient." In other words, his was largely a readership impelled by a very different interest in China, its people and culture as well as its commercial ports and military resources, than that which had directed his observations during his first travels inland, as part of Lord Amherst's embassy to Beijing in 1816. It was with the aim to establish more extensive commercial relations that Amherst had been sent as ambassador extraordinary to the court of China. But on arriving in the Peiho, he was informed that he would only be admitted to the emperor on condition that he performed the *kow-tow*, what Davis was to describe in an almost tongue-in-cheek way as the "Tartar Ceremony," "all quite à la Chinoise."[1] Following the advice of his second commissioner, Sir George Thomas Staunton, Amherst refused to consent, as Lord Macartney had done in 1793, unless it was admitted that Britain's sovereign would, theoretically, be entitled to the same obeisance from a high-ranking mandarin. This admission was refused; the embassy was not allowed to enter Beijing; and like Macartney's, Amherst's mission was declared a notable failure. Yet surprisingly little need be said about it for a reading of the *Sketches*. Writing in the 1840s, Davis clearly considered at least its details a thing of the past. It is not central either to his nostalgic remembrance or to the military advantages he attempted to glean from his notes so many decades later. As such, it is pushed to the periphery of the *Sketches*. What is more, only shortly after the book's first publication, attitudes underwent another sea-change. The end of the war, the consequent opening of regions that had so far been rarely accessible to the traveler from "the West," and ultimately the creation of a semi-colonial China, necessarily changed the parameters of travel writing on China for good. It is therefore doubly important to remember that, published in 1841, Davis's *Sketches* appeared at the height of the First Opium War, before China's "opening," and yet decades after his youthful experiences. His recollections were hence at once mediated by changing perceptions of and attitudes to China and couched in an essentially nostalgic enterprise that was further to be co-opted by pressing concerns with military strategies. As the work's subtitle promised, the original account was supplemented with "Notices and Observations Relative to the Present War." An advertisement inserted in the first volume even more emphatically called up "the deep and growing interest which the present crisis in our relations with China has excited."[2]

Although his two-volume "collection of notes," *The Chinese: A General Description of the Empire and Its Inhabitants* of 1836, likewise purported to rework opinions he had made "as a very young man," Davis's subsequent publications focused much more insistently on the importance of China's strengths and weaknesses during the war and on growing interest in the Romantic traveler as a literary figure of the past.[3] If this strikes the reader as two diametrically opposed projects, this seeming imbalance accounts not only for the ambiguity that indisputably radiates through Davis's writing, yet also for an unusually balanced representation of occidentalism that came out of his oscillation between value-judgment and occasional orientalist rhapsody. Byron and Coleridge, for example, at once absorbed and newly illuminated the Celestial Empire as part of a poetic orientalism that made more of the imagined than the observed exotica of a region at once remote and still largely off-limits.

As Nigel Leask has pointed out in his seminal study *British Romantic Writers and the East*, in Romantic writing, oriental places began to "displace the Arcadian locus amoenus of neo-classicism from a Mediterranean 'Golden-Age' to a 'contemporary eastern site.' "[4] Oriental sites were used to contrast with, but most importantly started to rival, the classical "antique lands" of the Mediterranean that had informed so much of

Enlightenment thought and writing. Coleridge's fragment poem "Kubla Khan" (1816) is a dream vision of Xanadu (ancient Mongol China) that evokes China as a symbol: a "genius loci" significantly inspired by a dream over an earlier travelogue, distilling aesthetic conventions into the poem's "allegory of high romantic genius."[5] Despite the mock-Romantic elements of Jane Austen's fiction, the heroine of *Mansfield Park* (1814), Fanny Price, can likewise go on an imaginary trip to Lord Macartney's China. It is a place of "composure," in sharp contrast to the similarly off-stage, commercially exploited, West Indies. While the slave plantations on Antigua are connected, through a significant parallelism, to the micropolitics of the landowner's English Great House, China is at once the object of an educational venture and a dreamy escape. It is a predominantly literary space, reached through the reading of travel accounts, autobiography, and poetry in the tellingly named "East room." As such, it is identified with Fanny's "nest of comforts," where she can retire, as her cousin puts it, from domestic persecution: "*You* in the meanwhile will be taking a trip into China, I suppose. How does Lord Macartney go on?"[6] This imaginary space is pointedly invaded by peculiarly domestic concerns: "but there was no reading, no China, no composure for Fanny. He had told her the most extraordinary, the most inconceivable, the most unwelcome news."[7]

By the mid-nineteenth century, however, reading and writing about China had become increasingly complex, conflicted not only by imminent opium wars, but also by changes in perceptions and literary conventions of "the Orient" more generally. While orientalism remained a crucial shaping force in literary production throughout the nineteenth century, "the East" as an idealized locus amoenus, or lovely place, largely became supplanted once again. It was to a large extent replaced and yet also co-opted by Victorian medievalism and a revival in neo-classicism. Conversely, Romantic aesthetics might have exploited and distorted an "East" that was largely an Orient of the imagination, but mid-century orientalism became newly steeped in a more strictly stratified understanding of imperialist superiority. This discourse became additionally validated by Darwinian evolutionary theory. Where China had once supplied Utopian visions, it was now considered stagnant or backward. Symptomatically, the Romantic idealization of the old and ruinous, an idealization that was premised on an aesthetic appreciation of the ancient as well as the exotic, collapsed into discourses on cleanliness.[8]

There are two layers of orientalization in Davis's work, and their contiguity strikingly brings out this shift. Ironically, however, these discourses were to an important extent also generated by the very accessibility that had made China interesting in the first place. Especially concepts of commercial superiority on the part of the British were seen to waver, yet re-emerged only the more vehemently, in the face of ancient Chinese notions of civilization and barbarism. China's forceful opening to "the West" as a resource of commerce was necessarily accompanied by the revision of the Far Eastern tourist and the changing aesthetics of travel. More invidiously perhaps, this also had an enormous impact on changing concepts and representations of what was thought to constitute (ancient) civilization. It is in these ongoing re-conceptualizations that the traveler's contact with Chinese occidentalism consequently made itself felt most notably. Davis's adaptation of his early nineteenth-century perceptions to suit his audience at once encapsulated and made problematic this ambiguous enterprise of opening China to Victorian readers.

By focusing on his *Sketches of China*, this essay therefore also aims to assess critically Davis's resistance to discourses of superiority, both orientalist and occidentalist in nature. At the same time, it will stress the ways in which his self-portrait as a curious, adventurous, young traveler, even on a failing diplomatic mission, is embedded in an account of China as both "one great anomaly" that fascinates, as it is put in the first chapter of the *Sketches*, and as a military enemy.[9] As we shall see, while the analogies Davis repeatedly draws between China and Ancient Rome underscore his recourse to conceptualizations of the antique and the picturesque, the insertion of, however seemingly spurious, delineations of strategic advantages indisputably works against (Romantic) idealizations of fascinatingly "other," decaying, or even lost, ancient civilizations. As these uncertainties in his stance create generic breaks, *Sketches of China* can be seen to fall into a tripartite arrangement: once the burden of the diplomatic mission is lifted through its very failure, self-congratulatory critique makes way for a more leisurely experience of travel until a return to Guangzhou and commerce — "with the sounds so frequent and familiar at Canton [Guangzhou], *Fânkwei* and *Hoong-maou*, 'Foreign devil,' and 'Rufus' " — also marks, in the retrospective text, a return to the original intention to turn travel accounts into a document of military and commercial value.[10] Travel writing is, in short, appropriated, for a specific agenda.

## Sanitizing Chinomanie and the Opening of Victorian China

Interested in Chinese culture and literature (and Davis was an avid translator as well) and deeply appreciative of the beauties of the countryside in all his travels, Davis infused what Nigel Leask has recently diagnosed as a particularly Romantic curiosity into later works. The result of such infusion was often the creation of intriguing anomalies that ironically disrupt their retrospective representations.[11] The 1857 edition of Davis's *China: A General Description of that Empire and its Inhabitants*, for example, specifically addresses a "sort of *Chinomanie*" that works around the mid-Victorian domestication of collectable exotica. Instead, it retains a fascination with a Romanticized inscrutability or "otherness," and yet the book also demands an account of more recent events.[12] By the time the book was published, Britain was caught up in the Second Opium War. The British joined forces with the French, and led by Lord Elgin, they occupied Guangzhou in 1857. As part of the subtitle of Davis's reprinted *China* promised, the new edition engaged *With the History of Foreign Intercourse Down to the Events which Produced the Dissolution of 1857*. *Sketches of China*, I shall argue, the more effectively render apparent the far-reaching shifts in Britain's relationship with the Celestial Empire.

The fusion of picturesque description with pressing political concerns in the *Sketches*, in fact, engenders a manifold breakdown of the Romantic aesthetics of curiosity that fascinatingly indicates a rupture in European discourses on China. Victorian "Chinomanie" may nonetheless have helped the publication of Davis's later works, but only by recasting their original emphases. As a result, his accounts are multiply mediated: filtered through political conflict and changes in the ways in which newly opened visions of China's interior were being co-opted in political discourses at home in Victorian Britain. But precisely how did Davis adapt his account of China in the context of a revamped, differently defined, aesthetic on the one hand and an uncertain political situation on the other? How did his writing fit in with post-Romantic orientalism and specifically with a new awareness of occidentalist views of the barbarian from "the West"? If popular conceptions of an "opened," rather than colonized, China at once expressed enthusiasm about Far Eastern commerce and clashed with ideologies of imperialist superiority, how did Davis's rewritten Romantic China feature such clashes?

Once China was open to tourists, seasoned travelers, and professional travel writers as well as traders, they naturally began to compare China — and Chinese sanitation problems — to other destinations. The relative convenience or inconvenience of travel became defining especially for the globetrotter who set himself (and increasingly also herself) against the tourist.[13] Traveling inland, away from Shanghai and Hong Kong, meant leaving certain customary conveniences behind, and minute descriptions of "dirt" (in the widest sense of the term, and often used euphemistically in Victorian writing to refer to a spectrum of human and animal waste) could authenticate accounts of having experienced "the real China" beyond colonial or semi-colonial enclaves. As Susan Schoenbauer Thurin has pointed out, for the casual traveler and, perhaps even more importantly, for the professional travel writer, authenticity of experience outweighed disgust, although concepts of colonial cleanliness had by then begun to develop racial connotations.[14] This was partly due to the impact of Darwinian evolutionary science on popular thinking at the time; partly due to topical debates on the sanitary regulation of Victorian Britain. Still, within power relations, colonial or otherwise, Thurin adds, the rhetorical use of cleanliness/dirt "comes easily to hand as a method of defining and separating self and other, and consequently appears in various cross-cultural and interracial contexts."[15]

Such issues necessarily only came to constitute a regularly evoked topic in discussions of China's reputed backwardness once traveling into its interior had become the subject of travel journals more generally. If Victorian perceptions of China read it as mired not only in yesterday's culture, but also more literally in the piled up refuse of the past, the Romantic ideal of the Celestial Empire was still largely undefiled by such palpable concerns. For Davis, taking issue with Chinese toilets (or a lack thereof) was simply not an issue. He was part of a diplomatic mission, and faltering hopes of its success at least at first remained dominant at the expense even of much description. It is as if personal impressions could only take over after failure had become regarded as inevitable and undeniable. It was then that Davis seemed to have found time to indulge in, or find the freedom to explore, ventures further into new territory and to new sites, beyond the mission's immediate confines and their temporary accommodation along the way.

Subsequent Victorian globetrotters might have made an effort to immerse themselves in Chinese society, but that was not part of the agenda of early diplomatic missions. They were well provided not only with familiar food, but with other amenities or "impediments" that were deemed necessary. During the unloading of their provisions, Davis revealingly noticed the astonishment of the Chinese "at the immensity of our 'impediments' " and attempted to explain this as evidence of the "total contrariety of the Chinese habits and our own [, which] made it requisite for the general comfort that the stores, and other articles for the use of the English party during several months in a strange Asiatic country, should be numerous and bulky."[16] This way they were able to avoid the unfamiliar and also the unsanitary described by later travelers, though of course it also meant that as a young adventurous gentleman of the Romantic age, Davis soon felt confined, and his experience of China necessarily to be limited. He was longing for the dream spaces immortalized in Coleridge's China, published in the same year that saw Lord Amherst's mission.

Davis's retrospective accounts indeed register repeated complaints about the double confinement imposed by the strictures of his position within the embassy staff and the restrictions on their movements demanded by what he invariably termed "the Tartar-Chinese government" and their "jealous fears": "This was a state of tutelage which seemed by no means calculated to increase our acquaintance with the country; and I quietly made up my mind that by every legitimate means in my power I would break through it."[17] "It required some philosophy," he writes even decades later, "to bear these repeated checks and restraints upon our natural curiosity."[18] Whenever Davis managed to escape this "tutelage," an " 'army of observation' round our temporary dwelling,"[19] the focus of his accounts, in fact, shifts correspondingly. The description of the official mission is broken into twice. In fact, it strikingly brings out the double lens of mediation that engenders the China of the *Sketches*. A Romantic would-be explorer exhibits self-conscious interest both in observing and being observed, in the spectacles of "otherness," and a nostalgic Victorian seeks to rewrite his adventurous youth. Most remarkably, however, this doubly removed narrator focuses on the experience of becoming a spectacle to be consumed by Chinese occidentalism:

> When after events placed us in some measure at issue with the government, and it no longer seemed necessary to keep terms with it, the vexatious restraints now imposed upon us were soon broken through by a little determination on our part; and when the Chinese found from experience that we were really a very harmless and inoffensive species of wild beasts, they no longer attempted to interfere with our excursions, which carried us over all the country adjoining our frequent halting-places, as well as through some of their largest cities, as will appear anon.[20]

Although Davis's retrospective vantage-point necessarily puts a different spin on past incidents, there was undoubtedly more time for excursions once initial attempts at negotiation had come to a halt after Lord Amherst's mission had failed. The diplomatic breakdown could indeed be harnessed to provide useful information for current military endeavors and subsequent commercial expansion. "In our existing state of war with the celestial empire," Davis thus writes in the 1840s, what he noticed in 1816 may become "of some consequence."[21] A glimpse of Formosa (Taiwan), for example, "offers a tempting position to any European power disposed to try the occupation of it, as a means of pushing its trade with the empire," and excellent harbors "render it a very advantageous station for a naval squadron."[22] The conflation of aesthetic pleasure and the search for an advantage generates a peculiar effect, as when Davis describes "the prettiest and most picturesque-looking building that [he] had ever seen in the country": in order to highlight its aesthetic effect, he resorts to poetry, moves on to a brief discussion of a specifically, he implies, Chinese fondness for weeping willows and their function in Chinese poetry, and then seemingly without any transition whatsoever points out that "willow charcoal forms one of the ingredients of their gunpowder."[23] More significantly still, however, the elision of the travels' initial purpose allows the retrospective writer to leave it behind fairly quickly to concentrate on telling the story of the Romantic traveler. It is, as we shall see, a doubly curious post-Romantic self-portrait that is fascinatingly articulated in a corresponding break through the confines of the retrospective account and a rewriting of what Leask has termed the antiquarian aesthetics of curiosity.

The failure of the mission, in short, engendered a temporary limbo between tight control over the mission's movements and their expulsion. This very limbo made room for an unscheduled venture into a still "closed" China. Suffice to say that Davis's position as an observer was nonetheless significantly incidental in the sense that, in contrast to later professional travels and travel writers like Isabella Bird Bishop, he had not come out to China to produce either fiction or non-fictional popular travel books. Nonetheless, had it not been for both his intense curiosity, engendered by a Romantic travel discourse on an "Eastern" antique, his forays into spaces beyond the confines of what could be called his work experience in China might otherwise have not much exceeded Arthur Clennam's in Dickens's *Little Dorrit*.

It is indeed vital to consider Davis's retrospective reworking of his experience in the contexts of wider cultural shifts in the representation of China at the time. I shall therefore briefly touch upon the indisputably marginal, yet precisely therefore significantly representative, function of China in popular or "mainstream" Victorian fiction. These examples are particularly insightful when they attempt to cast, very much in the way in which Davis does, retrospective light on early nineteenth-century China and Britain's relationship with the Celestial Empire, and most importantly, whenever commerce and Chinomanie as a reductive exoticization of "the Orient" meet.

Dickens's mid-century novel *Little Dorrit*, we shall find, does all of that. In its emphasis on mundane commercial life, here or there, it dismantles cultural myths of "exotic" China and counterpoises the Romantic writing that had largely created them. Described as "an Englishman, who has been more than twenty years in China," Clennam returns to England disgusted with the failing family business and reticent about his stay in China, "an object on which I [Clennam] was never consulted and which was never mine; shipped away to the other end of the world before I was of age, and exiled there until my father's death there."[24] While the novel's serialization (1855–57) started before the beginning of the Second Opium War (1856–60) and was finished before its end, the main plot is set more than three decades earlier in the century. Clennam's business exile moreover needs to be projected twenty years further into the past. His barely evoked China is hence the same China Davis described. Indeed, if Davis was "greeted with the sounds so frequent and familiar" in Guangzhou, this eerily mirrors both Clennam's mixture of nostalgia and disappointment upon his return to an alienated, all too dull and familiar, commercial City of London and his elided commercial dullness in China. But if the family's business in China remains opaque, Clennam's former flame Flora expresses a curiously jumbled Chinomanie. Flora fears

> that you [Arthur Clennam] are married to some Chinese lady, being in China so long and being in business . . . I only hope she's not a Pagodian dissenter . . . I don't know where I'm running to, oh do tell me something about the Chinese ladies whether their eyes are really so long and narrow always putting me in mind of mother-of-pearl fish at cards and do they really wear tails down their back and plaited too or is it only the men, and when they pull their hair so very tight off their foreheads don't they hurt themselves, and why do they stick little bells all over their bridges and temples and hats and things or don't they really do it!²⁵

Although much has recently been speculated about the Clennams' possible business in the opium trade as a convincing source of the son's sense of guilt, the novel's emphasis is really on the dullness as well as the shadiness of all commercial enterprise.²⁶ As Thurin reminds us, "[a]s a rule, foreign merchants traveled little in China. They were notorious for not learning the language and avoiding the Chinese population. To some extent these patterns were a response to the treaty-port regulations in that foreign businesses and housing were confined to the concession areas."²⁷ If popular mid-century fictional references to China underline an important conjunction that set apart a new fascination with China at home — a Chinomanie, as Davis puts it — from the daily encounters with commerce that structured the newly opened ports, Davis's contrast between Guangzhou and travels into the interior captures the very basis of this dual perception of China. The interior, even described in retrospect in the 1840s, could still accommodate a Romantic traveler; commerce in Guangzhou had become familiar to the mid-century reader as an extension of the clerk's City.

In Austen's *Mansfield Park*, a novel published in 1814, the heroine may still have been able to read travels to China as part of her Romantic (or mock-Romantic) education in contradistinction to the much discussed function of West Indian plantations. But in Dickens's mid-century novel, Clennam's business in China embodies a different "dead silence."²⁸ Nevertheless, much as one might wish to argue that the seemingly working-class Amy Dorrit, the eponymous heroine of Dickens's novel, and her enclosed world in the East End might stand in for oriental — and orientalized — women and the East, it is nonetheless first and foremost the break-up of a commercial Empire and of a ridiculed consumable Orient (as in Flora's flighty fancies) that occupies the China of Dickens's novel.²⁹ The perceptual distance between *Mansfield Park* and *Little Dorrit* spans the Opium Wars, the "opening" of China, and the shift from a Romantic aesthetics of curiosity to the mid-century juxtaposition of orientalist Chinomanie and commercial preoccupation. The *Sketches* may seek to present Davis as a Romantic traveler, but at times he emerges more like the returned Clennam except when, in an enthusiastic triumph of having broken through confines, he describes himself as escaping from the bonds of the mission and governmental restrictions, oriental and occidental alike. Then considerations of war and commerce fall aside to reveal a Romantic traveler's fascination with an orientalist antique that is constructed precisely on a curiosity that needs to leave commerce behind, but cannot always achieve this.[30] What is more, as he shuttles between an appreciation of landscapes or temples on the one hand and a rhetoric of commercial speculation on the other, Davis's ambiguous perception of occidentalist reactions additionally permeates this otherwise binary structure.

## Occidentalist Spectacle: "A Specimen of English China"

While Davis's rehearsals of Romantic aesthetics might at times seem all too familiar, if not forced, his resistance to the prevailing discourses of the mid-century importantly marks out his writing as negotiating the significantly fluent lines of demarcations between Romantic and Victorian modes of orientalizing China. Even when retrospectively rewriting his travels, he remains dedicated to the "Eastern" locus amoenus Leask describes as the Romantic writer's generic space of "otherness." Leask's more recent study on the Romantic aesthetics of curiosity draws on material that stretches as far into the nineteenth century as the 1840s, and although he refers only to ruins to be found in "the torrid zones" (beyond "the East" in Mexico), much of his argument on antiquarian (or archaeological) travels can be extended to the attraction of Chinese ancient civilization.[31] Like the Romantic writers Leask discusses, Davis sees the ancient and the ruinous as picturesque, a word that regularly appears in the *Sketches*.

What is more, Davis not only repeatedly compares China to Ancient Rome, at one point even likening a "mandarin from the 'general of the nine gates' " to "a sort of praetorian prefect," or a pagoda's spiral stairs to those "in the well known columns at Rome, London, and Paris," but he also puts much emphasis on the fact that Chinese antique bottles had recently been found in Egypt. There were, symptomatically, "mixed up with the scarabæi and gems, and other small objects in the ancient tombs of Thebes."[32] "They might," Davis writes excitedly, "belong to the period of the Roman empire, when we know that there was a direct intercourse with China, or they might perhaps be brought as low down as the period of the Arabian commerce with that country."[33] Given the comparative thrust of early nineteenth-century antiquarian discourses, it can likewise hardly surprise us when Davis repeatedly likens Nanjing (Nanking) to Rome, yet what is striking is that the resemblance seems based on convention rather than experience:

> In the small proportion which the inhabited part bears on the whole area of
> the ancient walls, Nanking bears a striking resemblance to modern Rome.
> . . . As I stood at Rome on the Coelian mount in 1837, the resemblance of
> its deserted hills (setting apart the black masses of ruin) to those of Nanking
> struck me at once, bounded as they are in both instances by an old wall.[34]

Does he base his comparative description of Nanjing on what he has seen in Rome or *vice versa*? However that may be, the retrospective framework indicates shifts in cultural perceptions. The fascination with the antique has made way for a comparison with *modern* Rome — a place of past glory. The focus of the investigation is more on decay and desertion than on Romantic eulogies on the ruinous, instead tying in with mid-century conceptualizations of "backwardness" or degeneration. With a European historical model imposed on it that set the contrast between "an activist energetic West and passive Eastern timelessness," as Clifford puts it, Victorian travelers understood China as "mired in the past."[35] The Romantics may have idealized this very timelessness; for the Victorians, it came to represent lack of energy.

In 1859, writing during the Second Opium War, John Stuart Mill evoked China in *On Liberty* as "a warning example" of arrested or "stationary" development.[36] This of course does not mean that Victorian travelers never felt ecstatic over ancient ruins, and the growing significance of archaeology over the course of the century would suggest the contrary, but in the majority of mid- or late nineteenth-century travel accounts, discourses of modernization and civilization go hand in hand and tend to oust the appreciation of the very crumbling of ancient buildings that inform Romantic orientalist aesthetics. Especially descriptions of decay could of course be co-opted very easily into a new idea of policing "opened" China through enforcing the newly developed standards of sanitation — a topical problem in Victorian Britain and specifically in the East End of London, a dark Continent at home for which "Eastern" metaphors regularly suggested themselves.

Davis slipped into a rhetoric of backdating even as he attempted to praise Beijing or Nanjing by likening them to Rome. This is no simple parallelism or even elevation of the one through the other, for China's, as Ancient Rome's glories, are (it is implied) over, although Roman civilization might have been absorbed by new European Empires: "What Rome was to Europe, Peking is, or has been, to the large portion of Asia. . . . It was naturally with feelings of considerable interest that we approached this singular place."[37] Davis's re-conceptualization of the Celestial Empire he visited as a young man as both ancient (with a long past) and unchanging (without history) might have been seen as suitably tallying with emergent Victorian ideologies of progress and, with them, of the growing superiority of the "younger races," which became increasingly re-inflected by evolutionary theory in the second half of the century.

It is, however, important to remember that he was no missionary, archaeologist, businessman, or scientist, and that he both traveled and wrote before the popularization of Darwinian science. He was part of a diplomatic mission that had, or so at least he considered in retrospect, the additional value of opening up access to military information. While they had both a scientist and an artist among them, these were allocated occupations. When they were at work, Davis was reduced to an observer, watching the re-presentation of local fishermen, for example, with self-ironic enjoyment. Thus, early in the *Sketches*, he describes how the necessity of having to fill up on water "gave occasion to several visits to the land, being to most of those on board the squadron their first introduction to the celestial regions":[38]

> The two gentlemen who acted in the several capacities of naturalist and artist to the mission went on shore, the one with his scientific apparatus, the other with his pencils and sketch-book. . . . [T]he last attempted to seize with his pencil the various groups of the natives, as these crowded round him in all the eagerness of insatiable curiosity. This however was no easy task, for as each saw the eye of the limner fixed earnestly upon himself, he suddenly wheeled round to the rear to look over the artist's shoulder and observe progress; and as our excellent draughtsman was not the most patient of his profession, the effect became rather ridiculous. The sight of Europeans was to these people, mostly fisherman, a novel one.[39]

If the familiar spaces of commercial ports could be seen to generate a stalled meeting of "the East" and "the West," ventures inland meant mutual curiosity. There was "ample proof that the Chinese are naturally as curious as most other people."[40] While such curiosity undoubtedly manifested itself foremost in a disruption of the occidental artist's sketches, this gazing back could counteract orientalist distortion. Nevertheless, at times Davis resented curious spectators, "express[ing] by their looks the utmost surprise at the sight of such strange and unexpected visitors," however reasonably startled they might be, for "crowding upon the English party, and examining their persons and dress with the most unceremonious curiosity."[41] The display of scientific apparatuses and sketch-books became part of a spectacle in which the novel sight of Europeans put the doubly curious "Westerner" on display. It is a reverse of what Davis was to term "things . . . certainly calculated to puzzle us of the West" — a puzzled gazing that worked in two ways, a meeting of East and West that reminds us that Davis was thus one of the first to lump together "Europeans" as "from the West" in order to distinguish their commonalities from "Eastern" conceptions.[42] As I have argued in more detail elsewhere, the creation of "the West" in the nineteenth century was indeed both an occidentalist and an orientalist enterprise.[43] Nineteenth-century reactions on the part of the traveler could significantly range from discomfort or unease to appreciative self-irony, or as Thurin phrases it, from being stunned by the "overweening self-conceit" and intrigued by "the paradoxical lure of China's legendary xenophobia."[44]

When Davis reveled in the recall of a two-way experience of novel sights, or noted the mission's increasing freedom of movement, he exuded the enthusiasm of a young traveler inspired by a culture of exploration and aesthetics of curiosity. Although likewise tongue-in-cheek, his return to the familiar sounds of the commercial ports was not merely mired in dull commonness. Something more rankled: with the novelty all worn off, only awareness of hostility and contempt remained. "*Fânkwei* and *Hoong-maou*, 'Foreign devil,' and 'Rufus' " were by no means endearing terms. They reminded the returned explorer of his unwelcome presence and his perceived inferior status in Chinese occidentalist thought. Davis's translations succinctly capture these ethnocentric terms of abuse, and yet his interpretation of "Rufus" is peculiarly interesting here. The Cantonese word for "red-haired" (*hoong-maou*) often implies the "ghost" or "devil" metonymically. In Europe, red hair had of course been stigmatized for centuries as an ethnic marker. Its Anti-Semitic associations, for example, can be seen in depictions of Judas Iscariot as red-haired.[45] While Davis may have intended to soften his representation of the hostility he encountered by equating Chinese occidentalism with ethnocentrism at home, by showing that there is racism everywhere, he also supplied an accurate translation of the racial slur implied in the description.

But while travel accounts of nineteenth-century China register and in manifold ways respond to Chinese occidentalist concepts, occidentalism has only very recently attracted attention, and then often as linked to, if not a substitute for, postcoloniality. This necessarily reduces it altogether to a reaction to orientalism, to a mere mirror-image of the worst that ever came out of orientalist perceptions of "the East." Couze Venn, for example, speaks of "the aim of interrogating modernity from the standpoint of a postcoloniality that knows itself to be caught up in the history of modernity," although his approach is further complicated when he uses occidentalism somewhat misleadingly to describe "the process of the becoming-West of Europe and the becoming-modern of the world."[46] The majority of studies on occidentalism, however, agree with Chen Xiaomei's influential definition of occidentalism as "a discursive practice that, by constructing its Western Other, has allowed the Orient to participate actively and with indigenous creativity in the process of self-appropriation."[47] Judith Snodgrass without doubt most compellingly highlights the Orient's participation in orientalism when she argues that while the exclusion of an "Asian" agency was central to Edward Said's concept of a dominant "West" and a passive "East," this was only a partial description of the discourse's dynamics "suited to Said's own project of emphasizing the wrong done to the Middle East."[48] Orientalism is really only a particular example of numerous functions of alterity, one of which is occidentalism.[49]

Occidentalism had of course always been present in Chinese culture. What Davis, for example, termed, in one of his most jingoist moments, "their silly prepossessions concerning the universal supremacy of the celestial empire" at times had an important counterpoising force to European orientalist appropriation.[50] Exposure of ignorance could work in both ways: part of a curiosity of aesthetics that was nonetheless inescapably orientalist. Hence, while Davis met visitors to ships or to his temporary accommodation with disappointment and even ridicule when they displayed ignorance instead of feeding his curiosity, he also noticed to what an extent he had become part of an occidentalist spectacle: "they seemed to be sufficiently ignorant of matters relating to their own country. On observing any costly or ingenious objects of art, they immediately asked if it was not made at Guangzhou. Being shown a specimen of English china, they seemed surprised and almost incredulous."[51] Exploring a temple, Davis was similarly startled by "an old European print representing Jesus Christ, with a Chinese inscription" being worshipped among numerous "consecrated" religious icons, and when a priest offered to explain, it was only to inquire whether "there were votaries of *Budha* [*sic*] in England, and if the inhabitants of our country were likely to be converted by his going and teaching them!"[52] Davis otherwise uses exclamation marks sparingly. It is important to remember that the missionary enterprise was viewed with much skepticism in Britain at the time. There is, in fact, a twofold critique embedded in Davis's expressions of astonishment. As Leask importantly reminds us, not "all European travelers were uniformly racists, jingoists, or imperialists."[53]

But this does not mean that Davis's doubly enthusiastic account of the "marvels and apparent inconsistencies which China presents to the eye of the commonest observer" as an exotic space and as a commercial resource to be conquered is always free of jingoism. On the contrary, especially as his accounts move to a close and hence back to Guangzhou and commerce, with all the attendant ethnocentric confrontations that are apparently all too familiar there, he leaves the Romantic traveler behind to explode occidentalist notions of superiority with its orientalist counterpart. His sudden emphasis on "superior efficiency" even anticipates later discourses on progress and "backwardness": "Whatever may be said about the indifference or repugnance of the Chinese as to copying foreigners, I am persuaded that the superior efficiency of many things of the kind at Canton, compared with the north and the interior, is owing greatly to hints furnished by our example to them."[54] Still, even while he somewhat jarringly encourages imitation, suggesting that the Chinese would do well to copy foreigners, he qualifies such orientalist judgments by foregrounding differences. As he describes how an educated Chinese named Chang "often spoke of his admiration of the blunt integrity and straightforwardness of the English character," Davis argues that their own "best aim to acquire the respect of the Chinese [is] by acting in a manner diametrically opposite to themselves."[55] Emulation is indisputably a one-sided affair for Davis, and this discrepancy is at the heart of the ambiguities that run through his work. There certainly are greatnesses and weaknesses, marvels and apparent inconsistencies, in the observer's accounts as well as in the China he describes. But while *Sketches of China* presents a curious "specimen of English China," its manufacture, as it were, brilliantly brings out the collisions, clashes, and conflations of different orientalist expectations and aesthetics of curiosity in nineteenth-century travel accounts.

# 2

# Converting Chinese Eyes:
## Rev. W. H. Medhurst, "Passing," and the Victorian Vision of China

*Elizabeth H. Chang*

The Reverend Walter H. Medhurst (1796–1857) begins his travel narrative *A Glance at the Interior of China Obtained During a Journey to the Silk and Green Tea Countries* (1850)[1] with the following injunction: "In order to accomplish a journey into the interior of China," Medhurst writes, "it is necessary, if the individual undertaking it be a foreigner, to assume the Chinese dress, to shave the front part of the head and temples, and to wear what is commonly called a tail. The traveller should also be able to converse readily in the Chinese language; and conform himself, as much as possible, to the habits and manners of the natives."[2] If this opening sentence appeared daunting to a would-be traveler unaccustomed to shaving his head, unable to speak Chinese, and altogether unknowledgeable about how to conform himself to the habits of the natives, it was Medhurst's project in the rest of the book to enlighten that ignorance, using his own seven-week journey through the province of Jiangxi in the spring of 1845 as a model.

Medhurst himself came well-prepared to this journey. He had been anticipating the opportunity to educate the "heathen" since applying to join the London Missionary Society (LMS) in 1816. Educated at St. Paul's and Hackney College, Medhurst's initial service to the Congregationalist LMS was as a printer. He served in Southeast Asia for over twenty years, chiefly in Malacca, Penang, and Batavia, and received his D. D. shortly before establishing the LMS mission in Shanghai in 1843. Though compelled to leave China at the age of sixty-one for health reasons, he still refused to concede the effort, writing: "it is my earnest desire and set purpose to return to my work in this country as I am never so happy as when fully engaged in the Missionary field."[3] While he never fulfilled that desire, dying only a few days after making landfall in England, he left behind a legacy of evangelical engagement for the next generation of delegates that emphasized linguistic scholarship, respect for Chinese literary and historical tradition, and daily interactions with Chinese of every class, as well as a substantial body of published writings of which *A Glance at the Interior of China* remains a little-known, but compelling, part. The first half of *A Glance*, a meticulous catalogue of Chinese daily practice arranged in categories including "Dress Requisite for the Journey," "On the Food of the Chinese, and their Manner of Eating It," and "Complexion to Be Attended To," forms a theoretical counterpoint to the second half, a travel narrative composed largely of transcribed journal entries that detail Medhurst's attempted visit to a school of Chinese reformers sympathetic to Christian doctrine. The two parts work together to detail how, in abstract generality and in experiential practicality, a trespassing Briton can safely see and be seen by a then almost entirely unfamiliar category: the Chinese of "the interior."

Yet, even as his volume seeks to create a specific and authoritative record of this new view of China, Medhurst is at the same time attempting to revise this vision. As a delegate of the LMS, Medhurst devotes such attention to the details of "passing" for Chinese because he hopes ultimately to make his manual obsolete.[4] The opening of China's interior to Western eyes and bodies would, Medhurst and the LMS hoped, result in a large-scale conversion of the Chinese people to Protestant Christianity and the free circulation of European Christians to all parts of the Chinese empire. As Medhurst writes in his 1838 survey, *China Its State and Prospects,* "This then is *the* field for missionary exertions; the sphere where the most influential societies should direct their chief efforts, for until some impression is made upon China, it will matter little what is achieved in other more confined and thinly peopled regions. . . . [U]ntil China is evangelized, the greatest half of our work remains to be begun."[5] In *A Glance at the Interior of China*, Medhurst gives a foundational Protestant account of the people and geography of China, which implicitly responds to and reshapes the tradition of writings on China by Catholics that had, up to this point, dominated European ideas of China's interior.[6] Later missionaries like Hudson Taylor, the leader of the China Inland Mission who adopted Chinese dress without attempting to pass as Chinese, would build on the emergent Protestant travel genre that Medhurst begins to develop here,[7] as would a range of other volumes detailing Protestant travels and travails among the Chinese.[8]

Because of the many disappointments that befell the journey, however — the leader of the school of reformers is ill and cannot meet with Medhurst, the members of the school decline to convert to Christianity, Medhurst's guide destroys all notes of the journey for fear they will be found and used as incriminating evidence — the text's impact is muted. The narrative mentions generally a plan for "paving the way for the introduction of the Gospel into central China,"[9] but glosses over the widespread resistance to Medhurst's proselytizing. (Even Medhurst's guide, despite his remarkable willingness to risk himself to help Medhurst, does not convert.) Also detracting from the text's influence is the lengthy gap between the completion of travel in 1845 and the publication of the travel narrative in 1850; by the time the text appeared, the restrictions on foreign movement that the guide was intended to circumvent were beginning to be informally lifted. The journey, and Medhurst's narrative of it, have largely been relegated to the status of historical curiosities, relics of the brief period between the Treaty of Nanking (1842) and the Treaty of Tientsin (1858) during which foreigners could not travel beyond a day's journey from the five treaty ports.[10]

Likewise Medhurst himself, though considered by contemporaries a significant figure in nineteenth-century Christian mission work, has fallen out of recent view. Contemporary studies that do include him have largely discussed his significant linguistic and literary contributions — he authored more than sixty works, including translations of the Christian Bible into Chinese and translations of Chinese literary classics into English[11] — and passed over the literary hybrid that is *A Glance at the Interior of China*.[12] Too secular and unstructured to qualify as an example of the personal "missiography"[13] narrative or to join the ranks of scholarly contemporary ethnographies, less popular than other narratives on traveling through China in racial disguise,[14] perhaps it is not surprising that this work has been relatively ignored.[15]  √ *See note — contradicts this*

# I

It is my contention, however, that this fairly unknown and unusual text opens up for us a number of important questions about our understanding of Victorian travelers in China. By virtue of what it is, a guide to adopting "the habits and the manners of the natives," the text must explicitly write out what it must be to see and be seen as Chinese. And in this act of making plain, the text highlights the assumptions and conventions by which China was seen and imagined by Victorian travelers and readers. Proleptic declarations of China's familiarity were a rhetorical commonplace throughout travel narratives of the nineteenth century: "the curtain which had been drawn around the celestial country for ages, has now been rent asunder; and instead of viewing an enchanted fairy land, we find, after all, that China is just like other countries," claims Robert Fortune, for example.[16] That China, to the British, never has been just like other countries probably needs no further explanation. What I do want to discuss further is the way that Fortune, and many others like him, framed the encounter with China in such single-mindedly √ visual terms, even as they pursued varied economic, political, scientific and commercial ends. The deficient language skill of many Victorian travelers, who could stare at but not converse with the Chinese they encountered, plays a practical part here, but a larger theoretical construct is at work as well. √

China, for the majority of nineteenth-century Britons, was more than a distant empire. It also represented a way of seeing and being seen that proposed a radically alternative visual aesthetic to the European tradition. Medhurst's text is worth rescuing from obscurity, because it offers an unusual negative definition of that visual aesthetic; rather than diagnosing the content of what the Chinese *did* see, Medhurst describes √ China and the Chinese in terms of what they (apparently) *did not* see, that is, Medhurst himself. The successful conclusion of both his journey and his text depends on his correct negotiation of the outer boundaries of Chinese visual capacity. In our attempts to √ reconstruct the basic activity of looking at China in the mid-nineteenth-century, then, this text is particularly rich source material. The narrative, full of inspections, looks, gazes, stares, peeps, as well as, of course, the "glance" of the title, offers us an opportunity to engage with the debate about nineteenth-century visuality in Victorian terms. Recent historically situated accounts of nineteenth-century visual practice have often used a technologically driven approach to describing how Victorians saw and were seen.[17] Yet studies of Victorians who traveled in racial disguise rarely overlap with studies of nineteenth-century visuality, despite the possibilities of such cross-pollination. Though Medhurst's one-sided text must inevitably fail in its attempt to show us how the Chinese themselves "really" saw, it does succeed in refining the particulars of the Victorian visuality in ways that studies of secular or domestic observers cannot.

Medhurst's attention to the nature of Chinese visual difference returns us to the inextricability of aesthetics from social, political, and commercial concerns. Because the purpose of his text makes Medhurst unusually precise in detailing the visual rhetoric that defined "Chinese" and "English" separation, we find direct evidence here of what is implicit elsewhere: that is, the complex and contested acts of division and exchange between the two empires. While scarcely a handful of Victorians were following Medhurst in adopting a complete Chinese *habitus*, millions were taking on some sign or symbol of China in their china cabinets, wardrobes, tea tables, and beyond. I argue that these acts must be read on a continuum — placing a piece of blue and white china upon the mantelpiece carried, in however small a way, the same mental accommodations to a uniquely foreign aesthetic as Medhurst's complicated self-transformation.[18] Both acts make meaning from a concurrent delineation and erasure of difference — the china plate is at once exotic and domestic, Medhurst's body is both English and Chinese.

It is this interplay between essentialism — the plate *is* from China, Medhurst *is* English — and subjectivity — the plate becomes a part of a British décor, Medhurst gets seen as an "ordinary" Chinese — that I argue warrants a reading of *A Glance at the Interior of China* as a passing narrative, despite its difference from classic nineteenth and twentieth-century American examples of the genre.[19] While such narratives root the practice specifically in slavery and post-slavery structures of black and white racial identity, recent scholarship suggests that thinking about such border crossing is useful in a far wider sense.[20] Passing, as we now understand it, details the practices of a subject, who, though "really" representing a group marked out or separated — by law, by gender, by race, by physical or social condition, or by some combination of those — from a group established as dominant by those same criteria, manages to "pass" (intentionally or unintentionally) as a part of the dominant group. The tricks of language necessary even to begin to define "passing" practice suggest what a complicated and contingent thing it must be. Even if we exclude the many and important instances of disabled, gendered, or gay and lesbian passing narratives, the concept of racial passing alone requires hard attention to just what it is we think race means to begin with. Our task becomes still more difficult when studying historical constructions of race in the missionary context. If passing, as a concept and as a practice, depends on an essentialist, visually defined idea of racial identity, as Walter Benn Michaels has argued, then it must be at odds with a notion of religious identity that depends on the possibility of conversion.[21] And yet these discrepancies and difficulties are productive rather than destabilizing, because they force us to consider Medhurst's engagement with Chinese minds *and* bodies. To Medhurst, understanding how the Chinese looked and how the Chinese thought was a linked endeavor, making his own adoption of a Chinese look contingent on his engagement with a Chinese way of thinking. To put it another way, Medhurst was not so much interested in disguise as in visual, and spiritual, translation.

Yet the false equivalency between these two kinds of translation deeply complicates Medhurst's project. Part of the reason *A Glance at the Interior* cannot succeed as either a wholly secular or a wholly evangelical text, I argue, is because of the conflict between secular and religious ideas about vision in the Chinese context.[22] While many contemporary writers understood China in terms of visual difference, Victorian Protestant missionaries engaged with the Chinese through the spiritual, internal, and *invisible* process of religious conversion. Medhurst's Christianizing project and his attempts to "pass" as Chinese while in pursuit of that project make uneasy bedfellows, however. And Medhurst was not alone in this difficulty. The Protestant missionaries of the mid-nineteenth-century, newly entered into China and focused on the challenge of mass conversion, were hard-pressed to reconcile traditional rhetorics of Chinese fixity, usually framed in visual terms, with a mutable definition of Chinese belief that would allow for the penetrating and widespread spiritual alteration they sought.

For this reason, I suggest, we must read narratives of Protestant missionary travel in China differently than we read narratives of other travelers. Missionaries, unlike merchants or scientific explorers, were not contented with the single revision from closed to open, unseen to seen, that the Opium Wars brought to China. A parallel rebirth from heathen to Christian was necessary as well. For Medhurst, as for other visitors to China, the condition of being Chinese determined a wide range of ontological capacities, from visual perception to historical self-consciousness to spatial awareness. But unlike other visitors, who noted these capacities and either celebrated them as part of an appealing Chinese exoticism or deplored them as a token of Chinese stagnancy, Medhurst sought to renovate the ontological condition of the Chinese entirely.[23] To be a true believer, in the LMS understanding, meant not only adding on a certain subset of beliefs and practices, but fundamentally reorganizing an entire state of being consistent with belief in the Christian God.

Reading Medhurst's submerged narrative of hoped-for religious conversion alongside the foregrounded account of racial conversion and disguise in *A Glance at the Interior of China*, then, shows us both the problems and the possibilities involved in attempting to write about the space of cultural encounter and exchange in China's interior between the Opium Wars. The key elements distinguishing Chinese from English were not the same for a missionary like Medhurst as they were for, say, a horticulturalist like Robert Fortune, even though each man passed through China's interior disguised as "a pretty fair Chinaman," as Fortune put it.[24] In the next part of this essay, I will focus on the ways that Medhurst's descriptions of Chinese ways of looking give us, if not an idea of what it meant to see as a Chinese, what it meant to Medhurst to seem to see as one. It is in this difference that Medhurst's text reveals the difficulty of recovering a historically situated notion of the observer.

## II

In the opening directives of *A Glance at the Interior,* Medhurst emphasizes that mastering the particulars of Chinese dress (to which he has devoted many incredibly detailed pages) is not enough. Something far more complicated must be mastered as well:

> The dress and cue [*sic*] having been assumed, it must not be supposed that the traveller has done everything to screen himself from observation: he must sustain the character of a Chinese, and this cannot be done, without putting on and wearing the different articles enumerated, precisely in the same way as is done by the natives. Every thing is stereotyped in China; there is a certain order in the putting on of apparel, which must not be departed from. Certain articles must be put on first, and certain ones afterwards; they must be buttoned and tied in a certain way, and one over the other, according to established form; or it will appear strange; and the least departure from common usage cannot fail to attract observation and lead to discovery. The manner of sitting, standing, or walking; the way of carrying the arms, and moving the legs, must all be strictly attended to, or some notice will be taken of the stranger. The individual must especially avoid walking fast, or taking long strides, or pushing past others in the street; but must move along quietly and placidly, as if uninterested in passing events.[25]

This remarkable piece of instruction suggests how wide-ranging a transformation Medhurst imagines. Passing for a Chinese requires attention not only to the materiality of clothing choice but to a network of behaviors bound up in the many meanings of the word "passing" itself. "Passing" has already come to describe both bodily motion and a certain kind of looking that is in fact a non-look, a "passing" glance, a refusal of scrutiny that grants mute acceptance to the visual subject who himself is then "passing." In the last part of this passage it also points to an idea of history, both personal and general, reliant on forward motion and constant progress as markers of time's movement. The supposed Chinese disinterest in "passing events" has been expanded on by many authors in many places, but its recurrence in this example returns me to my central contention. I argue that Medhurst's process of passing *for* Chinese must be read in the context of his passing *through* China. Both movements sought to convert the inhabitants and geography of China, which was for many readers an atemporal and exotic landscape, into a people and a space both accessible and familiar. In all the multiple implications of "passing" — in history, in mobility, in racial and national consciousness — meaning clusters around the primary notion of the Chinese eye as a perceptual organ quite unlike the British. Medhurst's narrative, before being able to write out a Christian vision of China, must first account for, and incorporate, the theoretical and practical effects of Chinese visuality.

Thus Medhurst's text is everywhere concerned with scenes of Chinese seeing, and with describing what the Chinese see in these scenes. In his formulation, vision is a contested practice, and the organ of the eye is the central field of conflict. He warns: "Should the eyes of the traveller be of a light colour, it would be better to conceal them by spectacles . . . The foreign traveller had better be particular in this matter, as the eyes are the first things that attract notice, and may be the most likely to lead to the discovery of his origin."[26] Given that for the foreign traveler the public sphere constitutes the allowable scope of experience, there is no respite from the effort of self-concealment. Even when taking refreshment at roadside tea-shops, he comments: "there are generally half a dozen or more travellers, whose observation it would be advisable for a foreigner to avoid, by sitting on one side, or in the more shaded and obscure part. . . ."[27] Yet, despite his precautions, Medhurst finds in his own travels that he frequently becomes a display site. When his bearers stop to eat, he complains, "I was obliged to sit in the most public place possible, with hundreds of people coming and going, to the gaze of all of whom I was exposed, for about an hour";[28] when he travels by passage boat, he records that "Here we had to sit in very close contiguity with all sorts of people, face to face, and eye to eye, so that if any discovery was to be made of the foreign extraction of any on board, that was the time to make it."[29]

As much as he is concerned with being looked at by the Chinese, however, Medhurst often seems incapable of understanding how they will look at him:

> I was surprised, and in other circumstances would have been somewhat chagrined, to see the little notice which the women and children took of me, whenever I met them; . . . This appeared the more strange to me, as I had been accustomed, as other foreigners are, when walking about in the garb of my country in Shang-hae, to be stared at and followed from place to place; but, being clad in Chinese costume, the people did not seem to imagine that there was anything peculiar about me, and passed me as they would another Chinaman, a class by no means rare in those regions.[30]

Physical encounters are even more unaccustomed: "It excited a little surprise . . . to see how unceremoniously the fellows pushed along . . . indeed one man made me get out of the pathway, and descend into the paddy-field, in order to make way for him. Having been accustomed to see the Chinamen turn out of the way for Europeans, and even jumping into ditches to let them pass, I was for the moment little prepared to be myself driven from the pathway in my turn; but when I recollected that I was then personifying a Chinese, I was rather gratified to think that I had succeeded so well, as to be treated like one of themselves."[31] Medhurst constantly oscillates between two understandings of Chinese vision — either dangerously discerning, or unimaginative and unobservant. Thus Medhurst's passing, described in *A Glance* as a constant series of lapses and betrayals, noticed and unnoticed, relies on a malleable conceit of native vision. To see as a Chinese — as Medhurst understands it — is a practice at best intermittent, obscured, and incomplete, not only because Medhurst's passing practice is hampered by his inexperience, but because he understands the ontological condition of Chineseness to be literally and metaphorically blind to its own coming salvation. The narrative rests on a series of contradictions: the Chinese cannot see their own condition clearly, and yet, to succeed in reaching these Chinese, Medhurst himself must submit to and mirror the same visual ineptitude, even as practical concerns, and narrative interest, are better served by visual acuity. The visual conditions of the pass thus create a double-bind that the narrative constantly struggles against.

That Medhurst is at least partially aware of this shows in his narrative's obsessive return to scenes of *near*-detection, moments when Medhurst's failure to conform visually, in his looking or in his looks, to Chinese standards, results in especially heightened scenes of scrutiny. The rhetorical consequence of these foregrounded scenes, however, is the linkage of Medhurst with the most peripheral members of Chinese society that he encounters — servants, children, beggars, and thieves. For while these are the categorical endpoint of the stereotypical Chinese eye, their very marginality increases, rather than decreases, their visual perspicacity, as with, for example, the number of "idle people" assembled outside Medhurst's lodging-house who are heard "remarking on [Medhurst's] appearance, as having something singular about it."[32] As Medhurst describes it, the scope of visual possibility constricts ever more narrowly around its economically and socially central figures, who barely bother to lift their eyes to register the passing scene. He explains: "In many parts of the country, indeed, the people seem never to have dreamt, that there are such things as foreigners, and would as soon think of seeing a ghost, as meeting with a barbarian."[33] But observers on the outskirts see more keenly. Of a "party of beggars" at a ferry crossing, he writes: "They spoke excellent Mandarin, appeared to be acquainted with every step of the road, and could, from the appearance of each individual, make a pretty shrewd guess, regarding the origin and profession of all whom they met."[34] The outsider status of these beggars means that the code of blindness which Medhurst both condemns and relies on cannot function as an effective restraint; Medhurst's only recourse is to "keep out of their way."[35]

The act of taking notice of these border figures is in itself a focusing of attention inappropriate in Medhurst's embodiment of a Chinese viewer. This is apparent in his warning to readers about the bandits that frequent inns and taverns: "A foreigner should, of course, avoid such . . . rascals . . . and, as they are not easily distinguishable from honest people, except by their debauched appearance and villainous looks, the greater necessity there is for circumspection."[36] Here the traveler, in order to pass successfully, must detect a "debauched appearance" while simultaneously remaining aloof and circumspect; the paradox demonstrates the self-canceling nature of the passing subject. Forced to see, and be seen, in stereoscopic fashion, the race-passer is aware of multiple subject positions without fully inhabiting any of them. The very self-conscious understanding of one's own looks demonstrates the value of analyzing these passing narratives: because such narratives can never naturalize vision or visual effect, entrenched cultural differences must be explicitly stated rather than left to be assumed.

For to gaze openly and single-mindedly would reveal Medhurst's status as an *interested* observer, and so mark him as essentially different from a populace distinguished for the British by their uniformity. Medhurst's guide reminds him, for example, never to ask questions about food placed before him, "because the simple circumstance of making enquiry would show that the traveller was not familiar with what he saw; and, to be unacquainted with what came upon the table every day, would

be a display of ignorance, that would be unpardonable even in a child."[37] This caution
to "avoid seeming surprised at anything" indeed applies to the journey in general, and
Medhurst concludes: "Those who travel in China, therefore, must abide strictly by the
advice given children at home, viz. to hear, and see, and say nothing."[38] At stake is not
only the right to make observations in general, but also the terms by which vision will
be defined and described in the interior of China. Medhurst, writing dismissively of
the "inquisitiveness" of the Chinese and their "unpleasant habit of asking a variety of
questions,"[39] echoes the complaint of countless travelers writing before and after his
narrative; yet Medhurst's passing makes the matter particularly complex. Given his
attempt to appear as a respectable stranger — perhaps as "some literary graduate . . .
proceeding to the provincial city to try for higher honors,"[40] as he suggests at one point
— he is bound by both the desire to observe his surroundings and his assumption that
respectable Chinese, as he defines them, take no interest in such observation. In the final
section of this essay, I will discuss the ways that Medhurst attempts to transform these
scenes of failed seeing into a narrative, and the ways that such transformation attempts
reveal the possibilities of representational practice in China.

## III

Though much of *A Glance at the Interior* is consumed with concealing any visual
activity, much of it of course is also taken up with relating the sights revealed along the
journey. To take one example:

> Our course was westerly, amongst ranges of hills, which, as soon as the sun
> was up, were gilded with his vernal rays. Thus illumined, the landscape
> displayed its varied beauties . . . The windings of the river, presenting
> constantly a new prospect, the balmy breezes . . . the warblings of the
> feathered songsters . . . all conspired to fill us with pleasing emotions, and to
> render this the most delightful part of the journey . . . The whole scene was
> such as a painter would have been glad to sketch, and I could not but regret
> my inability to secure a more durable impression of it, that I might gratify
> others by its representation.[41]

In this final section, I want to discuss further the transmission of Medhurst's impression
of the country and the transformation of vision into more durable forms by travelers in
China more generally. Medhurst's impulse to convert his general Chinese surroundings
into particular scenes which might be reproduced and circulated seems to understand
the value of Chinese landscape to be purely aesthetic. Yet the contents of *A Glance at
the Interior* demonstrate how intertwined Medhurst's vision of picturesque landscape
is with his vision of economically productive landscape. Medhurst's *Glance* at China,
like other mid-century narratives of its kind, therefore stands for both a new way of
representing China and of "securing" its representation. Visual practice like Medhurst's,
both surreptitious and bent on conversion, permanently altered the traveler's vocabulary
of scenes.

To get at the contrast I am proposing, compare the visual set-pieces in *A Glance* with this scene from Medhurst's 1838 *China Its State and Prospects*, written before beginning his permanent residence in Shanghai. He describes his view of the South China coastline:

> The prospect from these heights was delightful in the extreme; . . . the great temple . . . basked like a basilisk in the rays of the noon-day sun. All the aids that could be collected from nature and art, were there concentrated, to render the scene lovely and enchanting. But to the eye of the Christian philanthropist, it presented one melancholy picture of moral and spiritual death.[42]

This description depends on the binocular vision of the prospect view kept separate from the lived experience of Chinese vision itself. Though the passage insists on the difference between the landscape admirer who finds the temple "delightful in the extreme" and the "Christian philanthropist" who sees only "moral and spiritual death," the two views are identical in their spatial and temporal remove.

    Such physical and mental separation becomes impossible, however, when the viewing subject is traveling disguised as a Chinese. Sights and scenes are framed contingently and subjectively, and vision can be abruptly and drastically limited or expanded at will. Compare Medhurst's 1838 prospect view with this incident detailed in *A Glance at the Interior*. Caught unawares by an inquisitive stranger while visiting his guide's native home and village, Medhurst writes:

> I soon perceived that he was a fortune teller, who pretended to ascertain the future condition of individuals by aid of the examination of their physiognomy. I could see, after a while, that he was surveying mine; then as mine, under the circumstances, would not bear too close inspection, I got up and retired into the inner apartment. Soon after, my host entering was accosted by the Fortune Teller, who, referring to me, said . . . the countenance was not of the common order. This startled my host, who got rid of him as soon as possible, and from that time took care that the outer gate of the premises was carefully barred. Thus I was immured for some days, between the four walls of my host's premises. . . .[43]

Here Medhurst can no longer describe his vision of China from a distance, as in his 1838 work. Instead he is immobile and vulnerable, subject to the surprise inspection of passing fortune-tellers and the precautionary imprisonment of his Chinese host. Chinese eyes, not Medhurst's, set the terms and viewing conditions within which China can be perceived. Yet Medhurst immediately qualifies his confinement, concluding: "I was not entirely abridged of liberty, however, as I availed myself of a back door which remained open, to take frequent walks into the woods and fields, where I enjoyed the fresh air, and the surrounding scenery."[44] Like the other scenes of near-discovery I described in the previous section, this encounter also works on a meta-visual level. Medhurst's translation of the vast expanse of China's closed interior into a succession of representable scenes depends on Chinese misprision and British physical mobility and textual proliferation.

The fortune-teller, for Medhurst, is blind in two ways: both individually, by dint of his specious profession, and generally, by being one of many Chinese who cannot successfully pinpoint the root of Medhurst's difference. Yet, as is clear both in this passage and throughout the narrative, the Chinese are not nearly as imperceptive as Medhurst would like to suppose. Instead Medhurst's eventual visual triumph in China comes from his ability to give value to the products of his sight. With always at least a back-door liberty, Medhurst can, freely and constantly, claim his views of China's geography as foundational. "The surrounding scenery" gains meaning and representational worth because of its proximity to the author. In a text where the natives are consistently figured as unable or unwilling to perceive properly, Medhurst's writing does more than transcribe a visual record. It also seeks to establish his descriptive scene-making as both more conceptually sound and more materially enduring than that of previous observers, be they Chinese locals or Roman Catholic missionaries.

Visual value, then, expands beyond the aesthetic. Medhurst's close attention to technological detail in his survey of the "Silk and Green Tea Countries" of the title — he inserts a translated Chinese manual on silkworm cultivation and production into his narrative — suggests that his vision of the Chinese countryside owes as much to British commercial concerns as it does to spiritual questions. Medhurst's physical work of travel gets converted here into the reward of a visual aesthetic that is both picturesque and thoroughly marketable. This is reflected by a changed emphasis in his descriptive views. He writes:

> The road which wound amongst these hills was exceedingly romantic, presenting an ever-varying scene of peaks and ravines, rocks and trails in succession. At length . . . we began to descend into the level plains . . . [and] found the country gradually opening, presenting on all sides cultivated fields and smiling villages. One change struck us as new in this region, with respect to that tea-cultivation, viz. the entire occupancy of most of the small hills by the tea-shrub, which was here planted in beautiful rows; and, as it happened to be the spring season, when the cultivators, men, women, and children, were scattered over the plantations gathering leaves, the whole presented a very lively scene.[45]

Though the description begins again with the same "romantic" view that featured in *China Its State and Prospects*, the concluding contrast is very different. Medhurst does not insist on the idolatry and eternal damnation of the population he observes; rather, he portrays them as active laborers participating in an industry with global penetration. That the British were deeply interested in replicating this scene of tea cultivation in British colonial holdings in India or even, as some optimists suggested, in Great Britain itself, is not overtly a subject of Medhurst's discussion.[46] But his understanding of the connections between visual labor, physical labor, and commercial product comes through clearly. In dividing what he sees of China into representable scenes, Medhurst relies on a logic as much economic as aesthetic. Of another climb, he writes:

> It was with much difficulty that we toiled to the top of this mountain, but when once there, the labour was sufficiently compensated, by the glorious prospect which presented itself of the Fowleang district of Keangse [Jiangsu] province; as its extensive rice-fields, interspersed with tea-plantations, stretched themselves as far as the eye could reach, glowing with the reflection of the western sun.[47]

In Medhurst's conclusion, even his own body stands as a commodity which Chinese eyes cannot convert or resolve into correct definition. At the end of their journey, Medhurst and his guide must await the arrival of the custom-house officer to grant passage to their boat through a canal-gate. The scene is anticlimactic; despite his guide's terror of discovery, they are met by a "low underling" who gives only a cursory inspection of the boat's contents. Medhurst writes: "He asked what merchandize we had, and being informed we had nothing but a box of clothes, he required to see it; on its being placed before him, he opened the lid, and rummaged it to the bottom; finding nothing particular, he took a glance around the cabin, to see if he could spy any contraband goods on board, and not heeding the principal contraband article that sat in a Chinese garb before him, he passed out through the stern of the cabin and we saw him no more."[48] The passing out of the customs agent marks the conclusion of Medhurst's own passing; a page later, Medhurst records that he "arrived . . . before my own door; where . . . [I] quietly walked in, those who had accompanied me not knowing who I was, and those at home not dreaming of the direction in which I had travelled, or the way in which I had reached home, except insofar as I chose to inform them."[49] Medhurst's actual and narratorial acts of self-smuggling are highlighted by this strange reference to the unreliability of his own testimony and his doubled deception of both his Chinese bearers and his English friends.

I suggest that Medhurst's linkage of himself to a traded commodity, whose essence and origin is both contingent and intermittently hidden, foreshadows later connections while also positing subversive challenges to those connections. In figuratively adopting the disguise of a piece of contraband, Medhurst proposes a linkage between an opening of China to commercial interests, and the spiritual conversion of China that the LMS sought, founded on the circulation of the trade object. Here, perhaps, questions of Chinese visual difference get incorporated into an anticipatory account of the commodity's transformative power. If Medhurst's struggles with paradoxes of essentialism, racial and visual difference, and religious conversion have rendered his narrative misshapen and, ultimately, forgotten, his engagement with these paradoxes also gives us grounds to pick his narrative up again. As we seek to reconstruct how the Victorian traveler saw the China that surrounded him, accounts like Medhurst's give us testimony to the shifting perspectives such viewers embodied.

# 3

## Traveling Imperialism:
### Lord Elgin's Missions to China and the Limits
### of Victorian Liberalism

*Q. S. Tong*

> Expansion as a permanent and supreme aim of politics is the central political
> idea of imperialism. Since it implies neither temporary looting nor the lasting
> assimilation of conquest, it is an entirely new concept in the long history
> of political thought and action. The reason for this surprising originality
> — surprising because entirely new concepts are very rare in politics — is
> simply that this concept is not really political at all, but has its origin in
> the realm of business speculation, where expansion meant the permanent
> broadening of industrial production and economic transactions characteristic
> of the nineteenth century.
>
> Hannah Arendt, *The Origins of Totalitarianism*, 125

James Bruce (1811–63), the Eighth Earl of Elgin, was a traveler, an imperial traveler.
In his professional life over a period of about twenty years, he was sent by the British
Empire on numerous "difficult and unwelcome" errands and traveled to different parts
of the world as a colonial administrator — governor of Jamaica, governor-general of
Canada, plenipotentiary to China and Japan, and viceroy of India.[1] Elgin's name and
reputation, however, are mainly built on his two missions to China, in 1857 and 1859
respectively, during the *Arrow* war or the Second Opium War, as it is known in Chinese
historiography.[2] Towards the end of his life, he recalled, not without some feeling of
ambivalence, that he had "been for many years very much, perhaps too much of a
wanderer" (*L&J*, 390).

In the context of historical imperialism, especially in its more adventurist early
period, "travel" was not just a movement from one place to another, but a required
action for discovery, conquest, and acquisition. Imperialism is by definition necessarily
"traveling," given its innate desires to extend its domains of control and to expand
its spheres of influence, primarily, though not exclusively, for economic interests and

trading privileges. Indeed, how could one speak of imperialism without at the same time thinking of travel as an essential part of its practice, as a mode of imperial action, as an embodiment of its materiality, and as a manifestation of its mobile attempts to explore and conquer, to colonize and rule, territories, near or far, for its self-realization and self-fulfillment? Empire has to be mobile, restless, adventurist, and aggressive; it does not know where or when to stop until it is forced to or is no longer able to move. J. R. Seeley, probably the most influential nationalistic historian of the British Empire, tells us that the history of Britain in the eighteenth century was written and enacted *outside* its boundaries, in America and in Asia;[3] in the nineteenth century, the British Empire merely repeated, though on an enlarged scale, this history of territorial and commercial expansionism. In that sense, the history of the British Empire is collectively written by the imperial travelers like Elgin, who, by the act of "traveling," turned England into Britain, and Britain into Great Britain, which was hoped to become "Greater Britain." Elgin's missions to China are metonymic of a traveling imperialism, of a collective imperial movement, driven and defined by the need to materialize the empire's vision of itself. No doubt, Elgin shared, endorsed and contributed to that vision.

# I

The Second Opium War evidences, more manifestly than the First Opium War (1839–42), the brutality and barbarity of British imperialism. It was a bloody war without justification, a war that started with a relatively slight dispute over the local Chinese government's decision to seize and confiscate the pirate lorcha *Arrow*. Even though its register with the colonial administration of Hong Kong had expired and the crew arrested were all Chinese, its seizure was nevertheless determined as a violation of British sovereignty and an insult to the empire's honor.[4] John Bowring, the governor of Hong Kong at the time, demanded compensation and an official apology from the Imperial Commissioner Yeh in Guangzhou and having received neither, insisted that the military option be taken and British troops be dispatched to punish the Chinese.

An ardent advocate of free trade and, as Marx called him, "a pet disciple" of the great patriarch of utilitarianism Jeremy Bentham,[5] Bowring had already made a name for himself in the public life of Britain, as a philosophic radical, a linguist, and a prominent traveler before he was appointed in 1854 as plenipotentiary to China and governor of Hong Kong.[6] Therefore, unlike other Hong Kong governors before or after him who achieved glory and fame in this distant land but remained obscure and marginal at home, Bowring was deeply involved in mainstream domestic politics and played an important role in Britain's public and intellectual life in much of the first half of the nineteenth century. He was, for example, the political editor of the influential publication *Westminster Review* and a driving force behind the Anti-Corn Law movement. Bowring's commitment to Benthamite utilitarianism and free trade shaped his understanding of international relations and determined his practice of colonial policy in Hong Kong. As governor of Hong Kong, he was in a unique position to propagate and spread what he believed to be the liberal principle of free trade in Asia. But the idea of free trade, when brought to the East, would seem to require extra efforts to put it into practice. The Imperial Commissioner Yeh refused to meet and discuss with him trade and other issues; Bowring's pride was hurt. Frustrated by Yeh's passivity and lack of interest in what he had in mind, Bowring became increasingly impatient and belligerent. In a letter to Lord Clarendon, the foreign secretary at the time, he wrote:

> I am convinced there is no course so safe nor so wise as to demand an official personal and becoming reception at his [Yeh's] Yamun within the city for the purpose of discussing face to face the grievance of which we have to complain. The demand for such a reception must be made in the presence of ships of war which shall be instructed to accompany and protect the envoy. . . . I do not believe access would finally be denied — though a show of resistance there would undoubtedly be. Such a measure would exhaust our efforts with the Imperial Commissioner . . . no doubt this would be excellent groundwork for a movement upon Peking. . . .[7]

Bowring must have been delighted with the opportunity the *Arrow* incident afforded; he seized upon it and readily escalated it into a full-scale war against China which lasted for two years. Bowring's desire to be formally received in the city of Guangzhou by his Chinese counterpart, with all the dignity and respect appropriate for a man of his status, sent him into the imperial heart of darkness.

That Bowring was vain and morally flawed was the opinion of many. In the House of Lords, Lord Derby, for example, was convinced that Bowring's "monomania" to be received at Yeh's *yamun* (*yamen*) was the only real reason for his recommendation that Britain should wage another war with China.[8] Critics of Bowring in both Houses including his friend Richard Cobden created a political storm, and Cobden's motion in the House of Commons in February 1857 brought down Palmerston, who, however, was re-elected after a nationalistic election campaign. A disciple of Adam Smith, Palmerston, like Bowring, was committed to free trade.[9] His triumphant return to power placed Britain on a path of hostility against China.[10] Elgin was thus called upon, and he was sent to China, according to Harriet Martineau, to "try what could be done to repair or to turn to the best account, the mischiefs done by Sir John Bowring's course, and by the patronage of it at home, in the face of the moral reprobation of the people at large."[11] Elgin traveled to China, not once, but twice. The objectives of his first mission were not completely fulfilled, and he accepted the task to travel to China for the second time in 1859, against his wish but with the conviction that it was his duty to guide "the Chinese situation out of brutalities and European exploitations into some future worthy of civilized, Christian virtue."[12]

## II

Of his various imperial errands including his two missions to China Elgin kept a record. His family letters and private journals were collected and published only a decade after the completion of his China missions in 1872. Whether this collection of Elgin's letters and journals should be considered an example of travel writing is not my concern here;[13] what they reveal is a man whose natural sense of humanity formed a striking contrast to many of those colonial merchants and administrators such as Bowring who rejoiced over the arrival of the British forces and imminent assault on Guangzhou. As manifested in these journals and correspondences, Elgin was deeply distressed, depressed and even saddened by the task he was about to undertake in the name of the British Empire.

At the preparatory stage of the military action, due to his intervention in the Sepoy Rebellion (also known as "Indian Mutiny"), Elgin himself was left with less than sufficient force to launch a full-scale assault on Guangzhou. Although he showed no hesitation in sending his troops to India and crushing the rebellion, Elgin was reluctant to execute the job awaiting him in Hong Kong. He was not so worried about the possible further delay in launching the military attack or whether he would succeed in the task assigned to him by the empire. "My greatest difficulty," he wrote, "arises from my fear that we shall be led to attack Canton before we have all our force, and led therefore to destroy, if there is any resistance, both life and property to a greater extent than would otherwise be necessary" (*L&J*, 210).

On December 22, 1858, just six days before the assault began, Elgin, accompanied by Commodore Elliot, inspected the deployment of the British forces in a gunboat. They went so near the city of Guangzhou that they were within "pistol-shot" of it. Seeing the British men-of-war lining up in front of the city, Elgin was seized by a powerful feeling of shame. In a letter to his wife, he wrote,

> I never felt so ashamed of myself in my life, and Elliot remarked that the trip seemed to have made me sad. There we were, accumulating the means of destruction under the very eyes, and within the reach, of a population of about 1,000,000 people, against whom these means of destruction were to be employed. "Yes," I said to Elliot, "I am sad, because when I look at that town, I feel that I am earning for myself a place in the Litany, immediately after 'plague, pestilence, and famine.' " (*L&J*, 212)

In front of him was a people and a land that did not seem to be so aggressive and insolent, and yet it was his task to organize and launch a military attack upon them. He felt indignant and resented those who dragged him into a war he did not want to fight. Cruising along the Canton River, and in an untypical moment of poetic expression, Elgin recorded what he saw with a pair of "tourist's" eyes:

> The weather is charming; the thermometer about 60° in the shade in the morning; the sun powerful, and the atmosphere beautifully clear. When we steamed up to Canton, and saw the rich alluvial banks covered with the luxuriant evidences of unrivalled industry and fertility combined; beyond them, barren uplands, sprinkled with a soil of a reddish tint, which gave them the appearance of heather slopes in the Highlands; and beyond these again, the white cloud mountain range, standing out bold and blue in the clear sunshine, — I thought bitterly of those who, for the most selfish objects, are trampling under foot this ancient civilization. (*L&J*, 212–3)

Who were those people eager to see this war go ahead for their own "selfish" purposes? Belligerent colonial traders and administrators including, no doubt, Bowring, who had a vested interest in this military action for opening the Chinese markets. On board a ship to China in his second mission, Elgin described to his wife in a letter what some British merchants expected of his mission to China: "The tone of two or three men connected with mercantile houses in China whom I find on board is all for blood and massacre on a great scale" (*L&J*, 325).

The kind of savagery and hatred Elgin found in his fellow countrymen contradicted his natural instinct for justice and equality. He was depressed as well as embarrassed. Knowing fully that these colonial administrators, functionaries, and traders in the East were empowered, supported, and encouraged by the British Empire which brought them to this part of the world in the first instance, Elgin started to question, though not openly as Richard Cobden did in the House of Commons, the moral foundations of his government's policy towards the East. While Bowring and Palmerston did not hesitate to exploit the opportunity the *Arrow* incident offered, for many including Lord Elgin it was scandalous and a major embarrassment to Britain supposed to be a civilized nation. Before the prepared full-scale assault on Guangzhou was launched, Elgin was reluctant even to use the *Arrow* incident as an excuse in his ultimatum to the Imperial Commissioner Yeh: "I have hardly alluded in my ultimatum to that wretched question of the 'Arrow,' which is a scandal to us, and is so considered, I have reason to know, by all except the few who are personally compromised" (*L&J*, 209).

In his second mission to China, traveling across the Indian Ocean, he found himself time for reading and musing. Among his readings, which included Tennyson's poetry, worth mentioning in particular is William Howard Russell's *My Indian Mutiny Diary*. He recommended it to his wife. "It has made me very sad," he wrote to her, "but it only confirms what I believed before respecting the scandalous treatment which the natives receive at our hands in India" (*L&J*, 325). Now on his way to China for the second time, imagining what awaited him, Elgin could not but feel depressed by the prospect of the war and its consequences: "Can I do something to prevent England from calling down on herself God's curse for brutalities committed on another feeble Oriental race? Or are all my exertions to result only in the extension of the area over which Englishmen are to exhibit how hollow and superficial are both their civilisation and their Christianity?" (*L&J*, 325) These private feelings could only be unconcealed before his wife. But Elgin's reservations about the British government's colonial policy, his bitter resentment towards those few who were "personally compromised" and "selfish," and his adoption of a restrained approach to "the Chinese problem" evidenced, for some, only his mental feebleness and his inability to safeguard the cause of the empire.[14]

# III

As a member of the British imperial elite, Elgin's professional trajectory was rather typical of British aristocrats in the nineteenth century. Born into one of the two most prominent Scottish aristocratic families,[15] he was educated at Eton and Oxford. It is said that he "had none of the frailties of youth, and, though very capable of enjoying its diversions, life with him from a very early date was 'sicklied o'er with the pale cast of thought.' "[16] In his years at Oxford, he became known as an outstanding public speaker and developed an intellectual receptivity to ideas and a strong interest in the political theories of Plato, Milton and Coleridge. He thoroughly "mastered" Coleridge's philosophy and was profoundly influenced by Milton's advocacy of free speech and equality. Milton's "soul-stirring treatises" "formed his constant companions wherever he traveled, and there are many occasions in which their influence may be traced on his thought and language." It was from Elgin that his friend Gladstone, later the Liberal prime minister of Britain, first learned that "Milton had written any prose" and Gladstone "remember[ed] his speaking of Milton's prose works with great fervour when they were at Eton together."[17]

Elgin considered himself to be a "Conservative," but he was a conservative "not upon principles of exclusionism — not from narrowness of view, or illiberality of sentiment." He was a conservative because, he said, "I believe that our admirable Constitution . . . proclaims between men of all classes and degrees in the body politic a sacred bond of brotherhood in the recognition of a common warfare here, and a common hope hereafter." Elgin's conservatism carries within itself a liberalism. He further explained what sort of conservative he was:

> I am a conservative because I believe that the institutions of our country religious as well as civil are wisely adopted when duly and faithfully administered to promote not the interest of any class or classes exclusively, but the happiness and welfare of the great body of the people, and because I feel that on the maintenance of these institutions not only the economic prosperity of England, but what is yet more important the virtues that distinguish and adorn the English character, under God, mainly depend.[18]

Elgin's consciousness of his political positioning is visibly informed and influenced by a liberal Benthamite utilitarianism, in particular by its principle of greatest happiness.

Elgin's years at Eton and Oxford "laid the foundations . . . of his own political sobriety, his liberal-conservatism, and his appreciation of sound and able administrative methods."[19] And it is perhaps his early moral and political formations that kept his humanity throughout his later career as a colonial administrator. He has been generally considered to be "one of those earlier sane imperialists."[20] It should be noted, however, that his sanity is defined and sustained not just by his liberal moral sentiments but also by his commitment to the imperial cause of Britain. He claimed that "[n]o human power shall induce me to accept the office of oppressor of the feeble" (*L&J*, 220), but his vision of universal humanity is intertwined with his vision of the future of the empire. As shown in his practice during his China missions, his moral sympathy with the weak and his distaste for the insolence and belligerence of his fellow countrymen were ultimately defined by his understanding that it would be best for the future of the empire to adopt a more humane policy towards its colonies and other nations subject to its imperial power including China.

Indeed, Elgin never lost sight of the most important task for a colonial administrator and attempted to make his office "the link which connects the mother country and the colony" and "his influence the means by which harmony of action between the local and imperial authorities may be preserved."[21] Military force could conquer, but could not rule. Elgin knew exactly what would be needed after the use of force: "WHEN FORCE AND DIPLOMACY SHALL HAVE DONE ALL THAT THEY CAN LEGITIMATELY EFFECT, THE WORK WHICH HAS TO BE ACCOMPLISHED IN CHINA WILL BE BUT AT ITS COMMENCEMENT."[22] He came to China with an interest in "extending the area of Christian civilization and *multiplying those commercialities which are designed to bind the East and West in the bonds of mutual advantage.*"[23] Therefore, Elgin urged all the colonial agents and functionaries — merchants, administrators, and even missionaries — to keep close to their heart the larger interests of the British Empire and to behave accordingly. During his first mission to China, on his way to Japan, Elgin stopped by Shanghai where his brother Frederick Bruce was posted as British Representative in China. He used the opportunity to "instruct the British merchants of Shanghai on their role in China" and to remind them of the importance to keep in mind the empire's long-term interests in this part of the world: "We have . . . incurred very weighty responsibilities. Uninvited, and by means not always gentlest, we have broken down the barriers behind which these ancient nations sought to conceal from the world without the mysteries, perhaps, also, in the case of China at least, the rags and rottenness of their waning civilizations."[24]

Elgin's early education implanted in him such ideas as universal equality and liberty that had already been established as a progressive ideology as part of Europe's ethical and political modernity. But within the context of British imperialism, those ideas would have to be limited to the sphere of personal belief when they were in conflict with the interests of the empire. Despite his reluctance to execute what he was sent to do in China, Elgin admitted: "it was impossible for me to do otherwise than as I have done" (*L&J*, 212). He understood his China missions not just as military operations but also as a beginning to find a political and ethical solution to the Chinese problem. As mentioned above, he accepted the task to travel to China in the hope that the practice of European brutalities and exploitations might be replaced by the effort to promote Christianity and a Western value system more generally in China.

But Elgin's missions to China led to devastating consequences, especially his second mission that concluded with the burning of the imperial palace Yuan Ming Yuan in Beijing, an atrocity about which Elgin and most of the liberal thinkers at the time kept silent. Did it ever occur to Elgin, one wonders, that he, too, was "personally compromised" in authorizing the destruction of the palace considered to be the most beautiful garden in the world? This act of barbarity placed him side by side with his father, the Seventh Earl of Elgin, who stole the sculptures from the Parthenon on the Acropolis in Athens half a century earlier. The English public could not have missed the similarities between the two; what was taken from Yuan Ming Yuan was presented as "the New Elgin Marbles" in a cartoon published in *Punch* (see Plate 3). The Elgin Marbles created, for John Keats in particular, a moment of the romantic sublime, but the elder Elgin was more likely to be fixed on "the pedestal of scorn" by Byron.[25] Although this passage from the sublime to the ridiculous that characterizes his father's life is not to be found in the younger Elgin, he suffered from a more severe moral schizophrenia that directs our attention to the complicity between imperialism and liberalism in Britain.

In a recent article on Lord Elgin in China, John Newsinger asks: "How did Elgin sustain the lifelong contradiction — in many ways so emblematic of a liberal England — that left him lamenting in private actions which he relentlessly pursued in public, while simultaneously bemoaning the character of those who would benefit from his deeds?" And Newsinger's answer is: "it was self-interest," or at least "partly."[26] Reductive as it is to attribute this contradiction of Elgin's to his personal interests, the question Newsinger raised here is nevertheless an important one, given in particular that it is posited in relation to a similar contradiction England itself experienced in much of the nineteenth century. How could a liberal England co-exist with an imperial and colonial Britain? The temporal overlapping between the heyday of British imperialism and English liberalism at its most influential in the mid-nineteenth century cannot be thought a mere historical coincidence.

## IV

Admittedly, Elgin and Bowring cherished liberal ideas, and perhaps more than Elgin, Bowring was a visible liberal, not least because of his intimate association with the circle of philosophic radicals in London. What has brought them together in this essay is not just the context of the Second Opium War, in which they each played an important role in their own ways for the same imperial cause. Although they came through different political genealogies and they might dislike each other for reasons more personal than political, a shared set of values and beliefs enabled them to meet in Hong Kong for the same imperial project they worked for with commitment and dedication. They both were strong supporters of the principle of free trade, which, no doubt, was a form of liberalism in the domain of economic production. Before his career turned to colonial administration, during his short service in the House of Commons, in a speech considered to represent "enlarged and liberal commercial views," Elgin said: "I have always been an advocate of the principles of free trade, as those doctrines were propounded by Mr. Huskisson."[27]

For Bowring, free trade is the only norm governing international relations; indeed, more than an economic principle, it is God's will:

> Free-trade represents the pacific principle, not inert and slumbering, but operating in its full and vigorous energy. It breaks through the narrow and selfish circle to which a miscalled patriotism, and an egotistical nationality would confine the social affections. It is a practical recognition of that great and elevating declaration, that "God," the common, the universal Father — "God," the omnipotent, the omnipresent Creator "hath made of one blood"; that he wrought with the same materials — that he regards with the same affection — that he disciplines with the same tenderness, and will lead to

the same high destinies — "all" — all, without any reservation or exception
— "*all* the nations of the earth."

The principle of free trade, if universally practiced, was the force to promote and keep international peace. Bowring continues:

> Every vessel that quits our shores, in the pursuit of honest and honourable traffic, is a missionary of good; every article of manufacture which, by its cheapness or its excellence, recommends itself to the approval of a purchaser, conveys a moral lesson; every act of barter, by which enjoyment is conferred, or inconvenience provided against, or benefits in any shape rendered to the contracting parties, is a link added to the great chain of brotherhood which ought to encircle the world.[28]

It is only ironical that Bowring, a member of the Peace Society who advocated the principle of free trade as a regulatory force to keep a peaceful international order, should have become a warmonger and played a major role in bringing about an imperialist war against China.

Free trade as an idea and practice occupies a central place on the agenda of the British Empire and indeed, as some have argued, constitutes an important origin of modern imperialism.[29] In its historical context, free trade, behind its liberal façade, desires unhampered access to even the remotest markets in the world and extends the empire's space for acquisition of wealth and resources beyond its boundaries. Like imperialism, the principle of free trade has to travel to every corner of the world, or it would not be what it is supposed to be in theory or in practice. Rather than promoting and protecting international peace, free trade, as it was practiced in the mid-nineteenth century, constituted a major origin of international conflicts, precisely because it required promotion and protection by means of military force for its own operation. War and trade were inseparable. Seeley knew well the dialectic between them: "Commerce in itself may favour peace, but when commerce is artificially shut out by a decree of Government from some promising territory, then commerce just as naturally favours war. We know this by our own recent experience with China." And more blatantly, he explains the necessity of force in promoting and fostering trade:

> Now whatever may be the natural opposition between the spirit of trade and the spirit of war, trade pursued in this method is almost identical with war and can hardly fail to lead to war. *What is conquest but appropriation of territory?* . . . commerce and war were inseparably entangled together, so that commerce led to war and war fostered commerce.

The productivity of war, however, does not lie just in its protective function in carrying on unbalanced trade; "to England the war is throughout an industry, a way to wealth, the most thriving business, the most profitable investment of the time. . . . By conquest she made for herself an Empire and the Empire made her rich."[30]

For Richard Cobden, who lost his seat in parliament due to his objection to the government's decision to go to war for a second time with China, free trade was a political and ethical issue. Probably the most severe critic of the British Empire in his time, Cobden defended what he understood as the true principle of free trade that must be practiced without military intervention.[31] The Second Opium War ended the friendship between Bowring and Cobden, who once fought together in the Anti-Corn Law movement. In a letter to Bowring dated August 28, 1859, Cobden wrote:

> It was honest though painful in us not to resume our old terms on meeting at the Athenaeum after all that had occurred. But it will give me great pleasure to find on a personal explanation that I have been in any way mistaken in my judgments of what took place under your auspices at Hong Kong. It would be affectation if I were to attempt to disguise my opinion that your course was ill advised & very much at variance with the principles which we had long cherished in common, & on which indeed our mutual friendship was founded.[32]

Bowring seemed to have always stood on the liberal side in domestic politics, but as soon as he entered the sphere of colonial operation, as soon as he attempted to put his liberalism into practice in a place far from home, that liberalism started to contradict itself. The end of a twenty-year-long friendship between Cobden and Bowring, which was built on a common liberal cause in domestic politics, is already a critical comment on Victorian liberalism more generally. Bowring might have betrayed his liberal principles, but in the 1880s, the non-interventionist, non-expansionist, and pacifist position that Cobden advocated was to be replaced, within the Liberal Party, by "Liberal Imperialism — also known as New Liberalism — which sneered at the Radicals as 'Little Englanders' and regarded their pacifism as naïve in a world where Germany and Russia had emerged as aggressive new powers."[33]

The two Sino-British wars took place in the mid-nineteenth century, at a time when the British Empire was at its most aggressive and English liberalism at its most formative and influential. John Stuart Mill's *On Liberty* was published in 1859, right in the middle of the Second Opium War. The publication of *On Liberty* was a significant moment in Mill's intellectual trajectory as it was intended to instill some human warmth into the bloodlessness of utilitarianism. But in no sense is Mill's liberalism an uncompromised defense of individualism in society, much less so when it comes to the freedom and sovereignty of a nation or a state. For Mill as well as for other liberal thinkers at the time, the most important principle for a well-ordered society was the constitution of a system of values that would perform a function similar to, if not the same as, Christianity in regulating that society. The practice of liberalism was conceived as a political and ethical basis on which to build an ordered society. Maurice Cowling's argument that Mill's liberalism is put forward as a form of religion — "a religion of humanity" — is made on the basis of a different political and ideological commitment — his intellectual Toryism,[34] but Mill's faith in the liberal principles as universally applicable provided support and justification for the cause of the empire.[35] His mentor and the great patriarch of utilitarianism, Jeremy Bentham, who had been advocating and promoting the "liberal principles" of utilitarianism for much of the first half of the nineteenth century, occupies an important place in the history of the British Empire. His direct contribution to the building of the British Empire, in Australia, North America and India, is considerable. "It is hardly too much to say," Ogden asserts, "that but for [Bentham's] influence all the reddest patches on the Map would long ago have gone as pale a pink as those of the United States."[36] Witnessing the empire's spectacular ascendancy, Bentham and his disciples were largely uncritical of or remained silent about its operations. Active as they were in their attempts to reform British society for the creation of a more liberal and fair community in which the principle of greatest happiness could be constituted in practice, "[c]olonization," as Elie Halévy asserts, "is a fact before which their logic capitulated."[37]

Liberalism, just like the empire itself, must travel afar to validate, legitimate and prove itself. Its internal compulsion to expand, extend, and enlarge its presence and influence in all parts of the world is generated by the conviction of its universality, as imperialist expansionism is driven by its innate anxiety over the limits of its growth. The complicity between liberalism and imperialism must be considered and examined as an aspect of liberalism's internal contradiction and in terms of its totalitarian and authoritarian proclivity, which is manifested in and evidenced by its unquestioned doctrines that attempt to impose uniformity on spatial diversities. Imperial claustrophobia — its constant fear of being unable to reach a larger space and of getting stuck where it has been — is a primal force of traveling imperialism. Imperial travel is then symptomatic of territorial and national claustrophobia created by both a desire to expand its space of existence and a fear of losing what is in its possession. In no radical way, therefore, does Victorian liberalism stand in contradiction to the British Empire. While it is for the good of democratic development within Britain, the extension of its application beyond its spatial-temporal conditions would have to be delivered by the gunboat and constituted under the force and authority of the sword. In its expansion, liberalism has already set its own limits.

At the time when most liberal thinkers in Britain accepted the universality of capitalistic modernity in its various forms — whether it is Bowring's idea of free trade, Bentham's principle of utility, or Mill's theory of liberalism, Marx and Engels presented a strikingly different picture of what the globalizing forces of capitalism would mean for humanity. In a splendid passage of *The Communist Manifesto*, they wrote:

> [The bourgeoisie] has resolved personal worth into exchange value, and in place of the numberless indefeasible chartered freedoms, has set up that single, unconscionable freedom — Free Trade.... [F]or exploitation, veiled by religious and political illusions, it has substituted naked, shameless, direct, brutal exploitation.... All that is solid melts into air, all that is holy is profaned, and man is at last compelled to face with his sober senses, his real conditions of life, and his relations with his kind. The need of a constantly expanding market for its products chases the bourgeoisie over the whole surface of the globe. It must nestle everywhere, settle everywhere, establish

UNIVERSITY OF WINCHESTER
LIBRARY

connections everywhere. The bourgeoisie has through its exploitation of the world market given a cosmopolitan character to production and consumption in every country …. It compels all nations, on pain of extinction, to adopt the bourgeois mode of production; it compels them to introduce what it calls civilisation into their midst, i.e., to become bourgeois themselves. In one word, *it creates a world after its own image.*[38]

*The Communist Manifesto,* published in 1848, about ten years before the publication of *On Liberty,* predicted what the Victorian liberal thinkers failed or chose not to see about the expansionist policy and practice of the British Empire.

## V

Elgin's China missions elevated him to the level of a social and political celebrity. He was praised in both Houses of Parliament by those who denounced John Bowring for the conflict with China, such as Lord Derby and Grey. More honors followed: he was invited by Palmerston in 1859 to join the cabinet, "feted at the Mansion House and made a freeman of the City of London," and elected as Lord Rector at the University of Glasgow.[39] The public celebration of his victories must be understood in its context as a nationalistic endorsement of the empire's overseas operations; but Elgin knew too well that it would not last long and understood what he wanted after his twenty-year service for the empire in various parts of the world. In a speech at an assemblage of his old friends and neighbors at his hometown Dunfermline, Elgin expressed a profound desire not to travel any more and to spend the rest of his life at home:

> I have been for many years very much, perhaps too much of a wanderer, and it has been my fortune to receive from our countrymen established in different parts of the world tokens of their regard and consideration. But allow me to say that among all these tokens, those most grateful and agreeable to me are those which I receive from friends and neighbours at home. And, perhaps, I appreciate these tokens the more highly, because I am conscious that the very fact of my having been so much of a wanderer, had prevented me from acquiring some of those titles to their personal regard which I might have hoped to establish if I had been constantly resident among them. (*L&J,* 390–1)

But Elgin's wish to stay home could not be fulfilled. In 1862, less than two years after his triumphant return from China, he was again dispatched, this time to India, to succeed his friend Canning as Viceroy. This was to be his last imperial journey, a journey from which he would never be able to return home. Elgin died in India the following year; his burial in the Himalayas completes his career as a professional "wanderer."

Elgin was one of those men whose destiny was to be "citizens of the empire" without any "abiding home in the lands which they govern," and whose life was defined by "a kind of eternal homesickness for a country which exists only in their dreams and through their services." While they enjoyed almost sovereign authority in the land they governed, they had "little share in the social distinctions of the centre" back at home.[40] Elgin's "best memorial," we are told, "is the young Canadian nation."[41] Alongside this memorial, however, are the ruins of Yuan Ming Yuan in Beijing, which, like the fragmented grandeur of the Elgin marbles in the British Museum, will continue to tell a different story about the family history of the Elgins, which contributes to and is shaped by the history of British imperialism.

# 4

# Mirror Images:

## John Thomson's Photographs of East Asia

*Thomas Prasch*

## Introduction

A revealing verbal slip occurs in the preface to John Thomson's *Straits of Malacca, Indo-China, and China* (1875), his summary of ten years' travel with camera in East Asia. "It has been my care," Thomson writes, "so to hold the mirror up to his [the reader's] gaze, that it may present to him, if not always an agreeable, yet at least a faithful, impression of China and its inhabitants."[1] If what Thomson held up is a mirror, however, the reader would see himself, not the Chinese.

Thomson spoke more accurately than he intended. He shared with most of his contemporaries a firm belief in the straightforward realism of the photographic image. "The faithfulness of such pictures," he claimed, "affords the nearest approach that can be made towards placing the reader actually before the scene which is represented."[2] Thomson's photographic practice, however, was far from neutral, encoding Western assumptions about hierarchies of race and civilization. His central project was to capture "characteristic scenes and types."[3] This concern with "types" is reflected in the photographs themselves — in Thomson's selection of images and in his compositional techniques. The supporting texts reinforce the message by underlining Thomson's very Victorian English beliefs about race and race mixture, class, progress, and civilization. The mirroring of England in the East is further underscored by both overt and indirect comparisons between China and England, and especially between the lower classes of both nations.

Thomson's project reveals the ways in which Victorian photography was employed to define, delimit, and categorize groups at the margins of nineteenth-century culture. Victorian photographers imposed their own categories and hierarchies on marginal groups (whether imperial subjects or the domestic poor), using photography to present these classifications to Victorian readers as "natural." The messages about social and racial hierarchies were reinforced within the photographs themselves by rules of composition borrowed from more traditional arts (especially painting), and further underlined by supporting texts. The "natural" status of these typologies further depended on widely accepted premises about the objective, merely transcriptive character of the photographic image — what led Henry Fox Talbot to call photography "the pencil of nature" — that obscured the mediating role of the photographer in selecting, posing, and composing his subjects.

## The Image of Empire

Born and bred in Edinburgh (where he completed his education at the University of Edinburgh), Thomson traveled to Asia briefly in 1861, but set out for a more sustained period of travel and residence there in 1862, at the age of 25. Stephen White has usefully traced the course of Thomson's travels. Setting up a studio first in Penang, where he remained for ten months, he then moved to Singapore, where his brother already worked as a ship chandler; the two briefly established a photographic business together there. Thomson journeyed to Ceylon and India in 1864, to Siam in 1865–66, and to Cambodia in 1866. After a short return to Britain, where he shared his photographs and observations of Cambodia and Siam, he returned to the East, settling in Hong Kong in 1868 after visits to Singapore and Vietnam.

Aside from studio photographic work, Thomson began to find other outlets for his photography, including appearances in *China Magazine* in 1868, and published albums of the Taiping Rebellion (during which he was embedded with Lieutenant-Colonel C. G. Gordon's troops) in 1868 and of the visit of the Duke of Edinburgh to Hong Kong in 1869. In the following years, he traveled extensively through China, assembling the photographic images that would provide the material for his *Illustrations of China and Its People* (1873–74).[4] In the introduction to those volumes, Thomson wrote of his Chinese travels that "my journeys . . . extended over a distance, estimated roughly, of between 4,000 and 5,000 miles,"[5] including not only major northern cities like Beijing, Shanghai, and Nanjing, but also trips up the rivers like the Yangtze, Pearl, and Min. Returning to Britain in 1872, Thomson continued to publish photographs and travel writing about his decade in East Asia through 1876. In the course of that decade's travel, Thomson's distinctive photographic techniques were honed.

The implications of Thomson's practices are particularly evident in his East Asian work, where he explicitly links his quest for a comprehensive photographic portfolio to the extension of scientific knowledge and of Western commerce and control.[6] His account of the spread of empire is glowing: "At last the light of civilisation seems indeed to have dawned in the distant East; with its early rays gilding the little island-kingdom of Japan, and already penetrating to the edges of the great Chinese continent, where the gloom of ages still broods over the cities, a dark cloud that lifts but slowly, and yields unwillingly to the daylight that now floods the shore."[7] The imagery of light and darkness not only reiterates a cliché of imperialism, but takes on added significance when recurrently used by a photographer, whose own project depends on light.

The double meaning seems more than accidental, since Thomson regularly linked photography, scientific progress, and imperial expansion. "The evolution of photography has kept pace with the progress in discovery in almost all departments of Science," Thomson wrote, "and contributes its full share of usefulness in extending knowledge."[8] Knowledge in turn contributed to the progress of commerce. In his discussion of Guangzhou (still referred to as Canton in Thomson's text), for instance, Thomson suggested that manufactures of "superior English make" could easily supplant locally produced goods if the English producer would "make himself acquainted with the exact form of all the different kinds of tools in use among the Chinese."[9] Only the lack of such knowledge delayed Western commercial domination. And Western commerce would bring prosperity, interest, and even history itself to the "long-sleeping" East — and incidentally would provide better photographic opportunities.[10]

The project incorporated photographic images of both the people of China and the landscape itself, with a common imperialist agenda for each. As James R. Ryan has pointed out: "Landscape was thus a form of imperial prospect in Thomson's work. As such, it also became a symbolic manifestation of different racial attributes. Thus the foreign settlements were beacons of light in an otherwise dark moral landscape."[11] From the land to the people themselves, China was presented as territory to be remade by the forces of English power and commerce.

For Thomson, the role of the photographer in this imperial enterprise was clear: his pictures of China and the Chinese "shall convey an accurate impression of the country . . . as well as of the arts, usages, and manners . . . and of the types of races."[12] As light dawned in the East, Thomson would make use of it to make photographs — following the opening of new trade routes in China, with "the camera the constant companion of my wanderings."[13] Thus, given his firm belief in the scientific truth of photographic evidence, Thomson would make his contribution to the extension of knowledge; given his equally firm belief in the equivalency of empire and scientific enlightenment, Thomson would also be contributing to the extension of the British empire. We, looking back on Thomson's project, can see it in another way: Thomson used his manipulative skills (selection and composition), masked by the contemporary idea that photographs were unmediated transcriptions of the real, to create a China in his own image, imposing familiar classifications and hierarchies on the unfamiliar Other at empire's edge in a way that would facilitate and justify the extension of the British empire.

## The Anthropological Eye

The practice of imposing typology in the interests of Western commerce and rule was by no means uniquely Thomson's; it can be seen as characteristic of the developing "social science" of anthropology in the same era. The 1860s and 1870s were a period of intense concern in anthropological circles with the development of classificatory schemes, above all else of racial categories, but also of levels of civilization, social hierarchies, and material culture. Thomson, writing about Cambodian races in the *Transactions of the Ethnological Society of London* in 1869, shared the journal's pages with John Crawfurd, whose obsessive ongoing series of pieces on racial type covered everything from broad categories like mental and physical characteristics to such details as hair, eyes, and skin.[14] Thomson's speculations about races in East Asia were contemporaneous with those of Alfred Russel Wallace on the racial history of the Pacific.[15] In 1875, the same year Thomson published his photographs of China, Francis Galton was beginning to publish his systems for scientific measurement of humans, British schoolchildren providing his first guinea pigs, and Augustus Pitt-Rivers was detailing the principles of classification, based on stages of evolution, that he had developed for his museum, which had opened to the public in Bethnal Green the year before.[16] Pitt-Rivers was also engaged at the time with the compilation of a handbook for ethnology, *Notes and Queries on Anthropology*, to ensure that anthropologists, travelers, and missionaries would know how to gather information scientifically, in a form that could be used comparatively.[17] In 1876, E. B. Tylor, in a review of a German "ethnological photographic gallery" just reprinted in London, noted that: "The science of anthropology owes not a little to the art of photography," especially in regard to "race-portraits."[18] Within such a social scientific milieu, Thomson's own typological photography, and his blurring of social and racial categories, found a ready audience.

Though presented at the time as "scientific," and thus objective and neutral, such social scientific concerns directly supported the formation of an imperialist ideology, and even in specific ways abetted imperial administration. The linkage of classification and imperial rule was already a significant subtext in anthropological writings of the 1860s and 1870s. For instance, W. L. Distant, writing about "The working of a large sugar estate by means of European capital, European appliances, and European superintendence, with the manual labour of some hundreds of Asiatics," put the "science" of racial typology to the service of plantation agriculture, drawing conclusions about the best racial types for "coolie" labor;[19] similarly, G. W. Leitner, insisting on the importance of anthropological methods in settling border disputes at the edges of the Indian subcontinent, praised the collaboration of the British-imposed "Local Indian Government" with anthropologists.[20] By the end of the century, such declarations had become *de rigueur*. Thus, C. H. Read, in his preface to the revised edition of *Notes and Queries on Anthropology* (1899), noted the "immense service [anthropology] would render, first to officers governing our distant possessions, and second, to the central government at home."[21] Henry Balfour, as president of the Anthropological Institute, declared: "With our Imperial and Colonial interests and responsibilities, the study of comparative and local ethnology is of prime importance to us . . . if we are to govern justly and intelligently the very heterogeneous people who have come under our sway."[22] And the first published guide to the British Museum's ethnographic collections noted both "how much easier the administration of native territories becomes when administrators can appreciate the reasons for native points of view" and "The possible advantages which merchants trading amongst primitive peoples might gain by studying their material wants and artistic predilections."[23]

As in Thomson's case, the anthropological alliance with imperialism made use of the new "transcriptive" art of photography. In 1869 the London Ethnological Society called on its president, T. H. Huxley, to develop guidelines for "the formation of a systematic series of photographs of the various races . . . within the British Empire." Huxley drew up a photographic method that, insisting on nude full-figure portraits against standardized grid backdrops, underlined physical and racial typology over any concern with cultural context.[24] The *Journal of the Anthropological Institute* published its first photograph in 1877, decades before photographic illustration was common even in illustrated journalism, and the journal regularly used photographic illustrations in the years that followed.[25] As late as 1893, contributors to the institute's *Journal* continued to urge the use of photography as a tool to distinguish racial types.[26]

Thomson's photographic practice coincided most closely with the concerns of contemporary anthropology in his own typological portraits (Plate 5): heads, in profile or full-front, against blank backdrops, employing "a lens longer in focus than that used for landscapes and groups" in order to facilitate "scientific" comparison, since "with a lens of short focus the features are so distorted as to render the photograph useless as a basis for measurement."[27] The emphasis on heads reflected both popular phrenological and physiognomic notions and a developing anthropological emphasis on craniometry as a measure of race.[28] As James R. Ryan also notes, "Thomson's use of full-face and profile views of isolated, individual heads . . . is clear evidence that he was influenced by the conventions of anthropological photography and phrenology."[29] His writings show a similar concern with the fine points of racial typology, carefully differentiating racial subgroups wherever he traveled.[30]

Thomson's writings also reveal other racialist preconceptions of the period, especially concerning racial purity. The "purest" of the races he encountered, the Papuan ("Pepohoan," Thomson called them) aborigines he met in the interior of Formosa (Taiwan), were "tall and well-formed, with large brown eyes kindling at times with savage lustre that told of a free untamed spirit," "a gentle and inoffensive [race], in spite of a sort of haughty savage manner not wanting in dignity and grace."[31] In contrast, Thomson traced the course of racial degeneration in the descendants of Portuguese settlers in Macao: "Influences — local, social, climactic — and a fusion of races have dealt unkindly with these descendants of the early Portuguese . . . one seldom meets with a well-formed and attractive countenance."[32] Thomson employed a double explanation for such degeneration, partially environmental, partially the ill results of miscegenation. Thus, on the one hand, "Naturalists tell us that long residence in a certain region is apt to transform the physical appearance of an animal."[33] At the same time, that they "are darker than the Portuguese of Europe, and darker even than the native Chinese" suggested to Thomson a history of racial mixture — which he, in keeping with his times, thought of as a history of degeneration as well.[34]

To his observations about the degraded Portuguese Thomson added, however, an important qualification: "This, it must be understood, is applicable to the lower orders of the population." Such blurring of the distinction between race and class was also a familiar pattern in mid-Victorian racial thought.[35] And it was upon this distinction that

Thomson grounded the greater part of his photographic practice, the portraits and group photographs of Chinese social types. Thomson's innovation was to substitute the streets for the studio, adding to the existing "truth value" of his photographs the heightened realism of naturalistic settings.[36] But in taking his camera into the streets, Thomson by no means left his compositional rules behind: as simply "realistic" as his works still may appear, they are strictly governed by the artistic conventions of his day. And his practice also underlined the importance of the class divide, for his portraits of Asian "gentlemen" remained indoors, and followed conventions more closely associated with those of the genre of European portraiture.

## Art and Nature

The importance of artistic conventions for Thomson derives from his view of the artistic character of photography; "Every portrait," he claimed, "should be a work of art."[37] In one case, faced with trying to make a photograph of the execution grounds in Formosa, he even concluded that it could not be done: "I tried to make a picture out of it, but there was nothing to lend pictorial grace to the scene."[38] Such a view might seem to conflict with Thomson's insistence on the scientific, transcriptive character of photography, but his position was characteristic of many of the art photographers of the period. That photography was a "mechanical" process did not negate its art possibilities, especially in an age in which concern with naturalism was dominant. The artistic eye and training of the photographer remained important, even if limited to selection and a more restricted control over composition.[39]

The heart of the issue is the notion of "nature," and a blurring between positivistic notions of photography as a "pencil of nature" and a notion of human "nature" founded on *type*. Thomson was looking for "true types," not individuals.[40] The point for the artist was to "concentrate his spirit on the essential nature of his work."[41] The essence was conceived as unity, and Thomson found his authority for composition in Ruskin: "The great object of composition being always to secure unity."[42] Such an aesthetic justified compositional intervention. In Thomson's case, the idea of compositional unity was wedded to his enterprise of capturing "true types." The reality Thomson sought was not the reality of unmediated transcription of street scenes; it was instead the "essential" character of "street types," which could best be captured by intervening, by selecting and composing groups, in order to create the "unity" that comprised their essence.

Getting those poses, Thomson noted, could present problems. Writing of his photo session with the King of Siam, Thomson noted: "Here was a difficulty. How to pose an Oriental potentate who has ideas of his own as to propriety in attitude."[43] Thomson's solution was to let the king choose his dress, but to convince him to follow directions in posing. Thomson clearly recognized that his subjects had an entirely different aesthetic, but he was not about to let it shape his own practice.

That Thomson recognized a sense of "propriety in attitude" in the East that differed substantially from Western aesthetic conceptions becomes even clearer in his discussion of indigenous Hong Kong photographers. He described the standard locally produced photographic portrait: "The majority wore the Buddhistic expression of stolid indifference, and were seated all of them full front, with limbs forming a series of equal angles to the right and left." Curiously, Thomson recognized that *other* aesthetics transmitted cultural statements, even though he seemed unaware of the premises behind his own. The Chinese pose was adopted for a reason, Thomson argued: "A Chinaman will not suffer himself — if he can avoid it — to be posed so as to produce a profile of a three-fourth face, his reason being that the portrait must show him to be possessed of two eyes and two ears, and that his round face is perfect as the full moon."[44] Faced with such objections, it must be emphasized, Thomson made no attempt to alter his own aesthetic but instead imposed his ideas about form on his subjects.

## Composing the Subject

Ironically, Thomson's compositional strategies can be seen to negate his move from studio to street. Selection and composition work to isolate subjects from their contexts, removing them from the street life of which they are part. This is clearest in an overall view of the pictures: street types exist in isolation from other street types, not in the active interaction that is part of street life (Plate 6). Sometimes vendors do in fact vend, but more typically they exist in Thomson's photographs outside the realm of exchange, offering goods to no one. Thomson's most isolated figures tend also to be his most exotic, the most unfamiliar made also the most removed from any social sphere — as in the case of the prisoners punished in the cangue and the cage (Plate 7).

Several compositional strategies operate to reinforce this isolating move. One is a matter of focus: in contrast to the practice of many of his contemporaries, whose photographs featured sharp focus throughout the image, Thomson tended to put his foreground figures into sharp focus and to let his background blur.[45] Secondly, Thomson made heavy use of triangulation, a standard compositional means of creating unity, where groups of figures are arranged in pyramids or inverted pyramids. Thomson often underlined the triangulation with strong use of diagonal lines and shadow, the lines of the picture echoing the group's composition. He also regularly used background doorways to frame his subjects, and by framing them to isolate and remove them from their social context.

Another of Thomson's strategies was the pairing of "type" to labor. In almost all his photographs of street types we see figures wedded to their means of sustenance, linked absolutely to their work (see Plate 8).[46] In the labels of the photographs, their work defines them, their labor is their "type." As Ryan puts it, "these scenes picture 'types' through a sense of their 'natural' trades and occupation."[47] In the accompanying texts, Thomson reinforced the message with repeated digressions on "happy" laborers. In the case of the sedan chairs, for instance, he notes a European's initial reluctance to use the contraptions, but concludes that finally "he feels the necessity of rest after a hard day's work . . . and marks the happy and contented faces of the chair-bearers, who clamour, all unconscious of degradation, for the favour of his regal patronage."[48] Thomson justified the divide between wealth and poverty in East Asia, and the use of "coolie" labor not only in traditional occupations like chair-bearing but in newer industrial roles as well, by such assertions of the contentedness of the laborer, and parallel claims about the "industriousness" of the Chinese as a people.

In contrast to such images of labor, where both Thomson's photographs and his text underline their difference from familiar Western types, his treatment of Eastern elites closely followed traditional European conventions of portraiture (see Plates 9 and 10). Again, the text reiterated the parallels. "The Cochin gentleman," Thomson wrote, "like his prototype among other and more cultured nations, generally exhibits in his physique and manners evidence of superior breeding."[49] Of the photographs of ministers in Beijing, Thomson noted they were "as fine looking men as ever our own Cabinet can boast," and the Prince himself, though less "fine looking," "had what phrenologists describe as a splendid head."[50] They are photographed in interiors, clothed in and often surrounded by the accoutrements of their power and status, and posed in standard European portrait manner.

And with the form, he imposed categories as well. Beyond the broad categories of hierarchical racial types, even in the details of labels and motifs, Thomson found ways to make the Orient echo in familiar ways to the Londoner. A street in Guangzhou was "even more offensive than the most crowded alley of London,"[51] and of the street groups of China he notes that "in our terms we should class them as tinkers or costermongers."[52] Chinese pawn shops are compared to London's, and Chinese musical entertainments are labeled "music halls."

The same trend can be seen in broader thematics borrowed from contemporary English literature about the lower classes. Thomson echoes Disraeli's "Two Nations" theme in Beijing: "I could discover evidences of a liberal distribution of wealth . . . On the other hand, fearful signs of squalor and misery."[53] He divides the poor, as England's were typically divided, between "respectable" and unrespectable: in Guangzhou, "the more respectable and industrious of the labouring classes prefer a shore life" to living on boats.[54] Thomson echoes even the familiar Victorian theme of a conspiratorial organization of beggars, forming their own underground social order and counterfeiting their ailments, in his discussion of Chinese beggars.[55]

Thomson's method in East Asia thus can be seen as an explicit attempt, on a number of levels (formal, textual, intertextual), to impose on the lower classes of Asia the social categories applied to the working class of Victorian England. Such an imposition of categories served to justify Thomson's support for a program of continued imperial expansion in the East, the whole project identified with the dawning of a new age of industrial, free-trading progress. If the lower orders of China could be made to seem like those of England, it was reasonable to attempt to transform them into an industrial proletariat.

When he returned to England, he turned the same techniques onto the working-classes of London's East End in his classic *Street Life of London* (1875–76), and he there anchored his arguments with regular reference back to his Eastern experiences.

Openly modeling his work on Mayhew's, Thomson presents it as a form of exploration. Where his Eastern exploration was an encounter with the exotic, however, Thomson cast his London exploration as an encounter with the unseen but familiar: "Little is known concerning the street characters who are most often seen in our crowded thoroughfares."[56] And again he used the camera as a tool to identify "true types."

Thomson underlined the analogy between the lower classes of London and those of the East by repeated comparisons with the Chinese. The strategy can again be seen in the opening text of *Street Life of London*: the "stamp" of the London nomad "reminded me of the Nomades who wander over the Mongolian steppe."[57] Often, such comparisons work to the disadvantage of London's poor: as opposed to the poor in Lambeth, "the Chinese people get used to floods;"[58] and, when it comes to garbage, "The Chinese, who are an eminently agricultural people, turn the dust and refuse collected in their abodes to better use than we do in London."[59] Thomson deployed such comparisons in the interest of paternalistic reform, but did so in such a way as to underline again the great divide between the London poor and civilization.

## Conclusion

Both East Asian and East London dimensions of Thomson's photographic project reveal a common set of interests: in the use of artistic conventions drawn from art photography as a means to achieve a harmonious "unity" in portraiture aimed at capturing the essence of social "types"; in the meshing of art photography with the scientific claims of photography as "transcription," which served to disguise the subjective quality of Thomson's techniques; and in the employment of photography to justify and further Victorian imperial and industrial "progress." Such practices by Thomson and other Victorian photographers justified the "widespread Chinese belief" about photography that Thomson recounted for his readers' amusement: "that, in taking a photograph, a certain vital principle is extracted from the body of the sitter."[60] A vital principle was extracted by Thomson: the principle that his subjects could create their own self-images, that they could control their own destiny.

# 5

## Eating out East:
### Representing Chinese Food in
### Victorian Travel Literature and Journalism

*Ross G. Forman*

Writing in her 1899 travelogue *The Yangtze Valley and Beyond*, inveterate globetrotter Isabella L. Bird proclaimed to her readers, "Our ideas as to Chinese food are, on the whole, considerably astray."[1] Echoing the sentiments of the periodical *Temple Bar* — which, in 1891, had declared, "It seems, however, impossible to disabuse people of the idea that dogs, rats, and snails frequently appear on the bill of fare" in Chinese establishments — Bird addressed head-on prevalent misconceptions about the exotic nature of the Chinese diet.[2] These misconceptions were often advanced through travel writers' and journalists' experience primarily with aristocratic banquet foods and their lack of familiarity with everyday and regional fare. By contrast, Bird provided her readers with a much more visceral account of the manners and customs of the "Celestials" by describing her adventures in eating in such diverse settings as mandarin's palaces, rural inns, wayside restaurants, and markets. "It is true," she notes, "that the rich spend much in pampering their appetites, that the foolish extravagance of providing meats, fruits and vegetables, out of season at 'dinner parties' prevails among them as among us, and that such delicacies as canine cutlets and hams, cat fricassees, bird's-nest soup — a luxury so costly that it makes its appearance on foreign tables — stewed *holothuria*, and fricassee of snails, worms, or snakes are to be seen at ceremonious feasts" (300). But, she continues, not only is the Chinese food she saw and sampled during her visit largely wholesome and healthy in nature, it is also incredibly diverse, even amongst the poorer households: "The variety of food eaten by all classes in China is amazing. It would require four or five pages to put down what I have myself seen in the eating-houses and food shops on this journey" (298).

With its fin-de-siècle publication date, Bird's book appeared towards the end of a long period of fascination on the part of the British public with Chinese food. For decades, the exotic and sensuous fare of the Flowery Land had been elaborated for readers back home and from a distance by a multitude of writers and travelers who had tested the cuisine on their behalf — usually in China, but sometimes in North America, among the expatriate Chinese communities of New York and the West Coast. These Britons recorded their experiences primarily in the periodical press, but also in stand-alone travelogues, where a scene of ritual disgust *à table* was almost *de rigueur* — as it also was for the expatriate British community resident in China, whose antipathy towards local food Jay Denby immortalized in his hilarious *Letters of a Shanghai Griffin to His Father and Other Exaggerations* (1910).[3]

Like her Victorian predecessors, Bird's descriptions of Celestial foodways use them as an exemplar of a more general fascination with the radically different world of China that the travelogue, as narrative form, necessarily seeks to elaborate for its audience at home. She relies on her audience's unfamiliarity with the culinary ground she covers to make her descriptions exciting, even titillating. Yet her more accurate and more laudatory discussion of these foodways and her inclusion of edibles for eaters across the class spectrum — ranging from the preserved eggs she observes being made in a village in Sichuan to the bean curd of the more prosperous regions she visits, to the "itinerant piemen" of the towns who hawk "vegetable patties" at markets and "places where men congregate" (298) — bucks the trend for much of the Victorian era of overemphasizing Chinese cuisine as strange and antithetical to the British diet. Instead of stressing the difference between the British and Chinese diet and eating habits, as was commonly the case (especially in the work of male travel writers and journalists), Bird focuses on variety, ingenuity, healthfulness, and even the triumph over adversity as the hallmarks of Chinese cuisine. ("Cleanly cooking and wholesome and excellent meals," she avers, "are often produced in dark and unsavoury surroundings, and those foreigners who travel much in the interior learn to find Chinese food palatable" [300].)[4]

Whether wittingly or unwittingly, this vision of Chinese food turns its producers into reflections of model Britons. The Chinese, through their cooking, excel at the Darwinian traits of adaptation to local conditions, and they embrace the principle of diversity as the means of safeguarding the survival of the social whole. Moreover, and contrary to readerly expectations, Bird's travels demonstrate that proper standards of hygiene prevail against the odds, and nutritional benefit accrues even if the foodstuffs themselves lie beyond the pale of the British palate and thus would normally be assumed to be unhealthy — which in part explains the emphasis in many travel narratives on the consumption of rats, dogs, snakes, insects, and other "low" animals that "civilized" eaters would have excluded from their purview.

By embodying a dialectic of fascination with the exotic and a simultaneous rejection of it, Bird's book encapsulates some of the contradictions that govern the narration of Chinese eating habits and dishes during this period. Regularly appearing in the columns of the nation's press from the 1840s onward — a starting point linked to the conclusion of the First Opium War and to British expansion in India and in Asia more generally following the 1857 Mutiny — descriptions of Chinese dinners and diners became a staple of travel narratives, miscellanies, magazines, and fiction produced by British writers in China, as well as those who wrote about the Celestial Empire from bases in Albion.

Such descriptions formed a crucial part of the way in which the British public conceptualized China as foreign and inaccessible, while also offering cultural explanations of manners and customs aimed at making the inscrutable scrutable through common bonds of etiquette, eating, and after-dinner entertainment. At the same time, discussions of Chinese food paralleled the interest in the cultivation and preparation of that article of Chineseness which Britons ingested on a regular basis — tea. Over the course of the nineteenth century, tea was gradually transmuted from the strange into the familiar, from the foreign into the domestic — as new methods of preparation saw black tea eclipse the consumption of green tea and as new colonial plantations in South Asia shifted production away from China and into the imperial fold (thus removing the economic danger of tea consumption implicit in Britain's dependence on China for this commodity at the same time as opium exports redressed the overall trade "imbalance" between the two countries). Yet Chinese food continued to enthral and repulse with its alterity, exotic obsessions, and unfamiliar modes of preparation and consumption. Even the implements used to convey this "chow" from table to tongue were a source of wonder to many observers who visited China: chopsticks constituted objects that unified the sublime and the ridiculous and inhabited the basic contradiction of an ancient culture that staunchly resisted incorporation into Western systems of behaviour and Western patterns of material culture.

Thus Chinese food — raising, as did interpretations of all other foreign cuisines, questions about the boundary of the national, the natural, and the adaptable — became emblematic of Britain's relationship to China: it was alternately used to contain Cathay through a process of exoticization and to bolster Her Majesty's imperial designs by making that exoticization central to Britain's own efforts to incorporate Cathay within its vision of global supremacy. The travel writer's dual subjectivity as ingestor and raconteur both confirmed cultural boundaries and traduced them, turning culinary descriptions into a process of reaffirming cultural integrity while simultaneously promoting patterns of identification across cultural lines. The heavy reliance on analogies in these descriptions — comparing thousand-year-old eggs to ripe cheese, for instance, or regularly relating the elaborate table etiquette and the variety of courses served to French traditions — highlights the search for recognizable terms of reference in Chinese menus that would make both the food and the customs surrounding it comprehensible to readers who had never experienced it. At the same time, these writers put into operation a counter-process for familiarizing Chinese cuisine by making European food itself strange; for, when viewed in a critical light, Western delicacies were themselves as exotic and potentially unpalatable as snakes, birds' nests, and the like. A January 1887 article on bird's nests in *The Cornhill Magazine*, for example, quotes Charles Darwin's derisory comment that "[t]he Chinese make soup of dried saliva" but contextualizes it as follows: "This sounds horrid enough, to be sure; but when we ourselves give up colouring jellies with defunct cochineal insects, it will be time for us to cast the first stone at the Oriental cuisine."[5]

## A Diet of Delicacies

Historically, fascination with the specific topic of Chinese food, at least in the popular press, quickly followed the signing of the Treaty of Nanking (Nanjing), which began the gradual process of opening up China "oyster-like" to Western commerce and influence. Interest clearly followed from the overall attention paid to things Chinese by the British media during and after the First Opium War in the early 1840s, but also from reports sent back by the increasing numbers of traders and civil servants sent to the region, as well as from the establishment of Britain's official toehold in China, the colony of Hong Kong. The 1840s and early 1850s saw a series of articles about the collection of bird's nests and their use in soup in periodicals such as *Hogg's Instructor* and *The Penny Magazine of the Society for the Diffusion of Useful Knowledge*.[6] These reports, which were based either on journalists' and naturalists' own experiences in China or culled from contemporary travel literature, concerned themselves not with culinary details, but with economic issues that reflected Britain's concerns about its trade imbalance with China. They focused explicitly on the high cost of the nests and their "monopoly price" and saw them as a spectacular example of China's resistance to "traffic with foreigners" and its disregard for market rules: "There is perhaps no production upon which human industry is exerted, of which the cost of production bears so small a proportion to the market price," concluded the *Penny Magazine* in 1841 in reiterating a quotation from John Crawfurd's 1820 travelogue *History of the Indian Archipelago*.[7] That the bird's nests were a foodstuff was almost incidental; interest here was more purely scientific and especially economic. The concerns about the way in which the scarcity of the bird's nest as commodity dictated its value both fed theorizations of the Chinese as the one race of shopkeepers and traders in Asia that most closely resembled Britain's own imagined self and pinpointed the non-European monopoly as the appropriate site for Britain's entry into new markets and new structures of informal imperialism. The highly organized regional trading networks needed to acquire and transport bird's nests and sea cucumbers from their collection points outside China, in areas that culturally and often politically and economically were — or had been — tributary states, to their consumption points within the Celestial Empire, suggested a rival form of maritime imperialism. It was also a rival form that had successfully resisted incorporation into European trading pathways.[8]

More directly culinary — although no less directly related to the growth of Britain's impetus to imperially incorporate parts of China — was *Times* correspondent George Wingrove Cooke's description of "A Chinese Dinner" during his sojourn there from 1857 to 1858. Sent to China to cover the Second Opium War, Cooke recorded the experiences of his travels in a series of letters published in the *Times*. The letters were reprinted as a book in 1861 under the title *China and Lower Bengal. Being "The Times" Correspondence from China in the Years 1857–58*. Although ostensibly an account of the war, Cooke's book was structured like a traditional travelogue; it begins with a chapter on "The Journey Out" and culminates (if not concludes) with a chapter entitled "Adieu to China."[9] His letter on Chinese food constitutes the chapter "A Chinese Dinner" in this book.

Cooke's discussion of the meal he enjoyed in Ningpo (Ningbo) is important for four reasons: First, it sets a model of the "Chinese dinner" as banquet meal that later in the century would become the standard formula for depicting Chinese eating habits. Second, it demonstrates that as early as 1857, it was difficult for Europeans to sample "authentic" Chinese cuisine in Chinese homes. Cooke explains that knowing the tastes of their visitors, Chinese hosts inevitably hire their guests' own cooks, although whether this pattern results from Western intolerance towards foreign foodstuffs or Chinese perceptions of hospitality remains murky: "It is impossible now to get a real Chinese dinner at a Chinese private house. Your host thinks it an absolute necessity of politeness to serve his guest according to his country's fashion. I had looked forward to a dinner to be given by the Shantung guild of merchants to the English at Ningpo in the new temple; but, alas! the Shantung merchants hire the cooks of their English guests" (238). Third, Cooke's description indicates a more highly developed and aristocratic restaurant culture among the Chinese than back in Britain, where, in 1857, the range of possibilities for dining out lagged far behind France. By contrast, as John Dudgeon, a medical missionary who arrived in China in 1860, would later point out, "Restaurants are to be found everywhere in China." [10] Whereas the custom of inviting guests over for dinner prevailed in Britain at this time, in China, the situation was quite different. As Dudgeon explains, "In the large cities these [dining halls] exist on a large scale, and are the rendezvous of the higher classes where friends are invited to dinner. The Chinese family relations prevent as a rule social gatherings at their own homes. It is considered highly becoming to invite to one of these dining halls" (317).

Therefore, in order to sample "true" Chinese food in Ningbo, Cooke sets up a dinner at a restaurant run by a mandarin who is a graduate of the imperial examination system; rather than a bourgeois establishment, this restaurant clearly caters to the elite. Named "The Gallery of the Imperial Academician," it also "holds repute of having, out of Pekin, the best *cuisine* in China" (239). The later institutionalization of the restaurant as the key site for experiencing "the Chinese dinner" also understands Chinese cuisine as an urban phenomenon; in so doing, it naturalizes any foreign items or preparation methods that might dominate the menu. Chinese culinary exotica therefore become aligned with an urban tradition of importation and amalgamation that in many ways differs little from the Victorian predilection for turtle, imported from America just as birds' nests are from Southeast Asia, and the penchant for seafood restaurants, where oysters and other slimy foods that might be seen as antithetical to a notional/national diet of meat are consumed. These slimy foods were analogues to banquet foods such as sea slugs and birds' nests that made many observers comment on the Chinese fondness for the gelatinous. Fourth and finally, Cooke's "A Chinese Dinner" differs markedly from many other examples of the genre as it would later develop in its sympathy towards the foods on offer and willingness to experiment. Cooke's sentiments are more in keeping with those of eighteenth-century British imperialists, who adopted local cuisines as their regular diet, rather than late Victorian suspicion and often revulsion towards the foreign foodstuff.[11] Cooke, in fact, shows an acute awareness of cultural relativity in eating habits, arguing for open-mindedness towards difference in diet and a healthy sense of adaptability to change. Pronouncing a dish of sea slugs "succulent and pleasant food, not at all unlike in flavour to the green fat of the turtle," he goes on to conclude: "If a man cannot eat anything of a kind whereof he has not seen his father and grandfather eat before, we must leave him to his oysters, periwinkles, and his crawfish, and not expect him to swallow the much more comely sea slug. But surely a Briton who has eaten himself into a poisonous plethora upon mussels has no right to hold up his hands and eyes at a Chinaman enjoying his honest well-cooked stew of *bêches de mer*" (240–1).

Although depictions of Chinese food never went out of fashion, forming a staple element of most travel narratives about the region, they blossomed again in the 1880s and 1890s. The opening up of Japan following the Meiji restoration, the growth of the International Settlement in Shanghai, and the expansion of steamship routes that both linked the China Coast internationally to Britain and Australia and rendered China's rivers up to foreign commerce all played their part. In periodicals in particular, competition for readership meant that periodic bursts of articles about Chinese food appeared at this time, as rival publications jousted to best one another in their portrayal of eating out East. Fiction also had its impact: *The Leisure Hour's* serialization of Jules Verne's *Troubles of a Chinaman* in 1880 sparked a spate of articles entitled "the Chinese dinner" or "the Chinese menu," following from the elaborate description of a banquet given by the novel's protagonist King-Fo.[12]

The mid-1880s also saw China's first official participation in an international exhibition in Britain in 1883 (the International Fisheries Exhibition) and the opening of a Chinese buffet and teahouse at the International Health Exhibition a year later. These public displays about the Celestial Empire kept the issue of Chinese food in the public eye; they also extended the experience of banquets that had traditionally been typed as a male preserve to the women who flocked to South Kensington to sample the Chinese *table d'hôte*, which gave impressive French titles such as "Chaudfroid de cailles à l'Essence" and "Crépinette de Vollaile à la Cantonaise au Varech Violet" to its dishes. (Just what these dishes were is difficult to establish, but the former was a preparation of quail in aspic, while the latter was some sort of chicken sausage with seaweed "Cantonese" style.)

The exhibitions themselves constituted a kind of reverse travel experience, bringing the world of China to Britain. With spatial layouts and pavilions that, as many scholars have noted, aimed to telescope the experience of globetrotting, and with specially printed guidebooks to direct the visitor's path through the exhibits, international exhibitions not only provided a substitute for overseas travel, but were also a means of inciting it. Moreover, in many ways these exhibitions offered visitors a direct means to try Chinese food (however adulterated) that, for cultural reasons, the ordinary tourist to Hong Kong or the treaty ports might not actually have the opportunity to experience. Indeed, the few guidebooks to China that date from the late Victorian period offer scant information on local food and how or where to sample it. (Presumably, tourists were supposed to eat in the hotels and, except when traveling in rural areas, might never sample native fare.)

## The "Exquisite Absurdity" of English Dining

The late nineteenth century also saw the appearance of the more occasional sub-genre of descriptions of European-food dinners given by Chinese hosts. These descriptions emerge in travel narratives only towards the end of the century in part because it was an historical juncture in which the motives for imperial expansion itself increasingly came under question (especially given the history of the opium trade in China) and in which the hierarchical systems for classifying cultures, of which cookery experts such as Mrs. Isabella Beeton — who famously averred in her *Book of Household Management* (1861) that "dining is civilization" — had taken advantage, were increasingly open to criticism. Generally of a comic nature, these descriptions point to the way in which issues of diet identify problems of cultural understanding by shedding new and often unsavoury light on the heavy consumption of tinned meat and other imported goods by Britons in China. They often show, in a self-mocking way, how erroneous Chinese impressions of British food are, but in a manner that underscores how the Chinese could in fact legitimately see Europeans as "barbaric." In narrative method, they rely on the adoption of a Chinese subjectivity to contextualize the way in which custom dictates the constitution of acceptable behaviour. In so doing, they show how custom is both contingent on culture and not necessarily hierarchical between cultures. Humour diffuses the narrative upheaval of the reversal of the presumed relationship between author and audience occasioned by the narration from a Chinese perspective; humour is, in fact, the force that mediates between that Chinese perspective of the European dinner and the audience's own through the intervention of the British narrator.

Trader and traveler Archibald John Little's description of one such European meal he was served in Sichuan by a Cantonese merchant, for instance, hinges on the plain boiled fowl and the large and bloody leg of mutton served in contradistinction to the more refined fare of the Chinese dinner party. "In lieu of the chicken being neatly cut up, and stewed in a delicate sauce, all ready for serving to the mouth with the elegant chop-sticks, a rough, plain-boiled fowl was set on the table, with no carving-knife to dissect it with," he notes, putting himself in the place of the Chinese guests at this dinner, who are unable to stomach the lot.[13] Although the problem of the meal in Little's mind stems from the inept serving of the fowl and joint — namely, the lack of appropriate carving utensils and of accompaniments such as bread and potatoes which would make it palatable — the ironic tone of the passage works to reveal how the Chinese viewed British food: as unadorned, undercooked, and shockingly rude in its serving method. Little's conclusion is a reappraisal of the Chinese food of his travels: "After experience of this meal I began to think myself less a victim than I did before, in being generally restricted in my travels to a Chinese cuisine pure and simple" (306). In truth, it is the Chinese guests, not Little, who are the victims at the merchant's dinner — a fact he implicitly recognizes by "mak[ing] up for my fellow-guests' indifference by setting to as best I could" (305–6). Nevertheless, this ideology of victimhood was a standard trope for British impressions of Chinese food, converting food from pleasure into torture and through this process heightening the titillation of the descriptive powers.

UNIVERSITY OF WINCHESTER
LIBRARY

An even more compelling example of the ironic use of food descriptions to underscore cultural relativity, also through Chinese eyes and lips, comes from Arthur H. Smith. Smith was an American missionary based in P'angchiachuang (Panjiazhuang), Shandong, whose *Chinese Characteristics* (1890) was published after he had been living in China for eighteen years.[14] Based on a set of papers printed in the *North China Daily News*, *Chinese Characteristics* was, according to Lydia H. Liu, the most popular book about China until Pearl S. Buck's *The Good Earth* (1931).[15] Here, Smith relays some Chinese impressions of Western food to great parodic effect:

> A Chinese official who had been honoured with an invitation to a dinner at the British Consulate, narrated afterwards, how the English "Great Man" stood up at the head of the table, and with a gigantic sword cut into the huge mass of beef, that was placed before him. Ranks of servants stood all about, and, like the visitor, watched the proceeding, and all of them were too used to it, to appreciate the exquisite absurdity of the performance. Is there any good reason why a host should pass a practical examination in the presence of his guests, as to his knowledge of comparative anatomy? Is it a sublime duty of the civilization of the nineteenth century to wait, while a man does at an inconvenient time what his servants could have done better at a convenient time? . . . (24–5)

Again, humour forms the means through which to convey cultural reappraisal through the eyes of the other, thereby diffusing the unpleasantness or even unacceptability of being made ridiculous by the Chinese. Dining, as Smith acknowledges here, is about performance, and this performance has been misrecognized because what for one culture is an act of hospitality (cutting the roast beef) is for another a symbol of swashbuckling ineptitude. The ceremony of carving is therefore turned into an "exquisite absurdity," but the crucial point is that the servants serve as spectators to this farce: the act of carving displaces the appropriate roles for host, guest, and servant and offers a supreme example of household mismanagement. Smith goes on to prove this point by retreating from Chinese subjectivity back into a Western one with a direct appeal to his audience, but this, too, ultimately shows the mock superiority of the Chinese. He invites readers to think of guests of honour being asked to carve a goose at an English table "with the result of depositing it in the lap of the lady sitting next, who of course smiles, and says it is of no consequence" (25). British politeness courts absurdity by denying that a soiled dress is, in fact, of consequence. "Nothing of this sort ever takes place in China, and for this reason alone, we are prepared to maintain that in eating, in cooking, in carving, the Chinese are more civilized than we," Smith concludes. Smith's description of the Chinese official's impressions of the English dinner thus prompts readers to query, more broadly, what the duties of civilization at the end of the nineteenth century might be, and asks whether Britons are actually in a position to dictate or mandate such duties.

When the Chinese themselves were giving the dinner, as in Little's case, the host's decision to serve Europeans with familiar food certainly owed something to pragmatics and to cultural notions of hospitality. Dudgeon, in the essay he prepared for the 1884 International Health Exhibition entitled "Diet, Dress, and Dwellings of the Chinese in Relation to Health," compliments Chinese ingenuity in recalling a banquet meal he attended: "it may be interesting to remark, as exhibiting the culinary skill of the Chinese, and the many pleasant forms in which milk can be presented, that I was once invited to a large dinner of ceremony by some of the highest officials in Peking, and knowing the foreigner's predilection for, and constant use of, milk, the sumptuous dinner was composed almost entirely of articles of milk composition, and neither cheese, butter, *lau* [a soft curd], nor *nai p'i* (milk skin) formed a part" (276). Yet if Britons' resistance to Chinese food can be interpreted, on some level, as an antipathy to "going native," at the same time the Chinese propensity not to serve their own food functioned as a distancing mechanism, as a way of avoiding too much proximity and common ground for exchange.

## How Much Depends on Dinner?

This is not to say that descriptions of Chinese fare, especially in the context of these banquet dinners, were necessarily negative. Although the Chinese music that might accompany the banquet was universally condemned as "deafening noise," the dishes themselves were often reported as delectable. An 1880 account of "Chinese Cookery" in *The Pall Mall Gazette* presented the report of a correspondent of the *Journal des Débats*, who had attended a banquet in China given by a French official in the employ of the Celestial government. "Many of these dishes are known to us in Europe, and appear to be more eccentric than in reality they are," it noted. Bird's nest soup might be taken for vermicelli in chicken soup, sharks' fins are reminiscent of skate, and "everyone" who has tasted thousand-year-old eggs "says that they are excellent."[16] In *Wanderings in China* (1886), Constance F. Gordon Cumming discoursed on the "excellent, but somewhat lengthy dinner, in twenty-five courses" that she experienced in the home of one Mr. Ahok.[17] Cumming found that "everything was exquisitely refined, and of such unquestionable cleanliness, that the curiosity of tasting new dishes might be indulged without alloy" (220). "I may safely say," she added, "that I tasted *everything* uncommon, and indeed I thought all the special dishes very good" (220–1). Even when they did not like the food, they recognized the care and expense involved in the preparation and elaborate plating involved, and the custom of giving diners hot towels for their hands was much admired.

Above all, the ingenuity and refinement involved in conceiving of and concocting complex dishes like birds' nest and sharks' fin soups marked the Celestial's sophisticated and civilized notion of taste. Darwin had argued in *The Descent of Man* "how similar the nerves of taste must be in monkeys and man";[18] commentators on Chinese food proposed the same model for the diverse "races of men," especially those who were members of such an ancient and distinguished civilization. Darwin had proposed that differences in moral disposition between the "highest men of the highest races and the lowest savages are connected by the finest gradations. Therefore it is possible that they might pass and be developed into each other" (35). Similarly, Chinese food might be exotic or alien, but the very process of trying it and describing it for others meant that British writers perceived this mutability of taste and recognized a kind universality of human appetites.

Another traveler, Henry Spencer Ashbee — better known to posterity for his indexes of Victorian erotica — made this point even clearer. In *The Metropolis of the Manchus* (1882), his account of a visit to Beijing, Ashbee "made up my mind for a Chinese repast, served in Chinese fashion."[19] Although Ashbee reports that he did not actually enjoy his meal at a "thoroughly native rest-house" in the city, he places the blame neither on the restaurant nor on the food itself, but on the limits of his own cultural sensitivity: "It was not the first time that I had tasted pure Chinese *cuisine*, so that the food was not altogether foreign to me, nor were the viands in their way badly cooked, but the taste of almost everything one eats is more or less acquired, and a matter of education; as my tongue was unschooled in the language, so my palate had not yet been taught to appreciate the cooking" (32).

Ashbee's analogy between the mastery of a particular language and the mastery of a particular aesthetics of eating is also a statement about the scene of narration. By focusing on the dual uses of the tongue — to speak and to taste — he again encapsulates the dialectic between experiencing food and recounting that experience; he not only recalls the embodied nature of the travel experience, but also calls attention to the travel writer's role as the translator of that experience for a reading public back home. Moreover, he draws an important distinction between the abstract appreciation of another culture through its difference (its food, its language, etc.) — an intellectual concern not necessarily grounded in personal pleasure or displeasure — and the ability of the traveler to concretely enjoy that difference — an experiential concern directly rooted in personal sensation. Most important to Ashbee's formulation, however, is the idea that education and schooling are the key factors for intercultural understanding. What transmutes displeasure into pleasure, distaste into taste, is knowledge and exposure.

This understanding that palates, like people, can be educated out of culturally limited worldviews helps clarify why commentators — particularly those from the 1880s onward who sampled Chinese food in a metropolitan British setting like the 1884 Exhibition's restaurant — saw such delicacies as sharks' fin soups as open to incorporation into the British diet. One writer, for instance, proclaimed during the Exhibition that he was sure that the birds' nest soup that he had sampled would soon be added to the repertoire of prominent London establishments. The idea that British palates could accommodate themselves to the best of Chinese cuisine also helps explain why the frame of reference used to describe Chinese banquet foods was so persistently that of French haute cuisine: for Britain, both models of taste and the aesthetic of the educable palate were of French origin, owing a debt to Jean-Anthèlme Brillat-Savarin, Auguste Escoffier and particularly to Alexis Soyer and other French chefs working in Britain, who promoted refined cooking and made fine dining fashionable. The enormous variety of soups, roasts, and palate cleansers that made up the menu of the banquets "to which foreign residents or travellers are sometimes invited by the Chinese" also formed a close parallel to Britain's valued French model of sophisticated cookery.[20]

Ultimately, all these varied and uneven descriptions of Chinese food boiled down to a question of taste, in the aesthetic sense of the word. Whether it was seen as *haute cuisine* or as the epitome of all that was vile and loathsome about foreign behaviour, nineteenth- and early twentieth-century travelers' and journalists' descriptions of Chinese cookery placed a heavy burden on it: to make China into an essence or a stock that could be intellectually sampled and appraised by those seeking to fold the Celestial into European systems of knowledge.

1. **Landscape in Sichuan**

Little, Mrs. Archibald [Alicia]. *My Diary in a Chinese Farm.* Shanghai, Hong Kong, Singapore and Yokohama: Kelly and Walsh, 1894, n.p. [1].

2. **The Rev. J. Heywood Horsburgh, M.A., in Traveling Dress**

Bishop, Isabella Bird. *The Yangtze Valley and Beyond: An Account of Journeys in China, Chiefly in the Province of Sze Chuan and among the Man-Tze of the Somo Territory.* London: Virago Press Limited, 1985, page 318.

**3. New Elgin Marbles**

"New Elgin Marbles." *Punch*, November 4, 1860, n.p.

**4. Chung-king Soldiers, Customs Guard**

Bishop, Isabella Bird. *The Yangtze Valley and Beyond: An Account of Journeys in China, Chiefly in the Province of Sze Chuan and Among the Man-Tze of the Somo Territory.* London: Virago Press Limited, 1985, page 484.

**5. Chinese Heads**

Thomson, John. *Illustrations of China and Its People: A Series of Two Hundred Photographs, with Letterpress Descriptive of the Places and People Represented.* Vol. 2. London: Sampson Low, Marston, Low, and Searle, 1873–1874, n.p.

**6. Street Scene**

Thomson, John. *Illustrations of China and Its People: A Series of Two Hundred Photographs, with Letterpress Descriptive of the Places and People Represented.* Vol. 3. London: Sampson Low, Marston, Low, and Searle, 1873–1874, n.p.

**7. Prisoner**

Thomson, John. *Illustrations of China and Its People: A Series of Two Hundred Photographs, with Letterpress Descriptive of the Places and People Represented.* Vol. 3. London: Sampson Low, Marston, Low, and Searle, 1873–1874, n.p.

## 8.  Vendors

Thomson, John. *Illustrations of China and Its People: A Series of Two Hundred Photographs, with Letterpress Descriptive of the Places and People Represented.* Vol. 1. London: Sampson Low, Marston, Low, and Searle, 1873–1874, n.p.

## 9.  Portrait 1

Thomson, John. *Illustrations of China and Its People: A Series of Two Hundred Photographs, with Letterpress Descriptive of the Places and People Represented.* Vol. 4. London: Sampson Low, Marston, Low, and Searle, 1873–1874, n.p.

## 10. Portrait 2

Thomson, John. *Illustrations of China and Its People: A Series of Two Hundred Photographs, with Letterpress Descriptive of the Places and People Represented*. Vol. 4. London: Sampson Low, Marston, Low, and Searle, 1873–1874, n.p.

## 11. Bound Foot

Little, Mrs. Archibald [Alicia]. *Intimate China: The Chinese as I Have Seen Them*. London: Hutchinson, 1899, page 139.

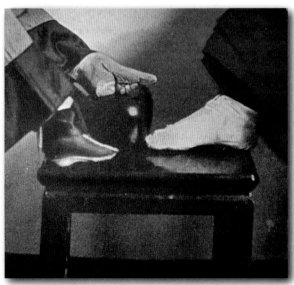

## 12. Alicia Little on Her Chinese Farm

Little, Mrs. Archibald [Alicia]. *My Diary in a Chinese Farm*. Shanghai, Hong Kong, Singapore and Yokohama: Kelly and Walsh, 1894, page 74.

## 13. Manchu Shoes of Silk, Linen, Wood and Leather

Courtesy of Northampton Museum and Art Gallery.

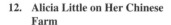

## 14. Little Girl, of Elegant Appearance, with Mother

Little, Mrs. Archibald [Alicia]. *The Land of the Blue Gown*. London: Fisher Unwin, 1902, page 48.

### 15. Isabella Bird in Manchu Dress

Bishop, Isabella Bird. *The Yangtze Valley and Beyond: An Account of Journeys in China, Chiefly in the Province of Sze Chuan and Among the Man-Tze of the Somo Territory.* In *Collected Travel Writings of Isabella Bird*. Vol. 11. Bristol: Ganesha Publishing, 1997, opposite page 352.

### 16. A Chinese *Wu-pan*

Bishop, Isabella Bird. *The Yangtze Valley and Beyond: An Account of Journeys in China, Chiefly in the Province of Sze Chuan and among the Man-Tze of the Somo Territory.* London: Virago Press Limited, 1985, page 475.

**17. Auden and Isherwood Leaving for China in January 1938**

Carpenter, Humphrey. *W. H. Auden: A Biography*. London: Allen and Unwin, 1981, opposite page 336.

**18. Agnes Smedley with Soldier**

Smedley, Agnes. *China Fights Back: An American Woman with the Eighth Route Army*. Westport, Connecticut: Hyperion Press, Inc., 1977, pages 42 and 43.

# 6

## Encounters with Otherness:
### Female Travelers in China, 1880–1920

*Julia Kuehn*

This essay looks at a number of female travelers in China between 1880 and 1920, and analyzes how these women experience and describe the country and its people.[1] However, rather than propose a synchronic study of history, I focus on a selection of encounters, or events, during that period.

Foucault, in *The Archaeology of Knowledge*, deconstructs the totalizing, linear, causal model of history. Instead, he establishes history as a series of "widely spaced intervals formed by rare or repetitive events," which "are juxtaposed to one another, follow one another, overlap and intersect, without one being able to reduce them to a linear schema."[2] For my context, I adapt the Foucauldian idea of episodic events for a taxonomy of the encounter in women's travel writing about China. The Foucauldian event seems a particularly appropriate model for travel literature, as the travelogue, like Foucault's concept of history, also often consists of a series of episodic narratives of particular incidents, or single episodes, which can rarely be reduced to a linear story. The American traveler Ellen LaMotte, who came to Beijing in 1917, introduces her travelogue *Peking Dust* with the confession that this book does not contain accurate or practical information, but consists of "gossip, — the flying gossip or dust of Peking."[3] Her advice, "Take it lightly,"[4] reminds the readers that travel writing can offer only a selection of incidents, and these are also often presented in the shape of personal impressions and related in an anecdotal, conversational way.

The Foucauldian event has both a temporal and a narrative dimension. Without losing sight of the event's temporality, this essay will focus on its narratological dimension, and specifically will examine what the women travelers say about certain Chinese institutions, and on the capital and the countryside.

## The Encounter with Institutions

*Hospitals*

Western medical support reached China throughout the nineteenth century, mainly through missionaries. Emily Daly (d. 1935), an Irish nurse, left for China in 1888 to take charge of a small hospital for Chinese women in Ningbo. The account of this woman, whom we might want to call a resident traveler, is of interest in so far as she not only discussed China's medical situation from an insider's point of view but also crossed paths with probably the best-known professional woman traveler in China at the time: Isabella Bird (1831–1904). In 1894, Bird visited Mrs. Daly and her husband in Newchwang (Yingkou) in Manchuria (where they had moved), and they bonded through their common interest in building hospitals. Daly's comment that Bird, "wherever she went encouraged and supported medical work," is no exaggeration.[5]

Bird's interest in the medical situation of almost all the countries she visited is admirable it itself, but it can also be read as a function of the prevalent Victorian belief in women's "civilizing mission":[6] women were expected to use their moral and domestic skills for the greater social good and engage in charitable giving and visiting. In the nineteenth century charity thus became both a lifeline for the underprivileged, and a duty and acceptable pastime for middle and upper-class women.[7] It is therefore not surprising that Bird, in her 1899 book *The Yangtze Valley and Beyond*, devoted an entire chapter to "Chinese Charities," however deficient she found them. Rather bewildered, she wrote, unaware that Western philanthropy had no precise equivalent in the Asian context: "I have not been able to learn whether the benevolent instincts of Chinese women find any outlet."[8] Bird's charity and practical goodness deepened after the loss of her sister Henrietta and shortly afterwards of her husband, Dr. John Bishop, both of whom she had assiduously nursed until the end.[9] On subsequent journeys in Asia Bird founded, with the money she earned from her travel books, a number of hospitals in memory of her family. She established John Bishop Memorial Hospitals in Srinagar (Kashmir) and Chow-fu (Zhejiang), Henrietta Bird Hospitals in Simla (northern India) and Paoning-fu (Sichuan), another hospital in Seoul, and an orphanage for earthquake victims in Tokyo.[10]

But even before Bird had the financial means to become actively involved in medical work abroad, she visited hospitals. On her first trip to China in 1878 she stopped at the Tung Wah Hospital in Hong Kong, built and supported by Chinese merchants. In it, Bird wrote, "nothing European, either in the way of drugs or treatment, is tried."[11] If Bird overall applauded the organization and work of the hospital, she felt bound to criticize the lack of Western medical erudition: instead of chloroform some "dark brown powder" was used,[12] which had apparently the same effects, but the Chinese doctors never used any disinfectants, she complained. Instead, wounds were dressed with "musk, lard and ambergris," and "powdered rhinoceros' horns, sun-dried tiger's blood, powdered tiger's liver, spiders' eyes," and ginseng was administered for other ailments.[13]

It was no wonder, concluded Bird, that because of the system adopted here, which was "one of the most antiquated quackery," the mortality rate was rather high.[14]

Bird's philanthropy, formidable energy and willingness to create an encounter is accompanied by a chauvinistic faith in the superiority of Western sources of knowledge. The desire to understand the encounter through a recognizable framework is not unusual for the traveler in a foreign land. Elizabeth Kemp (b. 1860), an English artist and scholar, also visited medical institutions while in China in 1920. Even more than Bird, she sought evidence of superior Western modernization, commercialization, and industrialization in institutions in Shanghai, Beijing and Hangzhou. She inspected, for instance, the Rockefeller Institution for Medicine and Scientific Research, the Red Cross, the Shantung Christian University with its School of Medicine, and the missionary Maternity Hospital in Hangzhou. Her complacency can be seen in her approval of Shanghai's Commercial Press, which was, wrote Kemp, to meet "the rapidly growing demand for handbooks in Chinese on all sorts of subjects of western knowledge."[15]

Miss Constance Gordon Cumming (1837–1924), Bird's rival in traveling remote places, but, in contrast, with an aristocratic background and connections which greatly facilitated traveling, also carried her upper-class duty to charity and a faith in Western superiority into a hospital in Fuzhou in 1879. Like her rejection of traditional Chinese medicines — acupuncture for dysentery, a concoction of scorpions for fever, pigeon's dung for pregnant women — her comments on the treatment of bound feet, in particular, display a superior air, but also the strategy of translating otherness into a framework that is familiar to the self. Cumming calls the tradition of footbinding "torture" and a "horrible distortion."[16] A woman's gangrenous feet which must be amputated will, luckily, through the "skill and tenderness of European and American trained nurses and doctors" soon be replaced, writes Cumming, by "American feet, which will be far more serviceable than the tottering 'lily feet.' "[17] Significantly, Cumming compares the "artificial beauty" which is at the heart of footbinding with the "tight-lacing in some countries nearer home," again translating a tradition foreign and other to her into something identifiable.[18]

Rather fittingly, Foucault, in the preface to *The Order of Things*, establishes a "Chinese" system of classification as the absolute other to Western thought and suggests that knowledge is always conditioned in a certain cultural system and built upon historical *a priori*, or *epistemes*. He quotes an entry from a Chinese encyclopedia in which animals are divided into "(a) belonging to the Emperor, (b) embalmed, (c) tame, (d) sucking pigs, (e) sirens, (f) fabulous, (g) stray dogs, (h) included in the present classification," and the list continues.[19] Ironically, this Chinese animal catalogue turns out to be a fictional invention of Jorge Luis Borges. Borges' taxonomic carnival of the animals is a little allegory of the way we experience phenomena through the matrix of our pre-existing, different, and sometimes arbitrary categories. It emphasizes the difficulty, perhaps impossibility, for these travelers to approach China in any other way than through the fundamental codes of Western culture be these ideological (moral), historical, or aesthetic.

*Footbinding*

The need to translate otherness into sameness becomes most obvious in the women's encounter with footbinding. In 1919, the Australian traveler and novelist Mary Gaunt (1861–1942) commented at length on the practice. Although she refused to be called a suffragette, she accepted that she was a suffragist, "realising that a woman is most valuable neither as an angel nor as a slave, but as a useful citizen."[20] Visiting a hospital in Shanxi province, Gaunt saw the misery and disease caused by bound feet, and she inquired into the origin of the tradition while at the same time imposing, like Cumming, her own judgments on it through a comparison with European waist-binding. "The reason for foot-binding is not very clear," she wrote:

> There is something sexual at the bottom of it, I believe, but why a sick and ailing woman should be supposed to welcome the embraces of her lord more readily than one abounding in health passes my understanding. Of course we remember that not so very long ago, in the reign of Victoria, practically the delicate woman who was ailing was held up to universal admiration. Look at the swooning heroines of Dickens and Thackeray. But let no man put the compressed waist on the same plane as foot-binding. I have heard more than one man do so, but I unhesitatingly affirm they are wrong. Foot-binding is infinitely the worse crime.[21]

Arguably, Gaunt's references to the corset can be interpreted, despite her own declaration, as the words of a feminist. Mary Wortley Montagu, two hundred years earlier, had experienced the "stark naked" freedom of a women's bath in Sofia.[22] The Turkish women in the bath tried to undress the foreign lady, but finding her tightly bound by her English stays, they gave up, believing that her husband had designed "that machine" for locking up his wife's body.[23] If Montagu's corset can be read as a metaphor for the constraints of a patriarchal society — especially since she regretted having to leave this liberated female society to perform domestic duties for her husband — Gaunt's bringing home of the experience might also be an illustration of how a foreign context is translated into a familiar framework, and, moreover, made relevant to the subject's own situation. The adventurous Isabella Bird, too, is often seen as an example of a Victorian woman's rebellion against domestic oppression.[24] On her journeys through China she wore an eclectic combination of Chinese gown, Japanese sun hat, and English gloves and shoes, not only to arouse less attention, but also to experience more freedom around the waist.[25] "Just as . . . Bird would enthuse over the comfort of her corset-free Chinese dress," writes Susan Thurin, "it was freedom from confining Western roles she sought abroad."[26] Arguably, in this case Gaunt, too, was protesting too much when she refused to be considered a feminist, especially as she complained at another point that a Chinese woman seemed to be a man's "favoured slave."[27] Introducing the comparable discourse of tight-lacing into their discussions of footbinding (if one is more damaging than the other), Cumming and Gaunt seemed to recognize that it was not only in China that women were pressed into unnatural shapes to conform to an imposed erotic ideal.

Continuing this line of feminists, the American travel writer and women's rights activist Grace Seton (1872–1959) came to China in 1922 with the specific aim to "throw a little light on . . . the 'dark places' of the 'woman's quarters' of New China, where the light of publicity has not yet beaten."[28] Her descriptions of Shanghai, Beijing, Guangzhou, and Hong Kong invariably end in a discussion about female emancipation, and her section "The Tai Tai Lantern" celebrates the emerging class of the New Woman in China: the suffragists, female doctors and philanthropists, women writers, and anti-footbinding activists. It is noteworthy that Seton repeatedly used the hardly appropriate phrase "New Woman," the term for the predecessor of the suffragette, signaling that she, too, used a Western framework to describe a new type of woman in China.[29]

The British novelist Alicia Little (1845–1926), another resident traveler, is probably the most recognized Western woman to comment on bound feet in China. In the first of two chapters in *Intimate China* devoted to the issue, she traces the historical and mythical origins of the tradition, explains the method itself, including its regional differences, and comments on its medical risks.[30] The next chapter is, as she writes, on "a cheerfuller subject,"[31] namely the Natural Feet Society she founded in 1895. This Anti-Footbinding Society had, by the time she wrote her account in 1899, gathered so many supporters, both Western and Chinese, that Little hoped, before long, "'golden lily' shoes [are] only to be found in the shape of Liberty pincushions."[32] Like Gaunt and Cumming, Little invokes Western concepts in her description of footbinding, including the conventional comparison with waistbinding, and, not least, the Liberty pincushion, and although her attempt to explain the tradition in its indigenous historical terms is laudable, it is more a question of speaking up for Chinese women than allowing them to speak for themselves.[33] There was some reciprocity, however, when Chinese women assumed leadership of the anti-footbinding movement and Little went on to use her success and experience to argue for women's suffrage in England, rendering her Chinese experience relevant for her English self.

## Orphanages

Many of the women travelers discussed here employ a strategy that is reminiscent of Mary Louise Pratt's "imperial gaze," in so far as they incorporate, in an ethnocentric gesture, otherness in a framework of familiarity and sameness.[34] However, although the "imperial gaze" is a suggestive paradigm for the colonial encounter, this essay is more interested in finding a paradigm that theorizes the first acquaintance between self and other in terms of the interaction itself, and the impact it has. To do this, I will now explore the woman traveler's encounter with orphanages in China (as a third Foucauldian event), introducing, within this model of the travelogue as a series of encounters, Hans-Georg Gadamer's phenomenological approach to alterity as a productive supplementary mode of analysis.

The evocation of Foucault's model of the closed and total nature of one's epistemic formation, and its expansion in Gadamer's philosophy which stresses the possibility of conversation and exchange between different cultural *epistemes* requires an explanation. Arguably, the moral categories available to our late Victorian women travelers might be sufficient to discriminate between prejudice and open-mindedness, particularly in the context of their contact with Chinese institutions, such as hospitals and orphanages. However, the latter part of this essay on the travelers' encounter with cityscapes and landscapes calls for a framework that transcends these women's moral situatedness and that taps into a dimension of their contact with alterity that cannot be adequately described in simple terms of conscious disapproval or open-minded tolerance, as the moral conscience dictated. Particularly the final section on our travelers' aesthetic response to the Chinese landscape necessitates a more inclusive explanatory model that can accommodate various manifestations of prejudice (moral, historical and aesthetic) and account for the possibility of dialogue with the other in *all* forms of the encounter. It is exactly this openness and expansion of Foucault that we find in Gadamer's model of the nature of human understanding.

Visiting orphanages and caring for abandoned children was another expression of female charity. Elizabeth Enders, an American librarian, who lived in China in the early decades of the twentieth century, met an orphaned girl while traveling with her husband in Jiangsu province. Seeing how the child lived in abject poverty and slave-like conditions with her cruel uncle, the American couple bought the girl for nine gold dollars. They dressed and befriended her during their journey, and later accommodated her in a mission school in Suzhou where they agreed to pay for her upkeep in exchange for communication about the child's progress. Such action, if not unusual among Western travelers and certainly well-meant, has imperialist and missionary undertones, as the couple "acquire" and possess the girl, as Enders writes,[35] and impose their own Western standards upon her by transplanting her into a Christian environment.

Enders of course did not see her own treatment of the girl as at all problematic. Generally, the women's encounters are informed by their own standards, conceptions, and frameworks — Foucault's *epistemes* — which are deeply rooted in history and ideology. For them, the image of China represents values that are the epitome of otherness. If knowledge is, then, based on what Heidegger calls the "fore-structures" of understanding, how is it ever possible to come to know the other as the truly other, and not just a reflection of the self? Gadamer's phenomenological model offers an approach to alterity that acknowledges these fore-structures and, indeed, argues that "the recognition that all understanding inevitably involves some prejudice gives the hermeneutical problem its real thrust."[36] His is a model that gets to the heart of the interaction between self and other during their encounter.

In her 1914 travelogue, *A Woman in China*, Mary Gaunt recounts visiting two orphanages in one day, one Christian and one Buddhist. Her first contact with the Christian mission for the blind illustrates what Gadamer calls the hermeneutical situatedness of the individual, which he understands as a complex web of prior ontological understanding, including self-understanding, which is determined by the individual's ideological position within history and tradition, and through which the subject approaches the unfamiliar.

Gaunt admires the mission, but rather than unequivocally praising the missionaries' work as a reflection of Western and Christian standards as many of her fellow travelers would have done, she criticizes the gravity of the blind children and wonders whether the missionaries "are a little too strenuous in inculcating prayer and praise, and exhorting to a virtue that is a little beyond the average mortal."[37] However, Gaunt's conclusion is, realizing that this severity might be acceptable in return for practical aid, "I, who do nothing, should be the last to judge."[38] Here, the other prerequisites of Gadamer's model for understanding become visible, that is, an Aristotelian faith in *phronesis*, or practical wisdom, and the willingness to engage in dialogue. Combining the hermeneutical situatedness, or "horizon," of the individual with the necessity for dialogue with the other, Gadamer establishes the self-other encounter and the process of interpretation as an ongoing process of mediation between what is familiar and what is alien. In this dialogue neither self nor other remains unaffected, but both engage in a so-called "fusion of horizons," in which what is otherwise unfamiliar, strange and anomalous is integrated into a new and changing horizon.[39] The key to approaching alterity is, then, neither "neutrality with respect to content nor the extinction of one's self," but the foregrounding and appropriation of one's own prejudices, which allows the other to assert "its own truth against one's own fore-meanings."[40]

In the Buddhist orphanage Gaunt judges the boys' shaved heads by her own standards of beauty, contemplating how it spoils "any claim they ha[ve] to good looks."[41] However, prejudice gradually gives way to dialogue, and what represented otherness to Gaunt in the beginning is incorporated into a new, changed horizon. At various points in her travelogue Gaunt mentions that after a first, biased encounter, her "eyes were opened," and she begins to see.[42] Once China is recognized as truly different, that is, not as an imaginary other with its history of imagery in the Western tradition, but as a country with its own history, and once the desire to know the other becomes part of the desire to expand the horizon of knowledge in the West, it becomes necessary to demythologize and engage in dialogue. At this point, Gaunt recuperates some of the real difference China represents, and does not consider the country any more as a mystifying, inexplicable, inferior, or exotic other but as something to be learnt and assimilated until it becomes part of her knowledge and experience of the world. In this way, the traveler crosses the bridge between the Western and Chinese systems of knowledge: rather than resorting to an ethnocentric use of imagery, stereotypes, or fiction to speak to and of alterity (and thus reveal the limitation of the subject's own system of thought, as Foucault suggests in *The Order of Things*),[43] Gaunt's encounter represents the attempt to be dialogic rather than monologic. Once she has seen how lovingly the Buddhist monks took care of their orphans, she regrets not being able to speak with them other than through non-verbal signs.[44] Despite this silence Gaunt's conclusion, after seeing both orphanages, that there are "many ways of doing good in the world" is an attempt to merge horizons, and it marks the beginning of what Gadamer calls a "*hermeneutical conversation*," in which self and other, ideally, find "a common language."[45]

## The Encounter with the City and the Country

*Cityscapes*

The temporal dimension of the Foucauldian event becomes visible in the following two encounters. One event at the turn of the century, in particular, marked the traumatic relations between China and the West. The Chinese hatred against foreigners came to the fullest expression in the Boxer Rebellion of 1900, and the siege of the European Legations in Beijing. The rebels were soon defeated by Western troops as European soldiers marched into Beijing and took control of the city, but in the process, many Westerners, and many more Chinese Christians, were killed. Not surprisingly, travel accounts of Beijing after 1900 are informed by the memories and the myths of this historical event, and our women take different positions towards it.

Constance Cumming and the American Eliza Scidmore (1856–1928) visited the capital before 1900, and both their descriptions show a relative lack of interest in, or failure to see, the sociopolitical unrest which had grown throughout the last decades of the nineteenth century. Instead, when describing the European legations (which were established after the Europeans first marched into Beijing in 1860, and afterwards were a part of the "concessions" extracted from the defeated Chinese), they focus on the pleasant side of expatriate life rather than its economic and political implications. Cumming reached the capital in June 1879 by land route from Tianjin, a journey which stood in marked contrast to the more comfortable travel arrangements by ship, which she normally preferred.[46] Repeatedly complaining about the "purgatorial process" of being driven in a Peking cart, and reminding the reader of her "bruised bones," Cumming finally arrived in Beijing. However, disappointingly, the "famous capital of the Celestial Empire" looked to this traveler like "a horribly hideous city built of mud and smothered in dust," and in great need of improvement.[47] The British Legation, a former imperial palace which the British government was now renting, found more approval with Cumming: the grounds were beautifully laid out, the state rooms were architectural masterpieces.[48] Overall, Cumming was glad to notice that the Russian, German, and American embassies were situated close to the British Legation, "so that while the Chinese authorities thus ma[k]e the best of necessity, the foreigners have the great advantage of being near together, and forming a pleasant little society of their own."[49] The many sources of entertainment (one of which Cumming swiftly attended at the American legation) were, according to this upper-class traveler, "a privilege in this horrid land of exile, which fully compensated for being apparently classed as tribute-bearers."[50]

Cumming remained, on the whole, uncritical of and unconcerned by the tension between China and the West. She admitted that "the necessity of admitting barbarians to dwell" within Beijing "must have been a bitter pill to the Chinese authorities,"[51] but was afterwards content to spend the remainder of her journey sightseeing, being entertained in the better-off colonial circles, and, characteristically, going souvenir-hunting. Cumming can be considered the prototypical modern tourist — it is noteworthy that she also complained that "nothing of the nature of a hotel for foreigners exists" in

Beijing — and Scidmore, although a professional travel writer and photographer, shows similar attitudes.[52] She, too, embarked on a sightseeing tour around the city, which also ended in a shopping spree, but only after she had commented at length on the presence of the Westerners in the capital.[53] More caustic about expatriate life than Cumming — this might be due to the fact that Scidmore's account of Beijing was written shortly before the Boxer outbreak, and unrest was visible — she understood that "[t]he whole stay of the envoys at Peking has been a long story of trial and fruitless efforts, of rebuffs and covert insults."[54] However, her allusions to current intrigues, secret conventions and concession-seeking, which European diplomats must concern themselves with (in addition to the "coup d'états before breakfast, executions overnight, rioting soldiers . . . mobs stoning legation carts and chairs at will, and telegraphic communication broken"), are balanced by a description of the sumptuous lodgings of the diplomatic corps and the many sources of entertainment the expatriates enjoy: "They have their club, the tennis-courts . . . their spring and autumn races at a track beyond the walls, frequent garden-parties and picnic teas in the open seasons, and a busy round of state dinners and balls all winter."[55] A reviewer in *The Literary World* was right to conclude that Scidmore's "sense is more artistic than political, [and] she is more occupied with the features of the present life of the people than in projecting the possible phases of the future."[56] On the whole, Scidmore's and Cumming's descriptions are rather similar in their disregard for the larger realities of politics.

Alicia Little's "Anniversary Study of August 1900" in her *Round About My Peking Garden* is, in contrast, a grim reminder of the massacres of the Boxer outbreak a year earlier, and the ensuing decay and desperation in Beijing.[57] Talking to Catholic nuns and their prefect who described in harrowing detail how many of their brothers and sisters were cruelly murdered — "killed by cutting [their] arms and legs to the bone, filling the cuts with petroleum and then setting them alight" — Little's description is of course partial to the Western perspective of the historical event.[58] If understandable in terms of Gadamer's prejudiced "horizon of the individual," it is disconcerting how Little's compassion is mostly reserved for the often trivial-sounding hardships Westerners endured during and after the siege, such as when she contemplated the disturbance of domestic arrangements:

> To live through eight weeks of a Chinese summer, bathless, with barely a change of clothing, on food that disagreed with nearly every one, some less, certainly, but most more! Then can one realise it! All of a sudden the thought that you are *saved*, and that you must now shift for yourself, provide for your wife and family and children, and that without a pan, a plate, a chair, a bed, a towel, without money to buy any of these things — without any one to sell to you if you had money. And first of all, to be without a roof under the August sun of China, virtually a houseless beggar, with some hundreds of Chinese, too, depending upon you! What would *you* have done?[59]

In Little's account, memories of the siege, such as murder and martyrdom, dead soldiers, orphaned children, and a city in ruins merge with a celebration of the collaboration of the victorious nations who, "in such close juxtaposition, harassed by such a worrying dust," have already managed to establish "so much order and decency."[60] Little, as a firm defender of the British Empire, translates the traumatic events of the Boxer Rebellion into a triumph of Western power. Her bias is untouched by any engagement with China's true otherness, and in her 1904 Baedecker-style *Guide to Peking*, the Boxer incident has been so far suppressed that Little merely speaks in passing of "the mad folly of the Boxer outbreak."[61]

It is to Scidmore's expatriate horse-races that Gaunt refers in her more impartial and tentatively dialogic 1914 account of Beijing in *A Woman in China*. Seeing that exiled Britons had a better life than "the men of the same class who stay at home," the Australian criticized the segregation that characterized the racing entertainment from which the Chinese population was largely excluded: "It was so expressive of the attitude of the Powers who watch over China."[62] Disregarding the post-Boxer and, more importantly now, post-Revolution problems (such as the National Assembly being in an uproar, the Premier openly accused of murder, everyone fearing that the North and the South would be at each other's throats soon, and rumors of war spreading), foreign Beijing, writes Gaunt sarcastically, "did itself well."[63] On a visit to the Legation quarter she reflected upon the city's foreign rule: "Suppose in London all the great nations of the earth took a strip of the town, extending say from Marble Arch to Hyde Park Corner, and from Park Lane to Bond Street, held it and fortified it heavily, barring out the inhabitants, not wholly, but by certain regulations that prevented them having the upper hand."[64] Her critique of the West reaches its climax when she labels the caption "Lest We Forget," written in bold letters on a wall in the British Legation, an insult to upper-class, educated Chinese as it is "a reminder always, if the nations needed a reminder, of the days of 1900, of the terrible days that may be repeated any time this peace-loving nation drifts into an anti-foreign campaign."[65] Gaunt, yet again, engages with the bias Gadamer sees in every encounter with otherness, and tries to represent both sides of the coin in a critical manner, defamiliarizing prejudice by attending to the other's point of view. Her conclusion about the West's influence in China is that the Chinese must hope to "oust these arrogant men from the West . . . who thus lord over them," a sentiment which is shared by LaMotte five years later when she explicitly expresses sympathy for the Boxers' attempt to get rid of the Westerners.[66]

### Landscapes

The description of landscape marks another moment in the travelogue which invites the traveler to engage with her cultural and historical *epistemes*, or fore-structures of thinking. The appreciation of landscape is sometimes considered as if it takes place in a rarefied isolation. Shirley Foster, for example, has argued that a heightened emotional response and momentary self-forgetfulness are most possible in the encounter with landscape, which is, she claims, entirely detached from everyday experience.[67] The final section of this essay argues against Foster's hypothesis and reveals the philosophical and historical depth of landscape appreciation both in Europe and in China by looking at four women's encounters with the Chinese landscape. The first two, Little's and Kemp's ideologically one-sided narratives of their journeys to the sublime Mount Omi (Emei) in Sichuan, in 1896 and 1908 respectively, are shaped by memories of the historical partitioning of China at the end of the century into spheres of foreign influence and economic activity. In contrast, Kendall's and Gaunt's descriptions are attempts to engage dialogically with the relations between China and the West.

After the Sino-Japanese War of 1894–95, one after the other, Britain, France, Germany, and Russia marked the bits of the country they would "buy" to help China out of its financial crisis following the large indemnity demanded by Japan. After a series of what were known as unequal treaties, the south of China was parceled out to France; Britain had a "sphere of influence" between Chengdu in Sichuan and Shanghai in the east; Germany had claimed parts of Shandong province; Japan parts of Manchuria; and Russia the far north-eastern parts of the empire. LaMotte's anecdote about the president of a big American corporation, who sought a concession from the Chinese government, was a critique of both the ignorance of her fellow Americans and the semi-colonized state of China. The American was presented with a map of China, with multicolored dots and sectors marking the foreign concessions. Unaware of this, the man pointed his finger at several regions on the map, stating "I'll do work here," but was repeatedly told by Western secretaries that the area in question was already in the possession of the Russians, the French, or the British. Exasperated, the American eventually turned to the silent Chinese and asked, "Where the hell is China?"[68]

Explicitly anti-colonial observations like LaMotte's are fairly rare. In contrast, and more typical in travel writing between 1880 and 1920, Little's and Kemp's descriptions of mountain views show how a partisan faith in the colonial mission and feelings of superiority are projected onto the landscape. Here, the potentially emotional encounter with the mountainscape (*vide* Foster) becomes, like the Kantian narrative of the sublime, a moment in which the mind successfully detaches itself from participation in the phenomenal world, and in an act of transcendental contemplation and self-analysis achieves intellectual mastery over the powers of nature.[69] The sublime encounter has been repeatedly linked to the colonial project. Both show the self's endeavour to define itself as a rational, superior entity; both include a struggle for mastery between two opposing powers; and both end in the subject's appropriation of what could potentially exceed and undermine it.[70] As soon as Mrs. Little had climbed Mount Omi, she took possession of it. She wrote in retrospect that she was "surprised and amused to find how easily and completely [she and her husband] could lose" themselves in the scenery, but this immersion in the landscape in fact took the shape of an imperialist fantasy. Little and her husband literally penetrated "the virgin forest," running their "spiked sticks" into the ground, and despoiling it, "breaking off here a twig and there a twig" and "gathering a profusion of ripe raspberries and sweetest large white strawberries as [they go] along."[71] The height of the couple's imperialist daydream is reached with the Littles' desire to colonize, or "people," the park "with happy boys."[72]

Kemp, on her six-month journey through the provinces of Shandong, Jilin, Hubei, Sichuan and Yunnan in 1907–08, also climbed the 11,000-feet-high mountain, but as in Little's case, her description centres on an assertion of the supremacy of the observing self. This leads to Kemp following almost to the letter the strategies of Pratt's colonial trope of "Monarch-of-all-I-survey."[73] Kemp, like Little, understands the landscape through the historical context of the Western semi-colonization of China. She aestheticizes and frames the landscape like a painting, and orders the description in (Western) terms of foreground and background: "Standing on the edge of the summit, you look down a precipice of more than a mile, and we could only feast our eyes on the ever-changing scene, the clouds looking as if they were boiling up from some hidden caldron, now concealing, now revealing the peaks of distant mountains."[74] The verbal painter thus renders momentarily significant what is, from a narrative point of view, practically a non-event.[75] Rich adjectives and modifiers endow the landscape with dense meaning: "On a *clear* day the *far-distant snowy* peaks of Tibet are visible, and the *glorious fertile* plain out of which the *limestone* peak of Mount Omi rises."[76] At the same time, the reference to limestone adds a material referent to the landscape, which sprinkles it "with some little bits of England."[77] The scene is fully mastered when the artist Kemp not only appreciates the mountainscape in her own terms and paints it verbally for others, but in actual fact takes out her sketchbook to capture the scene of "the neighbouring crag of the '10,000 Buddhas' " in a drawing.[78] If Little and Kemp both believe that the political and economic "redemption of China must come from the outside,"[79] they render their ideological superiority and cultural and historical situatedness visible in the descriptions of Mount Omi's setting. The description of the landscape turns into a historicized event, which abolishes the otherness of China in favor of a celebration of the imperial eye/I.

But what form might a Gadamerian landscape representation take, and how is it different from the monarchic Little and Kemp? Elizabeth Kendall (1865–1952), an American teacher of history and political science at Wellesley, traveled in Yunnan in the 1910s and, in contrast to the previous two travelers, she was rather critical of the Western influence there. She writes that

> [d]read of the foreigner underlies much of the present activity and openmindedness towards Western ideas. The willingness to adopt our ways does not necessarily mean that the Chinese prefer them to their own, but simply that they realize if they would meet us on equal terms they must meet us with our own weapons.[80]

Kendall summarizes Yunnan's history with the West — specifically with France from the 1880s onwards — as one that is characterized by "[b]loodshed and disorder," and she suggests that this history has "given the country a set-back from which it is only beginning to recover."[81] Her rejection of the colonial paradigm and her attempt to interact dialogically with the landscape around Yunnan-fu can be seen in her discussion of the region's history, geography, demography, climate, infrastructure, and trade. Rather than interpreting these features in light of how they could become profitable for Western traders, as Little and Kemp might have done, Kendall reads Yunnan's copper mines, its metal trade and its agricultural riches as possible means out of the region's post-Western economic and social crisis. The opium trade of the region, emblematic of the West's unequal, destructive relations with China, has been abolished — "not a poppy field was to be seen"[82] — and although Kendall predicts that Yunnan's road into the future will be a difficult one, she is hopeful that the region's emerging economic self-governance will soon be visible in a different, flourishing landscape.

If Kendall's travelogue foregrounds a more disinterested account of the countryside than do Little's and Kemp's, her bias in favor of the economic potential of an independent China may point towards an appreciation of the other's viewpoint and the possibility of dialogue but can hardly be called a "fusion of horizons." It is only Mary Gaunt's landscape description of the "holy mountain" near Tsung Hua Chou in Hebei province in Northern China that, arguably, comes close to Gadamer's ideal.[83] Approaching the mountain range Gaunt writes:

> I looked up to the hills that towered above us, almost perpendicular they seemed in places, as if the slope had been shorn off roughly with a blunt knife, and I saw that one of these crags [i.e. the holy mountain she will later climb], that must have been about a thousand feet above the valley bottom, anyhow it looked it in the afternoon sunlight, was crowned with buildings . . .[84]

Gaunt's initial comments show unease with the unfamiliar landscape that is so far from Europe "where rolling ridges and valleys are the norm" rather than "mountains and hills that rise sharply out of flat alluvial plains."[85] Her sense of alienation instinctively prompts her attempt to "grasp" and "possess" the mountain by capturing it in a photograph. However, this approach to knowledge and understanding through photographic realism fails her: "They say the camera cannot lie, I only know I did not succeed in getting a photograph of that mountain."[86] Gaunt's frustration increases. If she was from the start rather disinclined to climb the holy mountain and visit the Nine Dragon temple and monastery on its peak, her struggle to grasp the encounter through familiar parameters leads to her conclusion that "[even] if it were the most beautiful temple in the world I would not go up that mountain to visit it."[87] However, she has not reckoned on her Chinese servant Tuan. The rest of the encounter can be read as displaying a shift from Gaunt's reliance on Western modes of organisation, thought and authority to an engagement with Chinese ones. In the same way that Gaunt surrenders control and Tuan takes charge, "inappropriate" Western frameworks of seeing open up a space for Chinese aesthetic modes of landscape appreciation. Telling Gaunt that she has come at an auspicious time as the temple is hardly ever open to visitors, Tuan persuades the woman that the journey up the holy mountain is worth the effort, and when she still protests that she is too fatigued to attempt the steep climb, he organizes a sedan chair and carriers for her. Having convinced the traveler of his superior knowledge in dealing with this situation, Tuan then changes his role once more when they reach the peak: "Here Tuan blossomed forth wonderfully. Up till now he had only been my servant," writes Gaunt, "a most important servant but still a servant, now he became, on a sudden, that much more important functionary, my interpreter."[88] Tuan takes on the role of an artist who paints the landscape for Gaunt to appreciate, engaging her as an active recipient in the visualizing process. Seeing becomes a dialogic process put together in collaboration between a master who gives access to a particular mode of perception, and a disciple who learns. At the same time, the disciple's subjecthood is shaped through a process of self-examination.[89] Seeing how Gaunt's photographic realism has failed to "see" the landscape Tuan takes it upon him to give the Western woman what Jonathan Hay calls soteriological guidance, where teaching becomes a means to enlightenment.[90] Tuan purchases incense sticks and worships his gods in the little temple, knocking his head repeatedly on the ground, signaling to Gaunt the spiritual nature of this landscape encounter.[91] Gaunt, in earlier encounters, already showed a willingness to engage dialogically with alterity, but in this scene, by accepting the role of disciple, dialogue is taken to another level: a different mode of seeing otherness is enabled only when Gaunt is helped to open her eyes to the spirituality of the mountain by the example of her master Tuan who interprets the experience for her. In this process of dialogic seeing, the disciple is actively challenged and persuaded; the master might even have to stimulate doubts in the disciple (or prejudice in Gadamer's model) in order to build up the psychic pressure that will make enlightenment possible.[92] Gaunt's own description of the vista once Tuan, the painter, has channeled the divine through his own transcendent mental nature,[93] is as follows:

> Oh, ... I had something — something that I cannot put into words — for my pains; the something that made the men of five hundred years before build the temple on the mountain top to the glory of God, my God and their God, by whatever Name you choose to call Him. It was good to sit there looking away at the distant vista, at the golden sunlight on the trees and grass, at the shadows that were creeping in between, to smell the sensuous smell of the jessamine, and if I could not help thinking of all I had lost in life [i.e. her husband, whose death forced her to leave Australia to earn a living in England], of the fate that had sent me here to the Nine Dragon Temple, at least I could count among my gains the beauty that lay before my eyes.[94]

The student's resistance to understanding cannot be overcome by anyone but herself,[95] hence Gaunt's description is an active communication between Western and Chinese frameworks. Words of possession and representational concepts of shading — a concept alien to Chinese landscape painting and only brought in from the West — merge in Gaunt's description with a sensory component, the jasmine scent, and her religious deliberation which are, arguably, prompted by Tuan's religious acts of worship. The visualization of landscape here involves an *experience* of place and a meditative process which cannot be so easily captured by film. Gaunt has been given access to "seeing" beyond photographic realism, and she later refers to her trip up the holy mountain as her "pilgrimage," which has triggered an understanding of the spirituality of landscape, by whatever framework — Christian, Buddhist, Daoist or Confucianist — one might refer to them. Encountering a landscape (painting) has become a process of self-examination for Gaunt, where the hermeneutic process of encountering alterity leads to an active engagement with one's *epistemes* and, ideally, a fusion of horizons, shaping subjecthood.

Rationality and imperial authority, manifest in Kemp's possessive description, are in Gaunt's encounter replaced by the willingness to give up control and reason and enlarge one's capacity to perceive the world in a different way. Gaunt's little anecdote can therefore be read as an initially forced then willing dialogic engagement with the other's — Tuan's — mode of approaching the world. All in all, Gaunt concludes, the trip to the holy mountain was "something well worth remembering."[96]

## Conclusion

"The fundamental codes of a culture — those governing its language, its schema of perception, its exchanges, its techniques, its values, the hierarchy of its practices — establish for every [wo]man, from the very first, the empirical orders with which [s]he will be dealing and within which [s]he will be at home," writes Foucault.[97] This essay has looked at a number of female travelers in a forty-year period around the turn of the nineteenth century, and has tried to systematize their diverse accounts through a number of shared encounters with institutions in China, with the capital Beijing, and the landscape. I have approached these women's meetings with the Chinese other through Gadamer's phenomenological model of understanding in which initial bias and the dominance of the self, ideally, give way to dialogue and a merging of the individual horizons of self and other in an active hermeneutical process. The essay has shown that the responses range from the women's utter refusal to partake in a process of understanding that might threaten to deconstruct their notion of subjecthood and authority (but also might give them insights into otherness), to a more unguarded willingness to engage with their own situatedness and prejudice and approach alterity with open eyes and open minds.

Jorge Luis Borges' imaginary Chinese encyclopedia article on animals continued, further classifying them as "(i) frenzied, (j) innumerable, (k) drawn with a very fine camel hair brush, (l) *et cetera*, (m) having just broken the water pitcher, (n) that from a long way off look like flies."[98] And although it is impossible here to summarize the women travelers' diverse descriptions of China as anything but '*et cetera*', this essay has, it is hoped, given some sense of the possible avenues the enquiry into the moment of the encounter between self and other can take.

UNIVERSITY OF WINCHESTER
LIBRARY

# 7

# Travel Writing and the Humanitarian Impulse:
## Alicia Little in China

*Susan Schoenbauer Thurin*

Humanitarianism does not usually spring to mind as the subject of travel writing. In writings about nineteenth-century China, however, and in particular in the writing of Alicia Little, or Mrs. Archibald Little, to use the name under which she published her books and articles about China, it has a prominent position. By humanitarianism I mean efforts undertaken to alleviate the pain and suffering of others; subjects Little addresses in her books about China. Her positive attitude toward China and Chinese women and children in particular, and her work on their behalf, distinguishes her humanitarianism. What this essay attempts to do is examine the motivation for Little's humanitarianism, how her life in China aroused her humanitarian conscience, and the specific subjects that demanded her attention and action.

Two of the standard topics mentioned in nineteenth-century travels in China are missionaries and footbinding — the humanitarians themselves and an issue claiming humanitarian interest. The numerous works about China that missionaries themselves produced are often essentially travel and description books such as Rev. Virgil Hart's *Western China*, or those suitable for a shelf on ethnography and anthropology such as Arthur H. Smith's *Chinese Characteristics* and *Village Life in China*, and S. Wells Williams' *The Middle Kingdom*. Non-missionary travelers, on the other hand, typically describe visits to missionaries and comment on the cost and value of their work, thus weighing in with evidence from the field to fan the debate back in Great Britain about the role of missionaries in the last decades of the Victorian era. Humanitarian work in the colonial world goes beyond the work of missionaries, however, even as it follows in the wake of historical precedent.

Humanitarianism, as used in this essay, is the practical application of altruism, a subject probed variously in philosophy, social psychology, developmental psychology, and evolutionary biology.[1] A useful starting point for my discussion is Gertrude

Himmelfarb's interpretive history of humanitarianism, *Poverty and Compassion: The Moral Imagination of the Late Victorians*. Noting the shift from the eighteenth and early nineteenth-century connotation of compassion as a moral sentiment to a political principle and subject of scientific research, Himmelfarb explains that the Victorian idea of poverty as a social problem that could be eradicated differed from the earlier notion of destitution as a condition needing immediate redress. Mayhew's social exploration and novelists such as Dickens and Disraeli dramatized and popularized the image of the poor, while a large pantheon of reformers such as Booth and Rowntree, and later the theories of those such as the Fabians, contributed to the development of agencies and institutional change aimed at eliminating poverty. The humanitarianism of Alicia Little discussed in this essay incorporates these wide-ranging views of compassion, from making individuals the object of benevolent action to her colorful depiction of those in need of philanthropy, to her portrayal of those engaged in this work, and finally her description of an organized campaign addressing a specific societal need.

In the context of travel writing discourse, the analysis of scholars such as Mary Louise Pratt in *Imperial Eyes* develops an interpretation essentially antithetic to the humanitarian impulse. Pratt's evocative study of "the gaze," for example, argues that the rhetoric of travel literature exposes the goals of exploitation of peoples and appropriation of riches as an object of the traveler.[2] The obverse is that the humanitarian-hearted travel writer such as Alicia Little prefers to describe conditions and cultural practices with an eye to reforming them. Often critical of missionary endeavor *per se*, she may be seen as a secular missionary, one who aimed to change for the better the culture of those among whom she lived. Her activism in China does not announce itself until 1895, eight years after her arrival there. This long gestation period includes several critical events, as well as being a consequence of her work as a writer, a traveler, and resident of China.

## Biographical Information

The light of Alicia Little has dimmed over the course of a century, but in her own time she was a minor celebrity, significant enough to earn an acerbic description tinged with envy by Gertrude Bell, who met her at a dinner party in Shanghai in 1903. Bell, whose brilliant political work in the Near East would earn her the title of "uncrowned queen of Iraq," writes to her father:

> Mr and Mrs Archibald Little were there — she is a truly awful lady. She wore a mustard yellow dress which was exactly the same colour as her skin. So that for some time I did not notice she had a low gown on . . . ! She has a very vivacious manner and a heavy black moustache. Her husband doesn't count. Dr Morrison [a missionary] says her books are pretty feeble, but as they are popular he hopes she will write a great many more, for he rejoices to see any interest roused about China.[3]

Bell's pettiness followed by a grudging compliment indicates the sources of Little's fame, her writing and social activism. Before her marriage, as A.E.N. Bewicke, Little published nine novels, the most significant of which from a cultural perspective are *Miss Standish* (1883), which argues for women's suffrage, property rights, and the repeal of the Contagious Diseases Act; and *Mother Darling* (1885), which popularized and influenced the reform establishing the right of mothers to have custody of their own children. As precursors to her work in China, these novels indicate Little's longstanding commitment to social causes with her writing as a primary vehicle to promote these causes.

After her marriage in 1886, Little went out to China with her husband and under her new name published three novels about Westerners in China, five books of travel and description, and a biography of the statesman Li Hung-chang. After her husband's death she edited two volumes of his writings. One of her novels, *A Marriage in China*, earned her a level of notoriety in the colonial world as it rather too closely uses the character and circumstances of several Westerners working in China at the time. The scandal was exacerbated by the frankness with which she handles two contentious subjects, concubinage and Eurasian children. The novel was the subject of numerous contemporary reviews and went through several editions. Another of Little's China novels, *A Millionaire's Courtship* (1906), is a didactic story about how to be an ideal European in China. Little unabashedly uses both fiction and non-fiction to portray colonial-era life in China, humanitarian themes, and travelogue. For his part, Archibald Little had distinguished himself as a sinologist. He started his career in China as a tea taster with a German firm, and after the demise of the tea trade became a merchant, entrepreneur, and the author of several significant books about China. Together the Littles traveled widely, and lived in Chongqing, Shanghai, and Beijing until their final return to England in 1907. They promoted the modernization of China through their writings and their deeds.[4] In *Intimate China* (1899) and *The Land of the Blue Gown* (1902), Mrs. Little writes her story of life in China as a combination of travelogue, memoir, and commentary on society and politics, ending with a chronicle of her stunning work in the anti-footbinding movement.

## Development of the Philanthropic Spirit

Victorian travel writing about China often complains about dirt, disease, and cultural anomalies, about Chineseness, typically to characterize what was deemed a nation in decay. By the end of the nineteenth century, the image of China as a place of luxury and riches had given way under the weight of Western conquest and exploitation to that of a country beset by corrupt leaders, poverty, and general backwardness. In *Intimate China*, Little attempts to counter such views by presenting an authentic picture. She pledges to describe the Chinese "as I have seen them in their homes and at their dinner parties."[5] Under the spell of her role as a bride and the excitement of becoming a resident in China in May 1887, she dismisses prejudicial judgments of China. So to Little, the dreary muddiness of Shanghai and the rivers meeting there gives way to the image of it as a hurly-burly of East-meeting-West. Six hundred miles inland at Hankou, she again disputes the stories of dirt and bad smells so legion about China; she compares it favorably to East London and the South of France. When years later she disparages the reputation of the Chinese part of Shanghai for uncleanliness — "Shanghai Chinatown enjoys the reputation of being very dirty and disgusting, but that sunshiny afternoon we did not find it so, though we wondered a little at the dirt as we passed down one street of Chinese houses . . ." (BG 43) — what she most wants to draw attention to is the objectionable quality of water with which the poor must make do for washing, cooking and drinking, made all the more unseemly by the "abundant supply of wholesome, pure water" in the foreign concession nearby.[6] Little is not above complaining about the "dirt and smells, which make what might be so charmingly romantic, distressingly Zolaesque" (BG 90), but she never blames the poor for being poor nor the victim for being victimized, instead exhibiting a philanthropic spirit by faulting the conditions that make life miserable.

Little is mortified by instances of human suffering. Like many Westerners in China, she observes cruel punishments for wrong-doers such as the cangue, which prevented "the poor wretches" from lying down or even feeding themselves (BG 40). However, in contrasting the Chinese, whose culture trains them not to express feelings, to the "vehement Neapolitan," whose dramatic gestures demand attention, Little misunderstands the Chinese: "Did they wish much to say anything their whole physique must have altered long ago. But they are a long-suffering race, born, one would say, to be hewers of wood and drawers of water, and to bear things patiently" (BG 43). Despite her patronizing tone, Little's comment displays sympathy in the Dickensian spirit, as if to echo Joe in *Great Expectations*, "We don't know what you have done, but we wouldn't have you starved to death for it."[7] The humanitarian impulse implicit in such descriptions appears even when criminal events touch her personally. When the Littles lose all their worldly possessions in a riot during the Boxer turmoil, she does not dwell on the loss in a self-pitying way, never even mentioning treasured items lost as she might have done. What she does instead is tell the story of the riot, the behavior of the rioters and of the foreigners attacked, and suggests the probable cause for the event. Her China books always try to take the high road, being intent on fair-mindedness, of trying to understand political and cultural clashes. This is an attitude which made the far more popular Isabella Bird worry about her *Yangtze Valley and Beyond* competing with Little's *Intimate China*. Bird wrote to her publisher John Murray in February 1899 that Little's "will be a very clear and readable book and very well-illustrated."[8]

When Little's observation of life in China remains in the public sphere, her discourse is philosophical and ideology-based. In a chapter on marriage in *Intimate China,* she compiles several anecdotes, including a comic wedding mishap, another on an affectionate marriage, and a long story about an abused wife who poisons her husband in desperation and is executed for the deed (IC 184–96). The object of these stories is to show a broad range of marital situations that transcend time and place, to shrink the distance between East and West. Moving to descriptions of the private sphere, however, Little's magnanimity sometimes flags. In *The Land of the Blue Gown,* she reprints a diary from the early 1890s when she spent a summer on a farmstead near Chongqing in Sichuan. True to the diary genre, Little's account is an unadorned reckoning with cultural difference, probably the motivation for a comment in *Intimate China* in which she attributes the authenticity of her account to "living long, oh! such long summer days among them [the Chinese], and yet wearier dark days of winter" (IC 5).

The diary has many references to the abuse of women and children, to crime and cruelty, the darker side of family life. At first there is a discontinuity with the philanthropic spirit shown in Little's travelogue discourse which may be explained by her own sense of disorientation in unfamiliar surroundings. The result, at times, is an incoherent assemblage of details, as when she mentions child abuse in a sentence sandwiched between observations of pleasant daily life: "Air fresh and fragrant, reminding me of haymaking days. Mistress of the farm flogged little grandson, because he had a sore on his leg and had not washed it properly. She does her washing in the most delightful fashion . . ." (BG 144). A later paragraph contains an anecdote, again without comment, about a young wife being beaten by her husband for a clothing bill, and this is immediately followed by a description of Little's ride into the hills to observe the landscape and sunset. She neither commiserates with those abused nor contemplates what she might do to interpose, once even complaining about this same little boy as an inconvenience when he "kept me awake last night by his groaning — he has a horrible skin disease over both his legs" (BG 167). The early pages of Little's diary betray her disengagement with the Chinese family among whom she lives.

The diary dates from the Littles' early married life when they moved to Chongqing, then outside the treaty-port areas where foreigners were allowed to do business. Missionaries were the only other Westerners in Chongqing at the time, and Mrs. Little's command of Chinese was not good. Her sense of isolation is obvious but she attempts to dispel this by joining a group of farm-wives engaged in preparing the fiber for grass cloth, and once she allows them to playfully bind her feet. These activities succeed in helping her develop empathy for the local people, as indicated by her approval when the father intervenes on behalf of the farm children being beaten. As more time passes, Little's philanthropic sentiments become more frequently stated, for example in her frustration with the parents who refuse to allow their son to be taken to the hospital where the Western doctor could treat his skin disease (BG 208). At the same time, the situation defines Little's helplessness in the face of an immediate, difficult situation. Commiserating with pain and suffering in the abstract and contributing to an argument for change is the method of helping others more suited to her skills and position.

## The Feebleness of Good Will

Little's position on the country farm underlines the need for authority in order to be effective in a philanthropic effort, even on the personal level. As a tenant, a wife, and a foreigner, her position on the farm was ambiguous, making it difficult for her to assert any control over life there. Best intentions sometimes go awry, as when Little employs the daughter of her landlord to embroider an ornamental sewing bag. This was intended as a good-will gesture, but one day she is told the girl has "almost gone blind with ophthalmia" (an eye infection perhaps not accurately explained in Little's day) as a result of the fine needlework she is doing (BG 203). This event compounded an ongoing trauma due to the Littles having had their valuables stolen as they slept. Under torture the apparent thief accused the farmer's son of being the instigator; as a result, "the eldest son [is] in prison through us" (BG 203). Finally, "unable any longer to bear the thought of the misery we have anyhow been the means of bringing upon these poor people" (BG 208), Archibald Little attempts to intercede with the Chinese magistrates and give up all claim to their possessions so as to release the boy and spare the Chinese family further woe, but the son is bambooed and tortured all the same.

The Littles themselves become frightened and practice using their revolvers. Alicia Little's well-intentioned scheme to integrate herself into the Chinese community soured pathetically: "We feel too sad even to talk over things now" (BG 213). In time a rough justice is effected when the wrongly accused young man is exonerated, the real thieves exhibited in cages, the Littles' possessions restored, "and the honour of the farm family is intact once more" (BG 226). The thwarted goals of the summer, however, illustrate the precariousness of good works even on the smallest scale. In retrospect Little is able to place the events in a perspective that returns to the philanthropic spirit with which she is comfortable: "that great division of the human race, called Chinese, consists not only of China men but of real men and women with simple wants and wishes not after all so unlike our own" (BG 226).

## Missionaries

Missionaries play an important role in this discussion of the humanitarian impulse in travel writing, for many missionaries were engaged in educational and medical work in addition to their strictly religious duties. In a country in which education had been reserved almost entirely for men and which had little access to modern medicine, Western missionaries aimed to introduce knowledge that would better the lives of the Chinese. Yet in Little's day only opium surpassed missionaries as a controversial subject of Western concern about China. On the one hand the exploitation of China by the West was rationalized in the popular press, political commentary, and parliament as a justification for Christianizing the country. The treaties after the Second Opium War in 1860 made specific provisions for allowing missionaries access to all of China, gave them the right to own land there, and accorded them special protection. On the other hand, the role of the West in the opium trade, the influx of large numbers of missionaries after 1860, the cost of supporting missionaries in relation to the number of converts to Christianity, and the misgivings of both the Chinese and Westerners about the justice of altering the beliefs of this ancient culture, all contributed to the difficulties missionaries faced in China. Little is as conflicted by missionary work as anyone; she herself both praises and condemns it. Her chapter on "Our Missionaries" in *Intimate China* pairs a catalogue of criticisms with examples of high praise for individual workers. But the most affecting passages about missionaries in her travel books are those describing the sadness of the Italian nuns and French Catholic priests, all of whom went out to China as a permanent assignment with no hope of home leave. If those who would do humanitarian work are themselves the object of pity, the effectiveness of their work seems called into question.

Unlike the forlorn Catholic priests and nuns Little describes, the Protestant missionaries had the comfort of family in China and of regular visits to their homeland. Little dilates ironically on this topic in a chapter called "Cheap Missionaries" in *The Land of the Blue Gown*. The most volatile issue was strictly monetary and Little approaches this with trepidation. At Wuhu one of the more embarrassingly large and grand missionary houses, that of the American missionary Dr. Virgil Hart, gives "the effect as if the various missions sat down outside a Chinese city in fortresses to lay siege to it" (BG 295). Little finds the placement of Western-style mansions in the Chinese countryside disconcerting, though she is careful to mention their private funding, to help allay the criticism of missionaries exacting donations from home to lead a life of luxury abroad. Though the educational institution run by Dr. Hart is praiseworthy, to Little his manner of living undercuts the altruism of his work.

The reverse of the "Cheap Missionaries" debate is exemplified by several missionaries whose living standard does not trouble donors at home. First there is Mr. Horsburgh of the China Inland Mission who claims to survive on five pounds a month.[9] Another of Little's anecdotes describes the destitution of a lonely priest, his only luxury a small glass-paned window above his desk, his only furniture three chairs and a tiny bookshelf. A mission station at Ta-Chien-Lu near the border of Tibet, a week's travel from the next-nearest Westerners, shows cost from a different angle. Three priests there seem to have a prosperous farm and comfortable housing but evidence of their mission work is small, consisting of a school with only eight girls taught by a Chinese sister. The brave cheerfulness of one of the priests belies their isolation. Little understands that their account of the events and news of the outside world is a compilation of events over a ten-year period: "Truly a costly mission, we thought" (BG 128). To Little the monetary cost of missionary work shrinks in relation to the tax on individual lives: so few children taught, so many lives withering in obscurity.

In her chapter "What Are Missionaries Doing" in *The Land of the Blue Gown*, Little addresses another part of the missionary debate, the results of their labor. Not being particularly persuaded of the need to Christianize the Chinese in the first place, Little never approaches the issue of numbers of converts, but rather focuses entirely on the work of missionaries in education and medicine. In *The Land of the Blue Gown* she praises schools and hospitals as "probably the most satisfactory form of missionary work" (90), and she offers many descriptions of visits to both in support of her argument. A visit to the closing ceremony at one girls' school impresses her. The girls were "interesting, they were attractive, simply because the mind in them evidently had been aroused, and was working" (IC 239–40). At the AME girls' school in Zhenjiang, she praises the pupils for being well-educated, healthy, making great wives, all the more to their credit because they never had their feet bound: "That they are happier than most Chinese women I think no one could look at them and doubt" (BG 292). Little found the men's university at Nanjing modern, excellent, "with an air of excitement." The aura of the classroom was electric, the students' "faculties were at full stretch" (BG 293). What Little does not mention is any conflict between this Westernized education and a traditional Chinese one.

Little's unreserved praise for mission schools is topped by that accorded two American-trained Chinese women doctors then in the process of building their own hospital while carrying on a large country practice. Little singles out other missionary hospitals such as those in Nanjing for praise, too, especially for their cleanliness and surgeries. Westerners held traditional Chinese medicine in low repute in the nineteenth century, yet few would dispute the contributions of medical missionaries as a worthwhile humanitarian enterprise. The introduction of Western medicine was helpful in treating a number of endemic diseases in China and remains a subject for a broader study.

In Little's attempt to present a comprehensive picture of the work of missionaries, she includes two stories on the margin of typical humanitarian concerns. Noting that a goal of a good many Westerners in China is to collect material for a book, she pays attention to two "who had specially strange stories to tell, [but] have written no books," namely Annie Taylor and Mrs. Pruen. Readers of nineteenth-century travels likely know the harrowing tale of Annie Taylor venturing into Tibet with the help of a single servant, reaching within three days of Lhasa, then one of the most resolutely closed cities in the world. The near-starvation, perishing cold, and murderous ruffians Taylor survived indicate her "resource and imagination" (BG 263). She has no tent, her animals die. The details of the story astonish, but why does she do it? As full of admiration for Annie Taylor's fortitude as she is, Little is skeptical of her on two scores, first for her image of the Tibetans, "so unlike anything that I have yet read" (BG 271). Second, Little questions Taylor's understanding of her mission: "Whether because of their vices or their virtues, Miss Taylor returned with her heart as much set as ever upon carrying the gospel of glad tidings to this people who, if they do no wrong, yet at all events, as she says, do not conceal it" (BG 271). Little then uses Taylor's story to suggest that missionaries might be more successful in Christianizing people on the Indian side of Tibet, just as it "might be more remunerative" to try to convert the overseas Chinese, those in Canada and America, for example, where missionaries "would excite no opposition" and where "those who have lived for any time outside their own country must be aware how, whether for good or ill, prejudices drop away, habits become loosened, and . . . all life becomes an open question" (BG 272). For Little, humanitarianism has a distinctly *human* purpose, so to her even religious work should take practicality into consideration.

Annie Taylor's story of survivalism overshadows its faith-based rationale. The second missionary story Little tells, that of Mrs. Pruen who was a member of the China Inland Mission in Guizhou, Yunnan, is purely ethnographical. Mrs. Pruen felt privileged to have been invited to witness the annual spring festival of the Miao, a little known ethnic minority in China then (and known today in the United States for its connection to the Hmong who emigrated there in large numbers after the Vietnam war). Mrs. Pruen's description of dances and ceremonial clothing adds to Western knowledge of the Miao, and gives support to Little's claim that what sets missionaries apart from merchants and other Westerners in China is first that they like the Chinese and second that they have a deep knowledge of local culture. In this respect missionaries like Annie Taylor and Mrs. Pruen make significant contributions to humanitarian interests by acquiring knowledge and showing appreciation of little-known people.

## Anti-footbinding

There are times when an unexpected look or gesture gives great meaning to one's life. In *The Land of the Blue Gown* Alicia Little describes such an experience towards the end of her 1896 campaign tour to end footbinding. In Fuzhou she is introduced to a merchant who wants her to persuade his wife to stop binding the feet of their little girl. The mother allows Little to start the process of unbinding, but it has a horrifying effect:

> [T]he poor little girl, who had never had her bandages touched except to tighten them, cried out and looked at me with an expression of such hopeless agony as I had never seen on a child's face and hope never to see again. She looked me right in the eyes as Chinese so rarely do and her eyes said to mine, "I cannot bear it. I know I cannot. I am powerless to save myself from you. *But* — it is *more* than I can bear." That expression of helpless rage and agony and hate in the poor wizened child's face is more than I can ever hope to forget, and would spur me on to redoubled efforts to do away with a custom, that has been more than so many children can endure, and that must have saturated so many childish souls with bitterness, before they passed away from a world made impossible for them.

The emphasis on the brutality of footbinding, its physical and psychological torment, would be sufficient explanation for Little's campaign to end the practice, but she goes on to add an affecting personal motivation:

> Sometimes indeed I have thought, that God has denied me the joys of personal motherhood in order that all possible tenderness for childhood may be expended on the tortured children of China without the diminution from it of one iota, reserved for some sheltered, guarded child by my own fireside. (BG 351–2)

Little's personalization of her work on behalf of women in China adds poignancy to her activism, but by any standard, her contribution to the anti-footbinding movement is significant as it eventually affected hundreds of millions: China's population at the end of the nineteenth century is estimated at 500 million, about a third of the world's population at the time. A societal change of that proportion is truly consequential.

Little's attitude to footbinding developed over a number of years. In her early months in China, when all was new and interesting, she is not above using the unfeeling phrase "hoof-like feet" as a descriptor for bound feet (IC 38). She even takes naïve delight in Chinese women with "bandaged feet" investigating whether there really are feet filling up the big boots she wears. She also says that these women in central China hobble about "astonishingly well" on their bound feet, and she stereotypes the Chinese when she suggests that their tolerance of the painful practice owes in part to their indifference to suffering (IC 136). In later years, after Little has seen much more of China and met many more Chinese women, she is far less sanguine about the subject, often focusing on the worst outcomes of footbinding: the intense pain of the little girls robbed of their childhood freedom, the "poor little mutilated one, with her long stick and dreadful dark lines under her sad young eyes!" (IC 96); women unable to walk at all and carried piggy-back by their servants; mortification and loss of the feet; and the death of "more — more" than ten percent of girls undergoing the process (IC 140). There is an endless supply of horrific tales of footbinding. Little suggests an ironic good result, though, that those who survive this cruel practice show the "powers of their endurance" (IC 97). The toughness of Chinese women is legendary.

The history of footbinding and the process has been well-documented by Westerners who, despite uniformly criticizing it, felt as though they were presenting privileged information by conveying it to their readers. Few nineteenth-century travel and description books about China ignore the subject, and there is not a little voyeurism in early Western accounts of the practice. Victorians had their own foot and leg fetishes. The eroticization of the tiny Chinese foot encased in white bandages and a gorgeous silk shoe embodied a mystery that had Western parallels.[10]

The misty origins of footbinding in the late Song court gradually evolved from something ornamental to severe mutilation and a very widespread practice with marriageability as the rationale. Little notes that footbinding was far from being a sign of class rank in the 1890s, as even beggar women and farm women "walking on their knees" from south to north China had bound feet. The process of footbinding entailed first bending the toes under the sole, then forcing the heel and ball of the foot together by means of tight bandaging. It took about three years for the process to be completed, the ideal result being a three-inch foot. Little includes a photograph showing the shod and unshod bound foot (IC 139).

In her arguments against footbinding, Little points out that some rural women were only partially bound, that is, had only the toes forced under the sole of the foot, and the conquering Manchu women never bound their feet, but in the urge to conform to the practice, they adopted a platform shoe with a variety of tapering soles mimicking the effect of the bound foot that produced a tottering gait, and when worn with the traditional silk trousers gave the impression of small feet (Plate 13).

Today there is a continued fascination with the bound foot in the West, with numerous publications describing and commenting on the practice and entrepreneurs taking advantage of this interest. For a modest sum one can buy hand-made-in-China silk shoes of the type once used for the bound foot.

Many missionary groups including the American Episcopal Church and the Roman Catholics tolerated the binding of girls' feet both to make them marriageable and because it was feared parents would not allow their daughters to be educated by the missionaries if they did not follow custom. However, in 1891 the Catholic nuns in Hankou abandoned footbinding in their school. Although they had found the pain of the little girls excruciating, the Mother Superior shows surprising callousness when she complains about footbinding as an "endless trouble" requiring numerous yards of bandaging material and securing new shoes in ever smaller sizes as the foot was shortened (IC 141). The efforts of the many missionaries opposed to footbinding were successful locally, involving the pupils at their schools and religious converts. Some historians credit missionaries for setting the tone for ending footbinding and prompting the emancipation of Chinese women in general because of their introduction of education for girls. On the other hand, missionaries' association with Western authority compromised their work. Because the treaties after 1860 gave missionaries special privileges, they fell victim to anti-foreign sentiment.[11]

It was in April 1895 that Little acted on her conscience and desire to reform a custom so damaging to so many. She persuaded a number of other Western non-missionary women in Shanghai to join her in forming the "T'ien Tsu Hui" or Natural Feet Society. The society intended to change public opinion, and so they started their work, not in the private sphere as missionaries did, but by entering the public forum. They published writings by Chinese women, then wrote tracts that they had translated into Chinese. The Society demonstrated understanding of Chinese culture even if the members had no command of the Chinese language. They were well aware of the taboos against talking about the subject at all: "feet are the most *risqué* subject of conversation in China, and no subject more improper can be found here" (IC 150). Worrying about the implications of using one dialect or the other, the Society settled on *Wenli*, the language of the Chinese classics, to impart a level of decorum to the discussion and to associate it with the literati.

The next step was to turn anti-footbinding into a crusade, and to Little's credit she understood how to organize one. She held meetings for women in the largest cities and the treaty ports, places where there was a concentration of influential people and where the meetings could gain the attention of large numbers. She showed x-ray images of the natural and the distorted foot. She told stories of individual women who had unbound their feet and places where women were never bound, then encouraged audience members to tell their stories, got them to sign a pledge against footbinding, and to add an aura of serious support, charged a Society membership fee. Understanding that ending footbinding could not be done without the support of men, she spoke to both schoolboys and dignitaries. She made use of her husband's connections to seek the support of China's most powerful statesman, Li Hung-chang (Li Hongzhang), an intrepid act that called for a self-possessed, committed woman.[12] She also wangled free steamer passage from city to city for her speaking engagements.

In promoting anti-footbinding, Little advocated two courses of action, one to prevent little girls from having their feet bound at all, and the other to unbind the feet of those already bound. The latter was a painful process, and not always successful, but had the happy result of enabling women simply to walk in a normal way. Little took a positive approach in recounting specific instances of unbinding, naming specific schools that refused to countenance the practice, describing the happiness of the pupils there and the happy marriages they made. To counter prejudices, she took pains to include stories of Chinese fathers, brothers, and bridegrooms who spoke out against footbinding.

Serendipity played a role in Little's success when one of the examiners at Beijing wrote a pamphlet, the so-called Suifu Appeal, calling for an end to footbinding. Little distributed copies of this pamphlet to the thousands of students gathered in Chongqing for the annual civil service examination. The Suifu Appeal lent the anti-footbinding movement authority and inspired support from other well-placed, influential leaders, including the leading nationalist reformer Kang Yu-wei (Kang Youwei) and, according to Little, Kung Hui-chung, a descendant of Confucius.[13] The governor of Hunan banned footbinding altogether. At the same time, Little's Anti-Footbinding Society continued its work holding meetings with both women and men, and finally the momentum for anti-footbinding shifted to the Chinese themselves. By 1897 the Chinese "Do-not-bind-feet" society had opened an office in Guangzhou.

Indeed, Mrs. Little cannot be credited for single-handedly ending footbinding, and others had prepared the ground. The Taipings had advocated the equality of women, but their commitment to anti-footbinding was nominal, an ideological plank in the platform to replace Confucianism with Christianity.[14] Several feeble attempts by Qing emperors to ban footbinding had been ignored, but by the end of the nineteenth century, reform movements within China sought to bring the country in line with the modern world. What Little did was to popularize a cause whose time had come and for this she was recognized by the Chinese in several ways. She found herself called a "second Goddess of Mercy" and the subject of a flattering account in a Chinese periodical. More gratifying was that the anti-footbinding effort inspired further reform. She and the officers of her society were invited to help promote the founding of the first high school for girls in China, and within two years there were three girls' high schools in Shanghai. A more visible honor for Little was being made Vice President of the Women's Conference in Shanghai in 1900.

It is tempting when studying travel literature to focus on the Othering process of the traveler, to measure the travelers from another time by today's standards. What is lost at times in our contemporary effort to understand the meaning of the texts such travelers wrote is the transformative nature of their travel. Some were Kurtzes who went mad, became slavers and exploiters, but some were moved to remedy inhumane conditions they found. Alicia Little is one in the latter group, though she is no plaster saint. She is capable of making naïve-traveler remarks, for example, and she makes an astonishing admission at the end of *The Land of the Blue Gown*. In the course of her anti-footbinding campaign, she describes the women in Suzhou, "the Paris of China," as "decidedly pretty — and I have lived fifteen years in China disbelieving in the possibility of a pretty Chinese woman — and they were for the most part very piquante [*sic*]" (BG 363–4). If such a back-handed compliment reveals Little's true feelings about Chinese women, she has suppressed them to a large extent in her books. The humanitarian is one who chooses to rise above personal prejudices and act on what is morally right, to focus on what can be done to ease the suffering of others. For this is the mark of the true altruist, one who does good works at some expense to herself.

Auguste Comte coined the term *altruisme* to identify his idea that the only moral acts are those that promote the happiness of others. Alicia Little's personal story illustrates this definition of altruism as does her presentation of China. She subscribes to the tenets of the late Victorian humanitarian movement in Britain. Consequently, she emphasizes sameness rather than otherness: Chinese women have the right to walk freely like every other human being, Chinese girls deserve to be educated, children nurtured, wrongdoers humanely treated, disease, poverty, poor living conditions to be eliminated. For Little, travel writing is an opportunity to express the humanitarian impulse.

# 8

## The "Sphere of Interest":
### Framing Late Nineteenth-Century China
### in Words and Pictures with Isabella Bird

*Susan Morgan*

By the early nineteenth century the prevailing political notion in England of what constituted British interest in the "East" was typically represented, in imaginative if not in literal terms, as an overarching purpose which could unite a whole range of British activities in the region. Everything was somehow connected. What the British did on the Indian subcontinent and in the Straits Settlements, the Malay Peninsula, the East Indies and China, was all of a piece.

What connected these multiple, particular, and scattered British activities in the places the British called the "East" was, first of all, an idea. It was captured in the phrase invoked again and again to describe and defend British imperial enterprise: "the China trade." Within the spacious rubric defined at the beginning of the century by William Pitt the Younger, that "British policy is British trade,"[1] the "China trade" held a special place. The phrase functioned as a sort of lodestar for the whole notion of seagoing trade, as valued by the little island that was Britain. The "China trade" would be the best trade, the biggest trade, "potentially the most important in the world,"[2] with virtually unlimited consumers as well as goods. Stamford Raffles "founded" Singapore in 1819 and the British officially bought it from the Sultan of Johore in 1824 for a lot of reasons, the foremost being to provide a port between India and China for the sake of the "China trade." "The Malay Peninsula became a place of significance for the English precisely in terms of its geographic proximity to India, as the land fronting the waterway from India to China."[3]

There was, of course, a wealth of material and imagined purposes for the historical processes which we have come to gather under the heading of British imperialism. These purposes are as varied as the many places and economic, political, and cultural conditions in which the British were to be found. My point here is simply that a usually implicit but always present aspect of nineteenth-century British writings about China was that they existed within a particular pre-existing rhetorical and ideological frame. That frame was, in its largest sense, the magical notion of the "China trade."

Tied to that notion was another one, also a given in British writings about China. This was that China, as the endlessly repeated metaphor went, was a sleeping giant and, as Napoleon was said to have remarked, "when she wakes she will astonish the world."[4] If one of the tropes of British writings was that the "China trade" was the pot of gold which would reward ambitious British trading interests, another was that China itself was a place of almost unimaginable economic potential. Therefore, almost as a moral imperative, China should not, as well as could not, be left alone. While the Qing rulers of China did not seem to realize that the country needed to fulfill its commercial destiny within the global marketplace, other nations, first merchants and then governments, did. The question for these foreign imperial powers was how to persuade China.

There was always that bedrock of British policy, gunboat diplomacy. The British had relied on it throughout the "East" and throughout the nineteenth century in China. Beginning in 1839, the British navy was central to British victories in the Opium Wars. As late as 1898 Sir Claude M. MacDonald, Britain's minister at Beijing, pressing China to cede the port of Weihaiwei in Shandong to Britain, sent the warning that, "if not affirmative, matter would be placed in Admiral's hands."[5] But in the simplest practical terms, force and the threat of force could never hold together an empire, certainly not an empire of trade. As Thomas Richards so memorably put it, "an empire is partly a fiction" and "the narratives of the late nineteenth century are full of fantasies about an empire united not by force but by information."[6]

"Opening" China, then, became in part, to borrow James Hevia's insightful term, a "pedagogical project," a matter of teaching "the Qing elite and the Chinese people in general through various means of coercion and enticement how to function properly in a world dominated militarily and economically by European-based empires."[7] If the challenges were many, the rewards were, or surely would be, great. Implicit in the project was the need for the production of information, for what one can think of as textbooks for a course in the value, and inevitability, of the China trade. Nor were the Qing elite and the Chinese people the only prospective audiences who needed to be educated on the potential benefits of the China trade, and therefore needed information to be produced for them. British writings for audiences back home were similarly engaged in a pedagogy of imperialism. The lineaments of this pedagogy in regard to China included the two key rhetorical assumptions: first, of China's extraordinary commercial potential, as market and as supplier of goods; and second, of Britain's right and obligation among the foreign powers to take the central role in developing the China trade.

While there have been centuries of Western writing about China, it is fair to say that the British treaties of 1860 and 1876 particularly opened China up to foreign travelers and thus to a plethora of travel writings. During the late nineteenth and early twentieth century among the most well-known British accounts of China were the books of Archibald Little and Alicia (Mrs. Archibald) Little, Lady Constance Gordon Cumming, George Morrison (who was Australian), Archibald Colquhoun, John Thomson (verbal and pictorial), and Isabella Bird Bishop. There have been several critical studies of these and other writings about China. Two of the more recent ones which I see as particularly helpful are Susan Schoenbauer Thurin's *Victorian Travelers and the Opening of China, 1842–1907* (1999) and Nicholas Clifford's *"A Truthful Impression of the Country": British and American Travel Writing in China, 1880–1949* (2001).[8] His title is taken from Bird's "Preface."

Thurin has pointed out that one of the qualities of Victorian writings on China is "a high level of polemics,"[9] pointing particularly to the issues of the opium trade and missionary activity. This characteristic indicates a clear awareness of some of the political and economic debates about China and a willingness to use their writings to enter those debates. In other words, travel writings about China were not innocent or politically naïve. The writers saw themselves and their books as entering into, participating in, and taking positions on some of the major issues in the discourse on China that was occurring in Britain at the time of their writing. And their polemics took in other major public issues, as well as the opium trade and missionaries.

Moreover, in a way that I see as more true about books about China than about such less volatile areas of imperial enterprise as Africa and British Malaysia, travel writings had to be politically up to date, *au courant*, as it were. Events in China that had to do with the Qing dynasty, the advances of the other foreign powers, the activities of and treatment of the various foreign communities, new treaties, commercial activities, and incidents involving the missionary community, all these occurred with startling rapidity. And they could be read about regularly in the British press. One could not write with any authority, could not claim any superior knowledge from actually having been there, could not, in short, claim that "a truthful impression of the country" was of significant value, without first being armed with a clear awareness of recent events, particularly those events thought to be of interest to an international community and which would have appeared in British newspapers and periodicals. To "teach" British audiences, a writer had first to be informed. Travel writings had to combine the immediacy of personal experience with the detachment of political and economic knowledge.

In this essay I take up one of the more well-known Victorian books about China written for British audiences, Isabella Bird Bishop's *The Yangtze Valley and Beyond* (1899), with the purpose of placing its rhetorical strategies within the interpretive frame of an imperialist pedagogy for audiences in Britain. Bird introduces her travel narrative in language that clearly invokes its educational or textbook role. She is explicit in arguing both for the need for a course on China and for the educational value of her contribution. Bird begins her "Preface" by explicitly labeling her book as "a useful contribution to popular knowledge of that much-discussed region." She ends her preface by using the language of science to claim the pedagogical authority of this "honest attempt to make a contribution to the data." And she is careful to point out "the extreme importance of increasing by every means the knowledge of, and interest in, China and its people."[10]

Bird used not only words but pictures as tools with which to produce the information necessary to educate her audience. *The Yangtze Valley* was closely followed in 1900 by *Chinese Pictures: Notes on Photographs Made in China.* But before turning to these two works, some of the British rhetoric about China generally, and Bird's rhetoric specifically, needs to be placed within the historical frame of Britain's nineteenth-century economic and political relations with China. What follows is only the briefest sketch of a few of those complex and often contradictory relations.


## Treaties and Their Ports

The imperial history of China, like that of Thailand, is distinguished in part by the fact that it was never directly colonized by a European power. The nineteenth-century history of Britain's more aggressive relations with China had one beginning in July of 1834, when William John, Baron Napier, "the British Government's first ever representative in the Chinese empire,"[11] arrived in Macao just after Parliament ended the East India Company's monopoly and deregulated the China trade. In a general proclamation circulated that August in Canton (Guangzhou), Napier insisted that "thousands of industrious Chinese" needed and wanted trade as much as did Britain and that resistance on the part of the Chinese was an indication of corruption and repression. Napier's words point to the convenient moral frame in which British entrepreneurs could cast opium smuggling, as a step along the path of fulfilling the destiny of the enterprising English and the industrious Chinese. The happy future of the two countries, and British connections to China, would be defined by trade.

As many historians have argued, the Opium Wars, beginning in 1839, were about more than a matter of going "to war to defend and expand trade." Opium business in China was a complex matter. First, though there was no real attempt to stop the trade, and British merchants profited heavily from it, "at no point were the British authorities in favor of opium smuggling."[12] The British Superintendent of Trade in Canton, Charles Eliot, described the trade as "a traffic which every friend of humanity must deplore."[13] Second, there were real problems of jurisdiction. Selling opium was not solely or even primarily a British enterprise. The foreign merchants and Country Traders were British, but also "American, French, Dutch, Danish, and Spanish."[14] And finally, while the Chinese government was firmly against the trade, many rich Chinese, merchants and officials, were deeply involved in trafficking in opium, working with the smugglers and making huge profits.

The Whigs justified the 1839 war as a matter of defending "British national honour,"[15] an important moral defense when engaged in what looked like an ugly drug war. In the immediate sense, honor meant that the Chinese, like all other foreigners, could not be allowed to get away with confiscating British-owned goods or otherwise interfering with British merchants. It was an insult to British commercial practices and British traders, and a dangerous precedent. On a larger scale, such interference was an insult to the sacred goal of "the China trade," a goal which represented that noble future toward which Britain's present trade practices were the path. Trade practices may have included drug dealing and then making war to force another country to legalize a drug most Englishmen knew was dangerously addictive. But really the point was not the particular trade item but the principle of the thing. And in terms of the future greater good of both countries, did not the end justify the means? "The war had not been about opium . . . In British eyes, the conflict had been about how relations between China and the West should be shaped."[16] And it would be the British who did the shaping. From 1842 onwards those relations were to be shaped by a series of "unequal" Treaties which China was forced to accept.

The complex of arguments around the Opium Wars included questions of tensions and differences among the Chinese, questions of British competition with other foreign nations also eager for a piece of China, questions of legal jurisdiction and extraterritoriality (over trading rights, goods and people), questions of Chinese rights to legislate and tax, and questions of British "rights," defined as questions of national honor. These arguments reappeared with variations throughout the rest of the century, always seen and interpreted through the lens of British assumptions about the indisputable value of the China trade.

The resolutions to the Opium Wars, the Treaties of Nanjing in August, 1842 and its supplemental Treaty of the Bogue in 1843, then the Treaty of Tianjin in 1858 and its sequel, the Convention of Beijing in 1860, forced a troubled and fluid relationship between China and Britain which kept trade relations full of uncertainty and conflict. The Treaty of Nanjing included a large payment for both the seized opium and the cost of the war, the opening of five ports (Guangzhou, Xiamen, Fu Xian, Ningbo and Shanghai) to British trade and British people, including consuls, the elimination of the Co-hong (the Chinese guilds which had controlled all foreign trade), and the ceding of the island of Hong Kong to Britain. It also set low tariffs for goods. The Treaty of Nanjing thus "inaugurated a treaty port system that was to have very large consequences for China . . . until it was swept away by Japan in 1941."[17]

Next came the Arrow War, superficially occasioned by the execution of a French Jesuit who had clearly violated treaty terms about foreigners by traveling inland and by the Chinese police boarding a British vessel, the Arrow. The supposed violation on the part of the Chinese was questionable, since the Arrow was owned and manned by Chinese, though it had a British subject as Captain. It was registered as British but the registration had expired. Moreover, the point of boarding was to arrest the Chinese for a previous act of piracy.[18] These facts were mere pesky details. The war, as Lord Palmerston put it, was about protecting "a right most important to the whole British commerce between Hong Kong and Canton, a commerce which is continually growing."[19] The British had learned through the example of the Bowring Treaty of 1855 with Siam, arranged by Sir John Bowring, Governor of Hong Kong. Their goal was to correct the limitations of the Treaty of Nanjing so as to establish terms in China that would not hamper their grand commercial goals.

The Chinese government balked at the new commercial and political concessions in the Treaty of Tianjin. In 1860 the Sino-British Convention of Beijing saw China finally forced to ratify it, with even more unequal terms. The Convention again included massive war reparations. It also named the treaty port of Tianjin and added nine more treaty ports, including Niuchang, Tongzhou, Taiwan, Chaozhao, Qiongzhou, Zhenjiang, and three along the Yangtze River to be opened later. Effectively, the treaty established the "right to navigate and trade along the Yangtze River to Hankow."[20] The treaty extended extraterritoriality and gave missionaries full civil rights, including the right to travel in the interior and to own property, ceded Kowloon to Britain, and created foreign legations in Beijing. Foreigners now had the legal right to buy land and property, and to move inland into China. Also, rectifying an absence from the first treaties, the treaty legalized the opium trade.

By the 1890s, foreigners were no longer confined just to port cities or official settlements but could travel anywhere. There were almost twenty-five hundred Christian missions active throughout China and because of all the protections demanded for them by Western governments, "the treaties turned the emperor into a protector of a foreign heterodox cult."[21] The Chefoo Convention in 1876 had opened more treaty ports, and also six ports inland along the Yangtze for steamers. By the 1890s there were dozens of open ports in China, some with large foreign enclaves untouchable by Chinese law, virtually little independent states of their own.

The second half of the century also saw China losing its tributary states. France had moved into Vietnam, and officially took it over in 1883, also picking up Cambodia in 1887 and Laos in 1893. Britain got Burma in 1885. So China was particularly appalled by Japan's interest in Korea, and went to war with Japan in 1895 to keep at least this one of her traditional tributaries. The Sino-Japanese war was a humiliating defeat for China. The Treaty of Shimonoseki in 1895 imposed huge reparations, created more treaty ports, ceded Taiwan, and gave Japan most favored nation status.

There were worse consequences of the loss to Japan. First, China was forced literally to mortgage her future. Already burdened by huge reparations from previous wars and now taking on a huge debt to Japan, China not only had to give up territories but her future income and any hope for economic stability. In 1895, in order to pay the reparations, the bankrupt government had to accept loans from "helpful" consortia that were Russian, French, German, and British, the collateral being her as yet unearned customs revenues and internal taxes. Effectively, "China's dependable revenues were now under foreign control" and "China was not to escape this foreign financial grip" until 1949.[22]

Second, and at least as destructive as this permanent debt, was the conclusion the foreign powers drew that the Manchu government was so weak that now was the moment to get what one could. The efforts were driven more by issues of the international balance of power than by economics. As Yueh-hung Chen put it, "from 1895 onwards the Powers' primarily commercial motives diminished, as their political objectives became paramount."[23] The British government, responding to financial arrangements being made with China by rival powers, became involved in what had been the sphere of private finance. Prime Minister Salisbury turned from his long-held policy of government aloofness from private British companies in Asia based on the principle of non-competition and the open door, memorably described in Disraeli's words: "in Asia there is room for us all."[24] The Foreign Office began to offer government backing for war loans, for mining and, especially, railway concessions. The British goal was not so much to have China as to keep rivals (meaning France and, particularly, Russia) from having China.

Starting slowly in 1895 and 1896 with those loans to China, and in full swing by 1897 and especially the summer of 1898, the "scramble" for "concessions" in China was on. The powers sliced the country up into what were known as "spheres of influence," areas they could control (typically, by 99-year leases) and have virtual trading monopolies in. They simply forced the Chinese diplomats to agree. Chinese diplomats, for their part, realizing the country was too weak to deny concessions, brilliantly deflected their force by granting multiple "concessions in a way which interfered with the development of the exclusive control of an area by any single power."[25] Russia, France, and Japan all staked out pieces, yet never quite succeeded in controlling a "sphere." In 1898 Britain did stake a claim to trading primacy in the Yangtze Valley, compelling Beijing to open its inland waters, and also got a 99-year lease on land adjacent to Kowloon, thus expanding the territory of Hong Kong. John Hay, United States Secretary of State, was concerned that the principle of open international trading which was the basis for the operation of the treaty ports was going to be jeopardized, and foreign powers were moving to monopoly rights in "their" ports. In an echo of Britain's temporarily abandoned policy of open trade, he sent to the other powers his Open Door Notes in September, 1899, to make sure the United States would not be closed out of the commercial action.

## What Bird's Audience Needed to be Taught

Isabella Bird Bishop's book on China was careful from its very opening to imbed its narrative in the major issues of the moment. The change in British policies toward China before and after 1895 is the quite specific rhetorical frame with which her narrative can productively be read. To make this point is to approach her book in a different critical frame from the very familiar one of her own intrepidness, a frame which she herself rhetorically privileges in her self-deprecating way, and which generations of her interpreters have privileged as well. In the critical literature on travel writing, Bird is the poster child of the intrepid woman traveler, Pat Barr's "traveler extraordinary," even more so because of her bizarre personal pattern of being ill at home, indomitable abroad, and producing no less than eleven travel books about her impressive journeys. The critical limitation of this focus on Bird herself is that it effectively obscures analysis of the political function of her books.

The present essay does not use a biographical and psychological approach. Instead, it looks at *The Yangtze Valley and Beyond* within the historical context of differing British rhetorical positions on China in the 1890s, particularly in the years between 1895–96, when Bird (as I shall refer to her) made her trip, and 1899, when she published the book. Bird's China book offers a particular contribution to the 1898 debate in the British government and the British press about England's future policies toward China.

Bird opens *The Yangtze Valley and Beyond: An Account of Journeys in China, Chiefly in the Province of Sze Chuan and Among the Man-Tze of the Somo Territory* by herself placing the book squarely within recent public debate. The very first sentence of the book invokes the fact that the Yangtze Valley has been rendered a "sphere of interest" by Britain. But on the first page Bird describes the Valley as "the great basin which in the spring of 1898 was claimed as the British 'sphere of influence'." By page 11 Bird has established her credentials in terms of being particularly well informed and up to date. She knows contemporary public discussions, as she demonstrates when she quotes from the Parliamentary debates of May, 1899, referring specifically to a report by the British acting consul in Beijing, in which he writes of the Chinese "general love of law and order."[26]

Bird's rhetoric invites us to read her work as, first, another entry in an important public discussion of Britain's proper activities in China in comparison with those of the other countries trading there. Second, she places her narrative as an educational journey with a properly authoritative teacher who can provide readers with a knowledgeable basis on which to form their own opinions about the significance of the Yangtze Valley to Britain and what British activities there should be. Bird's authority is established initially by "her wide knowledge"[27] of China from her trip in 1895–1896, a knowledge drawing on direct experience of, as she puts it, "journeyings in three of the most important years in modern Chinese history."[28] That first claim to authority is then overlaid and enriched by a second, her informed knowledge of public debates in England in 1898–1899.

The first lesson to be learned, the lesson of Bird's opening paragraph, the rhetorical impact of placing two similar but not identical forms of words in quotations within the first seven lines of the book, is that there are not one but two operative phrases in Britain's relations to China: the "sphere of interest" and the "sphere of influence." Good readers, good students, will note the difference — made hard to miss by placing the terms so close to one another — and wonder what it entails. One can look at *The Yangtze Valley* as an extended exercise in teaching British audiences the differences between those two terms.

Having introduced the two terms, Bird goes on until page ten making one major point. She is describing the Yangtze Valley or great "basin" (a word preferred to valley in contemporary debates as less geographically limiting). What she would have us learn, our lesson in physical and economic geography, is its sheer enormity and commercial importance. We are told first that it "includes all or most of the important provinces," that it is 650,000 square miles, that the river's actual length is unknown but probably not more than 3,000 miles, that it can be "regarded as the most important of Asiatic waterways"[29] and multiple rivers feed into it, and that its "water volume at 1000 miles from the sea is estimated as 244 times that of the Thames at London Bridge."[30] She concludes that "it cannot be repeated too often that for its export trade, estimated at £3,300,00, and its import trade, estimated at £2,400,000, the Yangtze is the *sole* outlet and inlet."[31]

Having initiated her readers into the extraordinary physical and economic significance of the Yangtze Valley, and thus the importance of her subject, Bird returns to her opening theme. She takes up first the British "sphere of influence," which she immediately categorizes as "a phrase against which I protest."[32] Another writer on China also protested the phrase. Archibald Colquhoun, in his 1900 *Overland to China*, also wrote about that 1898–99 session of Parliament when the British "sphere of influence" was discussed, and the Foreign Office pressured to produce the document that guaranteed such a sphere. Colquhoun's point was a species of contempt, for the Foreign Office and the "sphere of influence," noting that Britain's claim was based on nothing so substantial as a treaty or an official declaration or any kind of signed document at all. In other words, it had "no concrete basis whatever." For him the sphere was a sort of "blank cheque, which a strong power might fill in as it found convenient."[33]

Colquhoun's comments highlight that the discussion in Parliament in that session of 1898–99 made clear that a specifically British "sphere of influence" in the Yangtze Valley was not a formal agreement. But neither was it a "blank cheque." It was a cluster of specific business contracts which, taken together, could have and hopefully did have the effect of creating a sphere of influence. For Britain that included building railways, supplying the engine and cars, and being in charge of running the railways (which company's goods were carried?, what were the fees?), an arrangement which guaranteed the railway managers significant commercial control over a region. "The railway concessions . . . in the Yangtze Valley, Manchuria, and between Canton and Kowloon" constituted "the major British gains during the scramble."[34]

Colquhoun's critique of the sphere of influence ignored both economics (the meaning of a "concession") and politics (Britain viewing its role as having to join a competition it neither created nor wanted, but could not afford to ignore). Bird is making a different point. For her the scramble to carve up China after 1895 is first of all "undignified,"[35] a sharp critique from a woman whose writings had long supported British imperial activities in the East on precisely the grounds of their nobility and general rightness. To be undignified is to lose the moral high ground, to allow doubt as to the justness of British imperial enterprise. Bird's other point is that the scramble is also blindered or, at the least, short-sighted, and therefore not worthy of the larger vision possible in British international relations. In thinking of that larger vision, Bird writes impatiently of all the terms current in the China debates, of " 'open doors' and 'spheres of influence' and 'interest,' in much greed for ourselves, not always dexterously cloaked, and much jealousy and suspicion of our neighbors."[36]

Bird's purpose is to offer British audiences a critique of efforts to establish a British sphere of influence, and at the same time to frame that critique in such a way as partially to undermine it. After all, Bird has no doubt that the British should be in China — just not in a "sphere of influence." The fault lies with other foreign powers, of course; Britain is caught up in an international competition and not in a political position to act with complete independence. The present process is destructive to China. Claiming the opposite of much contemporary rhetoric after 1895, which presented China as breaking up and therefore ripe and vulnerable to foreign commercial takeovers, Bird argued forcefully in her conclusion that cause and effect are reversed. China is not "breaking up." Instead, the cause of "foreign interference, . . . the shifting and opportunistic policy, enormous ambitions, and ill-concealed rivalries of certain foreign powers",[37] will lead to the effect of weakening the Central Government and breaking China. Bird quotes approvingly Lord Salisbury's June 28, 1898 reiteration of his long-term policy goal for China, "to maintain the Chinese Empire, to prevent it falling into ruins, to invite it into paths of reform, and to give it every assistance." She then puts his last point, that in "*so doing we shall be aiding its cause and our own.*"[38]

This language locates Bird on the side of those in parliament and in the British public who had difficulty after 1895 shifting to a notion of active government-involved commercial competition with other powers in China. As she put it so explicitly in the conclusion, she remains "a believer in the justice and expediency of the 'Open Door' policy as opposed to what I think is the fatal alternative policy of 'spheres of influence'."[39] The signs of this belief appear throughout Bird's narrative, the first sign the dedication, "to the Marquess of Salisbury, K. G." Here is Bird's declaration that her book is at the service of empire and that it also is an entry into the political debate on the side of the government point of view. For those who are informed of political events, the dedication signals clearly that Bird's book will reflect the position of the Prime Minister, who had long since come to stand for a measured China policy in which, of course, Britain had a rightful place in China, but as its superior and leader, not its occupier.

In a variation of the familiar trope of the "white man's burden," Bird represents China as a peculiarly British burden. Britain's historic role must be to place itself apart from the barbarism of other foreign powers and reject the low and greedy notion of "spheres of influence." Instead Britain's historic destiny lies in taking up the high and noble role of savior of a great civilization. In Bird's imperial logic, every insistence on the grandeur of China and the greatness of its history and culture leads to the conclusion not of China's right to independence but of Britain's obligation to be its leader. Britain's call to accept her burden is directly in proportion to China's worthiness, and to the inappropriateness of any other foreign contenders for the central leadership role.

Bird shapes her argument in part through presenting herself as an interested but open-minded observer of China, merely recording what she sees, with an uncensored immediacy. And what she sees with her imperial gaze includes other foreigners. The language is less than admiring, yet always presented as a traveler's politically innocent description. American steamers were "luxurious to a fault," and the "white enamel and mirrors were detestable."[40] The Frenchman is to be found in her pages "brutally" remarking "Good! there'll be some yellow skins fewer," when a Chinese junk with all its crew sinks. The treaty port of Sha-shih, "opened" and "first occupied" by the Japanese, she "was not prepossessed with":[41] it was very dirty.

Throughout these negative descriptions of foreigners from other nations, Bird balances her sense of British superiority with an argument that the British are not doing enough to stay competitive. Our merchants and manufacturers need to abandon their complacency and increase their business acumen if they hope to be competitive in China. And again the language is that of providing information and asking her readers, once properly informed, to draw the proper conclusions. Thus we are told that the foreign articles in Sha-shih are mostly Japanese, "owing to the energy or, as our merchants call it, the peddling and huckstering instincts of the Japanese traders." The objects of Bird's irony are clarified when the "huckstering" turns out to mean finding out "through their trained Chinese-speaking agents ... what the people want and supply[ing] it to them."[42] Of the hugely productive cotton weaving industry in the city of Wan, which she notes is supplied with material from Japan and British India, Bird's provocative question is "can Lancashire compete …?"[43] She observes that German and Austrian firms "in their practical way are spreading themselves through the country" and "the competition of Japan in the larger branches of trade" ought "not to be ignored by us."[44] Nor are foreigners the greatest worry. Bird's narrative is filled with examples of what she calls "the tide which is gradually sweeping business out of foreign into native hands." She assures her readers that though "job opportunities for young Englishmen in China are shrinking," nonetheless "actual British trade may not suffer."[45]

Bird's myriad accounts of businesses in non-British hands, be those hands foreign or Chinese, are balanced by her at least as frequent "observations" of the wonderful riches to be made in China. If her British audience needs to learn of the challenges and the competitors, they also need to learn the fullness of what is to be gained. At least one reason why the British should not weaken China is that it is in Britain's material interest to keep her economy and government functioning. This is more notable in the first part of the book when Bird repeatedly gives us the typically impressive commercial figures for the cities, particularly the treaty ports, she passes through. Thus we need to know that the "total value of the trade in Ichang for 1898 amounted to £2,298,437."[46] But Bird also feels obliged to point out commercial possibilities to her audience. As she travels further west upriver into the Upper Yangtze and then inland, she informs her readers about mining, salt, cotton, and the general richness of the farmland. British attention should not be limited to a "sphere of influence" not simply because it is greedy but because there are so many commercial possibilities in China that only a "sphere of interest," national rather than narrowly regional, can do justice to its potential.

While Bird frequently exhorts her audience to "push" harder if Britain is to be commercially competitive in China, particularly in the accounts of the early part of her journey in the more easterly ports, her narrative also has a more uplifting educational goal. This is to teach her audience a fuller valuation, in terms of more than just "markets, territory, and railroads," of the riches that China can offer the "West." Early in the book she makes her point by turning to a humanistic eloquence. There is a "risk," she says, of thinking only in material terms, of "ignoring the men who, for two thousand years, have been making China worth scrambling for." She then offers a veiled warning of the evil consequences of a "sphere of influence." Are we, "along with other European empires," breaking up "in the case of a fourth of the human race the most ancient of earth's existing civilizations, without giving any equivalent?"[47]

Bird's account, then, is framed in the first place as an attempt to offer to British audiences an enlarged vision of the Yangtze Valley (in her writing, virtually synonymous with China), one that asks the question of how much the British should really value China. That vision will be a corrective to the notion that China equals "barbarism" or "debased theories of morals." Instead, through the method of allowing us to travel with her and see China through her eyes, Bird will teach us that it is "an elaborate and antique civilization which is not yet decayed, and which, though imperfect, has many claims to our respect and even admiration."[48]

China, then, should not be read by British audiences as merely a venue for making money or an arena for competing with other foreign powers. Competition is important, and British merchants do need to do better. But China needs to be understood by the English as rich in multiple ways. It is a place of cultural and economic value and, therefore, of interest. Yet Bird's audience also needs to know that China is not ready for full economic exchange and cultural partnership with Britain. Bird's book will go on, for more than five hundred pages, to support, however implicitly, the notion of China's healthy future if Britain does not weaken it, and to offer an expansive picture of China as an appropriate British "sphere of interest" rather than "influence." It is this peculiar tension, between the enormity and range of riches China has to offer and the constraints Britain must practice, which informs Bird's narrative.

Bird's pedagogy also extends to ethnography. Rather late in her narrative, as she gets to the northwestern section of her journey, she switches for several chapters from a teacher of the wide range of China's trade potentials to a more scientific voice, and *The Yangtze River* suddenly becomes an ethnological narrative in the tradition of Alfred Russel Wallace in *The Malay Archipelago*. The familiar narrative conventions of the explorer/ethnographer appear, as Bird carefully maps her route and describes the physical and social contours of the "Man-Tze," the mountain people of Somo, living in what she refers to as "The Beyond," outside the western boundaries of China. Enough critical work has been done on this form of objectification, this version of the imperial eye as a disengaged scientist in narratives of travel. I simply point out here that Bird's narrative is somewhat split, breaking out in these Somo chapters from the authority of immediate experience and political knowledge — the terms that give her objectivity for most of the book — to the temporary authority of geographic explorer.

The Somo section reminds her readers that Bird's pedagogical authority is to be taken seriously not only because she is, to use a later term, an old China hand, but also because she is a trained observer of national stature. Bird "was the one woman traveler whose geographical credentials were well secured and not questioned by Victorian readers."[49] She had long been a fellow of the Royal Scottish Geographical Society and in 1892 was one of a very small group of women admitted to the Royal Geographical Society. She writes *The Yangtze Valley*, then, as a known and recognizable voice in her culture. She is an educated and personally knowledgeable traveler in China and, on a more abstract level already familiar to her audience, a distinguished British geographic traveler. The Somo section recalls her readers to the fact that this elderly lady riding around China in a chair and a little boat is also a scientist.

## Picturing China

Bird's narrative, and explicitly her conclusion, defends China against critiques of the country, its people, its culture and its way of governing. Yet Bird's defense always operates within her belief that, as she put it in her very last sentence of the book, China's future "depends very largely on the statesmanship and influence of Great Britain".[50] *The*

*Yangtze Valley* in the forms of its defense of China is also a defense of imperialism. It never doubts Britain's right, nay responsibility, to be in China. The only question is what kind of responsibility. Within the framework of support for the British imperial enterprise, Bird's narrative offers a series of pictures of China. If this complex representation of China's present conditions and future potential and what should be Britain's stance towards the country is Bird's topic, her method is primarily pictorial.

Bird's style had always been pictorial, with its vividness, immediacy, and rhetorical claims to objectivity and truthfulness. In *The Yangtze Valley* these claims are considerably simplified by the relatively new technology of photography. Bird's words are pictures and they are accompanied by more pictures — not creations of an artist but records of an observer. There are 160 accompanying illustrations in *The Yangtze Valley*, almost all of them photographs. And one year later Bird published her photography book, with the text reduced to an accompanying paragraph for each, of sixty *Chinese Pictures*, close to half of which had already been printed in *The Yangtze Valley*.

The view of photography as providing objective data, a scientific record, was already well entrenched at the Royal Geographical Society. From January 1886 John Thomson had been "the Society's photography instructor," training many explorers and travelers to use "the camera to document their journeys."[51] As well as his photographs in London, John Thomson was famous for his photographs in China, particularly the four-volume *Illustrations of China and Its People* of 1873–74.[52] His 1898 book, *Through China with a Camera*,[53] was a great success and immediately reprinted in a cheaper edition.

By the 1890s Thomson's own work and his job with the Royal Geographical Society had ensured that it was *de rigueur* for anyone with any claims to scientific observation to travel with a camera, most especially to China. Certainly, Bird would have known his work well. But in spite of being a Royal Geographical Society Fellow, she did not get her photographic training at the RGS. Before going on her trip to China Bird took "an advanced photography class at the Regent Street Polytechnic,"[54] then a recent outgrowth of the Young Men's Christian Institute and now a part of the University of Westminster.

Thomson's fame rested to a great extent on his photographs of people, including his extremely popular 1877 *Street Life in London*. Nancy Armstrong has written eloquently on how Thomson used his ethnographic photography to set people apart, be they poor Londoners or Chinese, and thus "not only to attach a class to racial difference, but also to affix a racial marking to class difference."[55] For my discussion it is enough to say that in Thomson's portraits people frequently become a generic type. His aim is to offer the representative, and his photographs have such titles as "Cantonese Girl," "Szechuan Hermit," "Chinese Sawyers," and "Native Actors." These are clearly a model of the kinds of portraits Bird offers of Chinese people in her books. From "The Cobbler" to "The Dying Coolie" to "Two Soldiers of Sze Chuan," Bird repeatedly presents and names the people she photographs as representative types. Together these types add up to one great prototype, not in any one photograph but present in composite form, which would be named "The Chinese." Bird writes frequently and explicitly of "The Chinese" in her texts, sometimes positively and sometimes negatively, but always generically.

This sort of essentialized terminology is a staple of nineteenth-century European and American travel writings, in words and in pictures. But there is another point to be made. One of the striking features of Bird's published photography about China is that, unlike Thomson's, hers actually contains very few photographs of people. In the photographs in both her books, China is represented primarily in terms of its architecture and secondarily in terms of its landscapes. People are a distant third.

*Chinese Pictures* is organized loosely into two major categories. The first I might call modes of travel, and includes photographs of carriages, carts, carrying chairs, wheelbarrows, boats and bridges. People in these are just the props. Even a photo in which I see two coolies, Bird has labeled "The Mode of Carrying Oil and Wine."[56] The other loose category I would call kinds of places. This includes examples of temples, shrines, forts, gates, houses and streets. If, as *The Travelers' Handbook for China* in 1913 assures its readers on its title page, "one seeing is worth a hundred tellings," what Bird's British audiences saw in looking at her photographs was an accessible China, an already culturally and architecturally developed China, and a China notably without many Chinese.

Writing of a country without much mention of its people is another familiar trope of imperial travel narratives, though it usually appears in explorer literature. But in Bird's pictures of China I think it also carries a unique significance. *The Yangtze Valley* and *Chinese Pictures* are both, in different ways, arguments in support in continuing British involvement in China, and of China as an appropriate "sphere of interest." One aspect of Bird's persuasive rhetoric was to present a China that was visibly manageable and therefore feasible for British companies to expand their investments in. If China was already being written of as a place with too many people, Bird simply photographed it without them. If her audience is concerned that China is decaying, her pictures portray it as tidy. If their concern is that it is wild, her pictures portray it as tame.

Bird's China is a fairly quiet place. There are fabulous mountains and wild people, but that is mostly "The Beyond." Mostly Bird's China is a place of fertility, cultivation and commercial opportunities. It has a wide range of landscapes and natural resources. It has roads and navigable rivers, lined with treaty ports, seemingly everywhere. There are some people, visibly hard-working, the representatives of a substantial labor force eager to be put to work. Yet it is all manageable, a quality which speaks both to its economic promise for British merchants and investors and to its appropriate international position as dependent "on the statesmanship and influence of Great Britain."[57] This manageable China is the country Bird teaches her audience to see.

# 9

## China Upriver:
### Three Colonial Journeys between Hong Kong and Canton, 1905–11

*Elaine Yee Lin Ho*

## I

The first decade of the twentieth century up to the outbreak of the First World War has often been considered the height of the British empire. During this period, accounts of journeys by British travelers to different parts of the empire often display self-confidence in the racial and cultural superiority of Western, specifically Anglo-Saxon, imperial rule, and belief in the progress that such rule would bring to non-Western cultures. These cultures are often perceived in states of lack, variously inert, primitive, barbarous, or in decline, and their subjugation to Western imperial rule is the necessary historical stage in their regeneration and eventual civilization; the only alternative is destruction and disappearance from world history.

As the passage of the uncivilized to civilization, world history takes shape as a prolonged journey of travel along routes laid down by Western imperial power, and the writers whose accounts help to inscribe this power on non-Western histories and cultures become, metaphorically, fellow imperial travelers. The provocation of Edward Said's *Orientalism* has generated numerous studies of colonial productions of knowledge within which European imperial travel writing, given the centrality of journeying as metaphorical passage into world history, has emerged into significant place. Taking up the radical challenge of *Orientalism*, scholars have shown how the discourse of European travel writing becomes complicitous with imperial conquest and colonial rule. But as critics have also pointed out, *Orientalism* critiques the totalizing power of Western imperial knowledge while enacting its own totalization vis-à-vis both Western producers of knowledge and non-Western others. Alert to these contradictions, scholars of travel writing are among those who have studied how the articulation of racialist and supremacist views on other cultures in imperial discourses is often incomplete, unstable, or disrupted. Under their stringent scrutiny, an apparently monologic discourse is broken up into numerous small acts, each asserting the truth-claims of its representation and each demonstrably perspectival. It is arguable that the enduring fascination of an orientalized discourse of travel for contemporary scholarship lies not so much in its power to represent the "East" but in how it can be emphatically disempowered.

This essay explores three accounts of travel by British travelers during the decade before the First World War, to an area on the edges of the Western imperial mapping of world history. The three sets of travelers — Frederick and Flora Lugard, Sidney and Beatrice Webb, and Charles Eliot — did not travel in order to write; they were officials or quasi-officials whose travels are part of larger professional schemes. Frederick Lugard was governor of Hong Kong, fresh from his previous posting in Northern Nigeria, paying a courtesy call on his counterparts in Canton (Guangzhou). The Webbs were Fabian socialists, well-established figures in British politics, who were interested in education and social institutions within and outside the British empire. Eliot was a colonial administrator, an orientalist and ethnologist, who was shortly to take up an academic post as the first Vice-Chancellor of the University of Sheffield, and after that, the University of Hong Kong.

The three accounts of travel are accounts of knowledge; the physical journeys between Hong Kong and the Chinese mainland are fact-finding journeys, and witness the attempted translations of observation into information, and information into cultural and social knowledge. On one level, these accounts appear to situate Said's argument at its most classic: that colonial power frames and is inscribed in texts and discourses about indigenous cultures and this is nowhere better exemplified than in the writing of colonial officials or those who enjoy official patronage.[1] Thus, one of the aims of this essay is to demonstrate how China and the Chinese take shape as others within imperialist and orientalist frames, and how the asymmetry of this engagement between the imperial self and the colonized — or colonizable — other is veiled by the familiar rhetoric of civilizational progress. What the travel writings show is a process of interrupted mobility in which steps taken towards cross-cultural connections are counteracted by retrogression into the security and complacency of Europe's disconnection. China as difference refracts Europe's supreme alterity.

But though British imperialism has established an outpost in Hong Kong since the middle of the nineteenth century, and secured footholds in various treaty ports along the China coast, its expansion into the Chinese mainland remains irresolute. In the Far East, China poses the greatest challenge to an expansionist British empire not least because perceptions of its weaknesses of rule, technology and military capability, and thus as a ready subject of Western domination, are thoroughly ambiguated by the recognition that its entrenched traditions are incommensurable with the Western cognitive mapping of world history. The travelers do not move fluently on the axis between arrival and departure; just as their itinerary of travel is often interrupted by unexpected events, their preconceptions are recurrently destabilized by actual encounters with China and Chinese subjects. Their writing inscribes their attempt to negotiate China as difference and as the same, negotiations which do not always issue in assurance of China's "civilizability" in

Western terms. This problematic outcome exceeds the closure of Western supremacist beliefs which notionalize the Chinese "race" as irredeemably degenerate and its civilization in terminal decline. The reader is not a mere armchair traveler; she is watching the multiple performances of the British imperial consciousness — and the occasional betrayals of its unconscious desires — in its contact with the phenomena of "China."

To some of the travelers some of the time, if the China they encountered appears "uncivilized" and "uncivilizable," the thought does occur that there is perhaps an alien historical and cultural logic at work which remains opaque to Western eyes. This essay aims not only to show the faultlines of British imperial rhetoric, but to explore an alternative, indigenous otherness which is recognizable even to imperial eyes at the very moment of contact, and leaves its traces in the travel writing as the discourse of hindsight. This alternative otherness is most discernible in Eliot's account of his visit to Canton; the model of civilizational progress he constructs co-exists with descriptions of everyday life and subjects in an indigenous life-world that demands engagement on its own terms.

## II

This discussion will begin with accounts of Lugard's arrival in Hong Kong and his journey to Canton. As colonial governor, his writing can be expected to show indelible inscriptions of colonial power, and this is clearly the case in his copious official memoranda and other publications.[2] But when we turn to the account of his arrival and travel to Canton, a rather more complicated picture emerges. The arrival is actually reported in a letter written, not by Lugard himself, but his wife, the former colonial correspondent of *The Times* in London, Flora Shaw. "One thing we both observed," Flora writes to Lugard's brother, Edward,

> was the oriental stillness of the crowd. The Chinaman may have learnt to use a Kodak but he has not yet learned to cheer. . . . Though the crowd did not cheer they looked profoundly interested. There was not an indifferent countenance in all those that we saw and the crowd as a corporate body had a curious intense way of conveying it was pleased.[3]

In this quotation, we see the first of many examples of empirical observation and the positivistic leap from observation to the construction of an internal logic in the observed. The Lugards were progressing on sedan chairs in the first stage of their journey uphill to the governor's residence. From their elevated vantage, the crowd's "stillness" is glossed as typically "oriental" but apparently without the derogatory meanings which the typification often entails. Instead, empirical signs are assembled and translated by the traveling subjects to produce a matrix of meaning which not only confirms their authority but also connects them with the observed. They are experienced in colonial travel, complementary about indigenous peoples as the latter are receptive to their presence; in the first moment of arrival, Flora's account enacts a bond between herself and her husband as seasoned actors and the crowd as satisfied audience in a street-theatre performance — pageant and spectacle — of benevolent colonial rule.

A significantly different vantage is offered by a report in the local English newspaper, *The Hongkong Telegraph*. In the report, the crowd is not homogeneously Chinese but variegated, and not voluntaristic in its stillness or pleasure but strictly marshaled:

> All the streets . . . were lined with troops, whose bronzed and business-like appearance must have been of reminiscent interest to the wiry, grizzled warrior who is now the head of the Colony. The mounted troop . . . never looked fitter, and the Indians might have been carved in grey granite. Among the spectators there was none of that crushing and impatient movements which have marked similar functions in the past, a fact which may be attributed to the admirable way in which they were handled by the police.[4]

The report associates Lugard with martial discipline, and with its own endorsement of the display of such discipline on the colonial streets.[5] Looking back from the vantage of this report, how should we read Flora's account? Did the Lugards not notice how the "stillness" of the crowd was extracted and maintained or have they chosen to avert their gaze from the realities of the colonial ground on which they were setting foot for the first time? Or did they see all too well but in the interest of their own liberal imperial beliefs and using their status as new arrivals, chose to gloss these realities positively so as to instantiate a new mode of colonial relations between the ruler and the ruled?[6] The two extracts above show how representations of indigenous others can inscribe different practices of colonial power. The questions also reopen the distance between the traveler and the indigenous ground of the journey, a distance which the Lugards' account of arrival, taken on its own, seems to have bridged. This is an issue which is recurrent in the three travels under discussion, and one which some of the travelers themselves become aware of from time to time. Positive appraisals about the Chinese other resonate in the Lugards' other writing.[7] Shortly after his arrival, Lugard traveled up the Pearl River to Canton, and he writes to Edward about the Canton crowd in a way which rehearses Flora's procedures of empirical observation, translation, and the semantics of approbation: "The thing that strikes one in the jostling crowd is the intelligence of their faces, their diversity within a common type, and the absence of wrangling and quarrelling. Generally speaking, you see a vast number of industrious folk, each in his own cell or pigeon hole, working hard, sallow and intelligent."[8] Lugard clearly approves of the industry and peaceableness which, together with intelligence, make up the characteristics of the Chinese type, and sees the typical confirmed amidst diversity and individuation.

As a newly arrived British political administrator, Lugard is taking the measure not only of his subjects in Hong Kong, but those Chinese who, given the free-flow of human traffic across the border, potentially fall within the compass of his rule. In typifying their industry and intelligence, he represents the Chinese's essential "civilizability"; this selective representation, in turn, blurs the boundaries between colony and hinterland.

His journey upriver has shown the prevalence and persistence of the Chinese type, and that there is little to separate the inhabitants of Hong Kong and Canton. As the governor of the former, this identification of his colonial subjects with those under Qing dynastic rule in Canton enables his projection as paternalistic guardian over both. This projection takes shape soon after his return from Canton in the scheme for a university in Hong Kong for Chinese students from the colony and the Mainland.

Thus, the travel accounts inscribe a complex process of differentiation in which Lugard can separate himself, on the one hand, from the militaristic colonial rule that *The Hongkong Telegraph* so enthusiastically reports, and on the other, from the coercive but far less efficient Qing government in terminal decline. His performance of benevolence was evidently highly convincing for he managed to gain considerable financial support both in Hong Kong and Canton for the university scheme. He also impressed none other than Sidney and Beatrice Webb who, as Fabian socialists, would normally be his opponents in British politics.

After traveling to Japan and northern China, the Webbs arrived in Hong Kong by steamer from Shanghai on November 20, 1911, and from Hong Kong took a side-trip to Canton. As social reformers, they had long campaigned for the poor in the London East End, and to promote the academic study of sociology and related subjects, founded the London School of Economics.[9] In their travel journal, the Webbs recorded visits to institutions and compared their development in the different Far Eastern countries. Written mostly by Beatrice, the journal contains Sidney's marginal comments, additions and amendments.[10] Everywhere in the journal, their professional observations about social organization are leavened by righteous comments on indigenous subjects and the present condition of the various "Eastern" races.

The Webbs' arrival in Hong Kong did not escape the notice of Government House, and an invitation from Flora to lunch resulted in their moving in as guests of the Lugards. For their hosts, the Webbs had nothing but compliment, praising Lugard extravagantly "as the best type of English administrator . . . inspired by a broad, sympathetic, open-minded determination to make the world better" (164). As a person, they did not find him particularly "interesting" but they had no doubt that "as a concrete justification and explanation of the British Empire," he "was full of significance" (165). As for Flora, Beatrice judged her to be "an imperialist of the somewhat hard type — a Tory, combining her husband's feudal faith" with a kind of "crude capitalist individualism" (165), though Beatrice also admitted to being quickly won over by Flora's "stately bearing" and "stimulating" conversations which made the latter "ideal" as chatelaine (165).

China dislodges the Tory Lugards and Fabian Webbs from their opposition in British party politics, and enacts a new rapport between them; in their empathy with the Lugards, the Webbs are displaced from their anti-Tory position in British party politics. This is the first of the three displacements which their travel journal witnesses. "China" is also the multi-valenced space where the imperiality of the Lugards and the Webbs becomes differentiated; it is the two couples' representations of China which define their distance from each other. In the Webbs' account of China and the Chinese, the journal witnesses their second displacement: the astounding retreat from their socialist sympathies for the plight of the underclass, so much so that they appear to occupy a political position even further to the right of the imperial Lugards.

In Lugard's treatment of "subordinate races," the journal observes — and here the Webbs reveal a familiar imperial prejudice — "he is essentially honorable and well-bred, considering that he has obligation to raise their status and to respect their customs and conventions" (164). By the time of their arrival in Hong Kong, the Webbs have had more than two months of exposure to various of these "subordinate races" in Japan, Korea and China, and they are in no doubt about the hierarchy of this subordination. Ironically, it is precisely their progressivist convictions which lead them to construct the Japanese as similitude, and the Chinese as irredeemably other. To the Webbs, the Japanese are definitely superior to the Chinese by virtue of their ability to modernize along Western lines. In contrast, the Chinese are "barbaric" and their primitive traditions ill-prepare them for the kind of political and social reformation the Japanese have embarked on in order to become a credible player in the European global map of nations.

The Webbs are also scathing about the preference of their expatriate informants for the Chinese over the Japanese, seeing this as the issue of habituation to the Chinese as servants who, in their servility, offer no competition or threat, as the Japanese do, to European supremacy. Lugard's expression of this "usual preference" (165) confirms a familiar failure of insight displayed by expatriates in the north, and the Webbs are equally disparaging about the European business leaders they meet in Hong Kong: "They were plainly men of great practical capacity but with amazingly little intellectual culture or curiosity, knowing and caring practically nothing about the Chinese" (166). Their contacts with the Chinese are entirely mediated by the comprador system, unlike the Japanese firms who dispense with intermediaries and require all their employees to learn Chinese. The English, the Webbs conclude, have "quite failed to realize the Japanese assidulty, intellectual humility and deliberate purposefulness" (167) which direct their corporate activities. Positioning themselves away from their colonial counterparts who cannot see beyond the familiar and the practical, the Webbs reach for a formulation of typical qualities which can be translated into a cultural logic of Japanese collectivization, and an historical explanation for that nation's emergence as an economic power and competitor.

Looking in another direction, the Webbs recurrently lament the failure of the Chinese to harness their industry in purposeful social organization. Traveling up to Canton, they record their impression of the city's teeming population as "a sort of nightmare":

> . . . this million of blue-clad human ants inhabiting apparently endless series of dark and dirty cells in which they lived and ate and worked amid gaudy decoration. Between the rows of these single-storied brick or stone cells open to the narrow street . . . there poured an endless stream of pedestrian life as in an ant-hill, through which our coolies forced their way with constant shouting, bearing our cumbrous "chair". . . . The whole city gave us the impression not of distinct houses but of a single construction of brick or stone cells built adjoining each other. . . . In these cells, deliberately made dark to exclude the burning sun, the whole population, rich and poor, seemed

to be burrowing with the animated motion, the uniformity and the perpetual
repetition of identical parts of an ant-hill. . . . Canton city is poles asunder
from Japan . . . namely, not really a social organism but an ant-hill. (169)

Elevated above the crowd like the Lugards, the Webbs' social sympathies appear to have yielded to the censoriousness of their progressivist ideals. And censuring the segregation from the Chinese of the colonial expatriate class, their own repudiation appears all the more acute because of their authority as sociologists and experienced social reformers.

If in their social Darwinian nightmare, contemporary urban China appears a primitive throwback, the sites of traditional China descend even further into inchoate primordial disorder. Unlike the pristine shrines and temples in Japan which they see as icons of a racially pure and morally hygienic culture, the Webbs find the temples in Canton "horribly squalid, neglected, and of the lowest barbarism, the images grotesque, the appurtenances tawdry, and the rites of the few worshippers degradingly superstitious." Glancing back on similar impressions up north, they judge that such a condition is "perhaps characteristic of China" (169). Occasionally, they glimpse an isolated remnant of ancient civility — an ancestral hall where families assemble to pay respects to their deceased elders, or a beautifully kept garden. But no single site is able, in their view, to escape its surrounding barbarity — the sobriety of Confucian ancestral rites contaminated by the "gaudily-painted and fantastically-carved" building in which they are held, an exquisite garden attached to a house elaborately furnished but "without any books or pictures to speak of" (170).

What is at issue is not the rebarbarization of China or a retrogressive teleology inverse to that of the successfully Westernizing Japanese; to the Webbs, Chinese culture is not so much in decline as innately degenerate. The failure to evolve a more advanced social organization and a higher intellectualized culture is deeply embedded in China's materialist heritage, where individual subjects have no collective consciousness outside of the family, and valorize sensuous pleasure as the highest good directing their industry and productivity. In their negative construction of China's alienness, the Webbs disclose the heights — or the hidden depths — of their own intellectualization and secularized morality. In a third displacement, the rigour of the scientistic sociology to which they are professionally committed seems to desert them. En route to Hong Kong, their summary reflection on their north China visit reveals the extent to which their progressivist sociology is shackled to a Victorian social morality at its most puritanical: "Is it possible," they ask, "that (a) the Chinese are and have been for centuries honeycombed by 'unnatural vice,' and (b) that this vice, as possibly among the Greeks, has some subtle deteriorating effect on character, far-reaching enough to destroy a whole civilization?" (154). An anxiety about the libidinous underside of their Anglo-Saxon scientistic rationality erupts into the discourse of the Webbs' Chinese journal. And not for the first time. Earlier in the journal, Beatrice, with barely concealed disgust, has observed:

> With regard to sodomy, ever since I came into China I have been wondering
> whether the vice did not prevail extensively because of the expression on the

faces of the men — the vicious femininity of many of the faces. We are now told, on good authority, that in every Chinese town there are streets of 'boys' homes', and that this form of prostitution is far more popular than the more material and healthy one of men and women. It is this rottenness of physical and moral character that makes one despair of China — their constitution seems devastated by drugs and abnormal sexual indulgence. They are, in essentials, an *unclean race*. (140, italics in original)

These observations reveal how — and how quickly — the Webbs' Victorian puritanism, which drives their reformist zeal at home, develops a downward spiral in its encounter with foreignness.[11] It is not just the nature of Beatrice's castigations, the collapsing of physical, moral, racial, and cultural categories into each other, which is truly startling but also the *speed* with which she leaps from impressionistic observation to supposed empirical information to judgment and finally condemnation of an entire people. What the specious logic and its ramshackle architecture betray is a betrayal of thought, or the corruptibility of that rationalistic process by which positivistic inquiry construes first causes and stakes its claim to truth. This betrayal is made manifest through its displacement onto a narrative of "China" as socially incoherent, morally disordered, and essentially corrupt.[12]

## III

Charles Eliot is equally interested in situating China in a narrative of world history. But in his travel writing, the discourse of civilizational progress takes shape differently, molded by an intense scholarly reflexiveness and further disoriented by fascination with the details of the Chinese indigenous life-world. Eliot arrived in Hong Kong in 1906, traveling south to north in the reverse direction from the Webbs. He made his way through Cochin China before arrival, and from Hong Kong proceeded upriver to Canton, and then northwards by land to the Yangtze delta and then Peking. From Peking, he crossed over to Japan, and the account of his travels is written in the form of letters which were published in the *Westminster Gazette* in London in 1907, and collected in *Letters from the Far East*.[13] Besides being a diplomat and colonial administrator in different parts of the British empire, Eliot was a scholar and polyglot who had cultivated a long-term interest in Buddhism as a historical, social and cultural phenomenon. As he states in the Introduction to the *Letters*, the object of his travel was "to study the curious development which Buddhism has undergone" because he realizes that his study of Sanskrit and Pali, while important for discerning the origins of Buddhism in India, cannot on its own "give a correct and comprehensive idea" of the part the religion played in the Far East (1). His comparative judgments between China and Japan, and on China and the world, exhibit far less righteous indignation and a great deal more thoughtful circumspection than the Webbs.

Eliot's *Letters* offers a discursive mixture of two kinds of travel: an intellectual journey into other cultures, and the record of the actual physical journey itself. Though the chapter divisions separate the two, they need to be explored in relation to each other for intellectual speculation and empirical observation are mutually supportive in his engagements with China, China in the "East" and "Far East," and China and Europe. Eliot's views on China are framed by a comparative discourse of civilizations which juxtaposes the secularism of Chinese and Japanese social traditions against Islamic theocracy and Hindu religiosity. He further distinguishes the "strong military spirit of a feudal type" which is propelling Japan into the modern world from the peaceable Confucian morality that underlies China's traditional institutions (6–7). Far from being homogeneous, Eliot's "East" is internally variegated, and this cultural variegation is also manifest vis-à-vis relations with Europe. Unlike "Hindus and Mohammedans" who are postulated as total alterity to Europe, both China and Japan are seen to share "many of the same aptitudes and aspirations as Europeans" and lag behind only in "material civilization and development" (7).

Japanese progress in catching up with Europe, and Chinese inertia are traced to their different traditional ideologies. Confucianism has provided "an excellent, sane, prosaic, moral philosophy" (7), and a stable basis to Chinese institutions under the aegis of dynastic rule. Confucianist values discourage individualism and aggressive endeavour, an attitude that counters "modern international ethics" (16) which promote competitive enterprise between subjects and states. On the other hand, the state and institutional culture that such values produce can lend itself to an "incredible conservatism retaining abuses when reform would be easy," or provoke a counter-logic of revolutionary change that denies all validity to tradition, "sweeping away at the bidding of government what one might suppose to be precious heirlooms" (8). In this, Eliot is clearly glancing not only at the past, but also at the Qing dynasty's vacillation between adopting and rejecting Western models of progress, and the mutual displacement of moderate and radical schemes of reform in the last decades of Qing rule.

Eliot offers a metanarrative that attempts to take into account ideological inheritance and the tradition of rule, and their correlative effects observable in contemporary events. He displays a wary scholarly reflexiveness that eschews — though it cannot entirely escape — reading culture as race and China's recent malaise as the cumulative effect of innate racial defects. It is the case, however, that the positivistic inquiry into first causes shapes his narrative as much as the Webbs' and other ethnological studies of his time. This is evident in his discussion of Confucianism as the singular source of both China's enduring strength and her embedded weakness, a doubled heritage he sees as manifest not only in the political and social domains, but also in Chinese philosophy, literature, and art. This vantage on Confucian cultural hegemony leads him, in turn, to question the extent of China's ability on its own to reform its ways, and to theorize on cross-cultural contact as a source of historical change.

History, Eliot submits, has shown that states "alternate between activity and quiescence" (18), the latter usually under the rule of foreigners, and China is no exception. The Manchu rulers of the Qing dynasty were themselves foreigners to China, and in their heyday, ensured or extracted "quiescence." Their decay is the sign of "national Chinese revival," or a return to "activity" which, fuelled by the "will, ambition, and ideals of the Chinese" will lead them on the road to progress (18). To Eliot, the Europeans have succeeded the Manchus as the latest foreign entrants into Chinese history. Although the current signs of this new contact are not auspicious, and are characterized much more by misunderstanding, hostility and rejection on both sides, the logic of historical progress, through contact and mixing, points towards a more pacific outcome in the future.

Eliot strives to be even-handed in his assignment of praise and blame. Though he is often critical of the "mental defects" (16) in those Chinese subjects he meets and the prevailing "conceit" (18) of the Chinese in thinking that if they wanted to learn from the Europeans, they could do so quickly, he is equally sure that European civilization is not so perfect that it should be "paramount." Deconstructing his own scholarly authority, he observes that no one really has "the impartial or cosmopolitan outlook to decide whether the European or the Asiatic character" is better (28). What his historical logic tells him is that out of the encounters between civilizations comes a kind of mixing, and in what ensues, the loss of distinctiveness is compensated for by rejuvenation and continued survival. The alternative — that is, when a civilization isolates itself — is senility, decay, and eventual disappearance. Once again, we hear a social Darwinian resonance although its temper could not be further apart from the Webbs.[14]

In crossing cultures, Eliot's intellectualization is the analogue of his physical journey, and also the informing spirit of his detailed record of sights and sounds in the *Letters*. Hong Kong presents itself to him as "a striking example of what European enterprise can do" (56); he registers the flourishing trade, public works, and signs of material prosperity. In agreeing that the colony would gratify "the patriot, economist, and politician," but "cannot be said to possess any special interest as a spectacle of men and manners" (57), Eliot appears ambivalent about the effects of European intervention on Chinese habitats and everyday life, or even ready to dismiss the latter, at least in Hong Kong, altogether. To view the "spectacle of men and manners," he contends, one must go to Canton which has for a long time been the only Chinese port opened to European trade. "It has not, however," he admits, "become cosmopolitan, like the ports of the Levant, but, in spite of centuries of European intercourse, remains in its life and customs purely Chinese" (57). This comment suggests that Canton, the foremost of China's treaty ports, remains recalcitrant to the kind of cross-cultural hybridization that, to Eliot, is the inalienable route to civilizational progress.

However, in describing what is "purely Chinese" in Canton, the premises of variety and mixture emphasized — and valorized — in Eliot's logic of progress are clearly observable. The spaces of Canton life are characterized by an abundance of activity and production that show uniformity in variety and variety in uniformity. Indigenous Canton appears dynamic and full of activity, which gives the lie to the earlier comment that the city is unchanging when it is seen in relation to the European presence. This is an interesting contradiction or a sign of mixing in Eliot's own discourse which he will try to address, as we shall see. Approaching Canton on the steamer, he finds the river life striking as a space where nature and culture interpenetrate. In Chinese tradition, he observes, boats are seen as "imitations of floating leaves," and the variety and profusion of river craft certainly "resemble the carpet of vegetation which obstructs sluggish water." The boats "are of all shapes, sizes, and colours — junks with sails like butterflies, painted house-boats belonging to rich Chinese, floating hovels inhabited by floating lepers and beggars . . . salt-boats, rice-boats, fruit-boats, and duck-boats" harboring "an amphibious population" who, "like the frogs, keep up a ceaseless noise and motion" (57). Abstracting himself from the empirical moment, Eliot reaches into history and tradition for perspectives that would unify the heterogeneous spectacle: the boats are mainly inhabited by "a tribe called Tanka"; they are the "aquatic" habitats of crime, especially of pirates, and only in China, "that museum of customs," does piracy continue to exist and enjoy the protection of a romantic aura going back to the resistance against the land-based military supremacy of the Manchus (58).

Similar alternations between the one and the many are evident in a number of other indigenous spaces. As he surveys the warren of streets from the elevated vantage of a sedan-chair, Eliot, like the Webbs, sees Canton as "an ant-hill," and while impressed by the "enormous" industry, remains dubious "that the output is commensurate with the labour" (59). But unlike the Webbs, he steps onto indigenous ground, and venturing from the dark and covered streets into the shops, is immediately captivated by the "brilliancy" of their interiors and the actual variety in the output of Chinese industry. He notes, for instance, the "extraordinary number of articles made of paper, gilt or painted with the crudest and most gorgeous colours — lanterns, fans, umbrellas, scrolls, and armfuls of artifical flowers. Besides this, there are piles of fruits and vegetables, green, yellow, and red, fish, fowls, and other eatables, which, if not always appetizing, are generally highly coloured" (59). Stopping by the residence of a rich Chinese man to whom he has a letter of introduction, Eliot moves from the dark, crowded, "topsy-turvy" streets into a house that is "open" and full of light. Inside the house, the same imbrication of nature and culture that he notices on the river is again observable: "I do not know," he muses,

> if it should be called a house in a garden or a garden in a house. Passages and pavilions were inextricably mixed up with a fantastic rockery, out of which grew small trees. . . . The rooms and pavilions were clean and decorated with landscapes painted in sober colours, diversified here and there with inscribed vermilion tablets. . . . There were no flowers in the garden, but out of a miniature lake nearly covered with the broad round leaves of the lotus rose a few red blossoms. (64)

If the temples are full of "idols . . . [that are] all gigantic and ludicrously inartistic" (62), he is also drawn, with a perspicacity much more refined than the Webbs', to the altar vessels, "particularly the great incense burners" that are "generally of good and sometimes of exquisite workmanship" (63). He cannot resist comparing the temple spectacle to "the stage of a pantomine," but rather than just abhorrence for this indigenous religious space, notes that he is like someone who has "wandered by mistake" onto this stage that is "intended to be seen by night and at a distance," and so appears "dismally absurd in the light of day" (63). The only Chinese subject Eliot seems to have had any interaction with on this occasion is his guide whose insistence that he follow a fixed itinerary of tourist sights frustrates his desire to "drift through [the] populous, many-coloured streets" (60).

But as he chafes against his guide's "remorselessly consecutive mind" (61), he is also intrigued by the latter's blend of "scepticism" which dismisses all religions as "folly" with compliant views on traditional burial arrangements (65).

In representing indigenous spaces, Eliot's own mobile perceptiveness functions to register mobility and multiplicity in the observed. "China" in these representations is differentiated from the "China" in his metanarrative where it appears apathetic to European influence, and, unlike Japan, dormant in a modern world of change. This seeming contradiction does not lead him to conclude that China is somehow "inscrutable and unfathomable" (21). Instead, he sees China's indigenous energies as a source of power that will move it on in its historical journey between "quiescence" and "activity." "If the race is not effete," he states, "it would be quite in harmony with its record in the past if the decay of the Manchu dynasty coincided with a national Chinese revival" (18). In Canton, and further north in his travels, Eliot did not see this "effete"-ness, and nothing of its related issue in "unnatural vice." Though there is much that he finds objectionable, there is also plentiful evidence that Chinese traditions continue to bond the disparate regions, and of continuous Chinese industry in everyday life. And if contact with foreigners "acts as a disintegrating force, it has sometimes the opposite effect, and calls into operation the national power of combination into guilds or societies for a particular object" (115). Eliot cites as an example the boycott of American goods that has spread from Canton north to Suchow (Suzhou) during the time of his visit. But beyond this immediate reference, the comment is a sanguine projection of China's regeneration under the stimulus of a new phase of foreign intervention. Eliot's intellectual investment in a particular historical logic is such that in order for China to be replaced in a global narrative of progress, its apparent recalcitrance in face of Europe is translated out of a discourse of incommensurability into that of contiguity. Being backward does not signify innate cultural degeneration or irreversible decline; China is simply lagging behind, and in time, given indigenous industry and the European presence, it will catch up with — or be caught up in — the irresistible metanarrative of progress.

## IV

Each of the three sets of travelers went on to develop, in their different ways, a reputation in Britain as experts in imperial and world affairs. A recent history of British imperialism confirmed earlier studies of Lugard as "the leading theorist of imperialism of his day".[15] Sidney Webb was a core founder of the British Labour Party, and was one of the main authors of its constitution in 1918. Eliot was appointed British ambassador to Japan in 1919–25 and authored a monumental study of Japanese Buddhism, published posthumously in 1935. To a large extent, it is their imperial reputation which lends authentication to their accounts of Hong Kong and China upriver, and confers upon these accounts the authority of truth. But if their accounts are small acts in the accretions of imperial discourse, they also show how this discourse devolves and atomizes in trying to contain the many-faceted phenomena of "China" it desires to incorporate.

The period before and after the First World War was one of fundamental systemic change in China when two millennia of dynastic imperial rule terminated in revolution, and amidst widespread national unrest, a newly constituted republican government struggled to establish its legitimacy. The three sets of travelers were journeying through populous urban centers on which political and social upheaval had direct impact on everyday life. The paucity of reflection, and cursory interest in the Chinese revolutionary movement as it might have been manifest in the daily lives unfolding around them, and the almost complete failure to imagine it as historical trauma, is symptomatic of the myopia of the global metanarrative of civilizational progress under the aegis of Western imperialism.

Of the three accounts, Eliot's seems much more sensitively attuned to the contemporary Chinese world it seeks to represent. His theory of external intervention and its resulting cross-cultural engagement as the source of civilizational change resonates with the ideas of Qing and Republican reformist intellectuals like Liang Qichao who sought to displace the orthodox view of Chinese cultural supremacy, and advocated an urgent rethinking about China as one among competitive nation-states. A detailed comparison of Eliot and Liang does not belong within the scope of the present essay, but it would be valuable to speculate on the possibility of a historicized cross-cultural imaginary that might emerge from this comparison, to study its internal dynamic, and think through its aspirational implications.

# 10

## With Harry Franck in China

*Nicholas Clifford*

## I

If we want an American equivalent of Isabella Bird Bishop (not that we are likely to find one), Harry Alverson Franck might be a candidate. Like her, he roamed through much of the world, often alone, though sometimes with his family parked nearby; like her, he was a prolific writer, publishing some twenty-three books on his travels between 1910 and 1943; and, like hers, his books promise his readers a direct apprehension of the reality of the lands through which he journeyed, seen through the eyes of a dispassionate observer.

In this last, of course, he and Bird fit into a particular tradition of travel writing. Their promise, implied or explicit, is that the travelers will report their observations directly and accurately, escaping the blinders of those whose long familiarity or experience with a foreign land — as settlers, expatriates, colonial servants, missionaries, or scholars — might actually impede them in their quest for truth. Travelers land unencumbered by any such baggage, enjoying the freedom to report the evidence of their own senses: what they see, hear, feel, and smell in the streets of Cairo or Kunming, Baghdad or Beijing, unmediated by research in dusty archives, untroubled by the earnest goals of missionaries, sacred or secular, by the desire to explain economic and social structures, or the need to wire home good copy for tomorrow's paper. Or, indeed, the need to produce "literature" (a question to be examined later). On her return from China, Bird, in a phrase far more ambiguous to us than it is for her, promises her readers "a truthful impression of the country," while Franck, without quite saying so, lets his audience know that the China he will show them may be quite different from the one they expect.

Here the resemblance ends, not simply because three thousand miles of open water separate the New World from the Old, but also because a catastrophic quarter of a century divides the two travelers. Bird was one of many journeying abroad in those still confident years before the West turned on itself in the sudden fury that left millions of dead scattered across Europe, ending forever the comfortable Whig dream of an enlightened and untrammeled Western advance. To her the British empire was a great agent of progress, and there was nothing ironic in her dedication of *The Yangtze Valley and Beyond* to Lord Salisbury for his services to that cause. A few years after the guns fell silent, Franck had no such framework within which to order any easy prescriptions for the salvation of less fortunate nations, and the idea that his books should be dedicated to, say, President Calvin Coolidge, or Secretary of State Charles Evans Hughes, would have seemed quite as absurd to him as it does to us. (*Wandering Through Northern China*, in fact, was dedicated, in a nice domestic touch, to his daughter, born in Beijing in 1923.)

## II

Harry Franck probably draws few readers today, and the plans of a British publisher to bring out reprints of his two books on China (at £125 and £135) no doubt reflect the recent respectability of travel writing as a subject of scholarly study. In his own day, however, he was not only a prolific but a widely read author ("the most notable traveler of our time," as a publicity flyer called him).[1] "His book is as interesting as the story of Marco Polo," wrote a reviewer in a Boston newspaper of *Northern China*. "Like the great Venetian traveller, Mr. Franck goes among the people and notes their manners, their habits, and their customs . . . [H]e has deservedly won for himself a reputation as the author of some of the best books of travel that have come from the modern press." A long and flattering notice of the same book in the *Nation* regretted the absence of an index, for its inclusion would have made *Northern China* even more valuable as a reference work. Some, however, wished on the author a less complaisant editor. "Can one sit down and read through practically 700 pages of close-printed words of detailed travel in a foreign land?" asked a reviewer in the *New York Herald-Tribune*. Yes, she concluded, "if one is a student of the matter and grasping out for everything on the subject. Otherwise, I fear the task will pall . . . As you progress you have much the same sensation as when you arrive at the fourth or fifth course of a Thanksgiving dinner; it is good, all awfully good, but there is too much of it!"[2]

Born in Michigan in 1881, Harry Franck graduated from that state's university in 1903, and presently set out on what he called his *Wanderjahr*, working his way around the globe with little money in his pocket, and publishing the account in 1910 as *A Vagabond Journey Around the World* (a journey which, incidentally, saw him spend a few days in Hong Kong and Shanghai before moving on to Japan).[3] After wartime service in France and Italy, he married Rachel Latta in 1919, and resumed his travels. By the time he turned his attention to East Asia a few years later, he had walked the length of Central and South America and traveled in the West Indies, publishing books as he went. *Wandering Through Northern China*, which appeared in 1923, was his ninth, and *Roving Through Southern China* (1925) his eleventh. In between came *Glimpses of Japan and Formosa* (1924), and immediately thereafter, *East of Siam* (1926) which recorded his trips through French Indochina.[4] His last travel work, the record of a journey through Mexico, appeared in 1943. There was still one more book, however, describing the operations of the Ninth Air Force in the last year of the battle for Europe in 1944 and 1945. For reasons not entirely clear, *A Winter Journey Through the Ninth* was not published at the time, and only in 2001 did it appear in print.[5]

A vagabond, Franck styled himself in his first book, and he continued to rejoice in the term later. "Inclined to stray or gad about without proper occupation," reads one of the definitions in the *OED*, "leading an unsettled, irregular, or disreputable life; good-for-nothing, rascally, worthless." These raffish qualities, exuberantly paraded to shock the respectable, carry with them a sense of freedom, not only from a fixed place called "home," but also from cares and responsibilities, from conventional ways of thinking, of conceiving the world and one's proper place in it. If, as has been said, "travel, with its timetabled arrivals and departures, provides a particularly acute experience of the relation between predestination and the free play of choice and volition,"[6] Franck's vagabondage claims to have been undertaken in a decidedly un-Calvinist manner. He embarked on his maiden voyage to prove to his friends that one need not be a millionaire to circle the globe, and his later books poked fun not only at cautious tourists, but also at those who set themselves up as authorities on far-away places and strange people, as well as those warning of the difficulties and dangers of travels in such uncharted regions. On the other hand, his Asian voyage strikes a familiar domestic note, for he brought his young family with him, setting them down in cities such as Beijing, Kunming, and Guangzhou while he struck off into the interior, and his vagabond nature did not spare him embarrassment at having to share public baths with naked Japanese of both sexes.[7]

*Northern China* runs to well over five hundred pages, and *Southern China* exceeds six hundred, to which one might add the roughly eighty pages describing Taiwan in the book on Japan, and all are copiously illustrated with Franck's own photographs. It is not easy to pin down the exact dates of these travels, or for that matter with whom he made them. Rachel Latta Franck's *I Married a Vagabond* is little more help, being almost entirely innocent of chronology.[8] Her presence, though, with their children, distinguishes Franck from the "almost imperative desire" of many travel writers, as Stephen Clark puts it, to abandon home and family. But he does not escape that other habit to which Clark points, the one — so annoying to historians and biographers — of writing family and friends out of their records,[9] and while the occasional references to "we" sometimes mean his family (apparently including, at one point, his mother as well), elsewhere the pronoun embraces a variety of unnamed companions in the interior — the occasional missionary, or American military or diplomatic official. Sometimes dates can be inferred from references to current events. After leaving Japan and making their way through Korea, the Francks appear to have crossed the Yalu into Manchuria shortly after Zhang Zuolin's defeat near Beijing, an event that occurred in May, 1922. They were certainly in Beijing for the celebrations ushering in the Year of the Pig (February, 1923), and they finally left Guangzhou for home shortly before the defeat of that city's Merchant

Volunteers by the Whampoa cadets, a clash that took place in October, 1924. *Northern China* appeared in late 1923, its foreword dated that summer from Guling, the retreat high in the Lushan mountains, where missionary families fled the steamy Yangtze lowlands, while *Southern China* was finished in August, 1925, in Philadelphia.

Placing him in China from the late spring of 1922 until the early autumn of 1924 will do well enough, with the first half of the time spent in the north and the latter in the south (his dividing line is at the 23rd parallel, and since this is roughly at the Huai River, it is a perfectly good traditional division as well). During those two years he left the country long enough to take passage on a small Japanese steamer from Xiamen (Amoy) to Jilong (Keelung) in Taiwan, and to make two excursions into Indochina, once alone and once with his family, whom he left in Hanoi while he went wandering.

Still, it will not do to toss chronology entirely to the winds. Not only was his China very different from that of Isabella Bird Bishop and her contemporaries at the turn of the century, but it was changing rapidly even while he was there. Had he arrived two or three years later — during the period of the May Thirtieth Movement, the Northern Expedition, and the dramatic break between Communists and Guomindang, for instance — he might well have found his observations colored by those events. (Here I may as well reveal my prejudice against the kind of postcolonialism that can be relentlessly single-minded in insisting on the subjectivity of the Western observer, as if the non-Western object, or its setting in time, has little or no reality apart from that granted by outsiders. "Real China" may exist only in the imagination, but it is worth remembering there is an actual country there, as well as the land produced by representation.)

## III

What should his readers expect, then? Let us examine his own admonitions to his audience first.

They are not to turn to him for light on China's politics, on its wars and uprisings, on the generals and others tearing the country apart. His interest in such matters "reaches only so far as it affects the every-day life of the people, of the mudsill of society, toward which, no doubt by some queer quirk in my make-up, I find my attention habitually focusing." Nor should they look for predictions about China's future — "I regret that I have not been vouchsafed the gift of prophecy and cannot tell you."[10] They must not take him as an authority of China; there are plenty of those at home, all too ready to mislead his own countrymen.[11] They are not to look for the comforting platitudes of "Young China's" spokesmen, who, living in America, and "hopelessly out of touch with their native land," spread their quite inaccurate promises of a progressive republic among credulous Westerners. Nor should they expect prescriptions for particular medicines to cure China's ills, as do the missionaries both of the sacred (Christianity) and the secular (science, technology, industry) stamp.

Finally, they are not to look in his pages for pretty writing. Instead Franck promises his readers no more than a record "of the things that most interested me, often things that others seem to have missed or considered unimportant."[12] For he claims to be no more than

> an average individual, with no particular bent for the scientific or the statistical, nor with an ax to grind, and, since even a vagabond must show some excuse for his existence in these energetic times, to try to bring that [record] home as intact as possible, in the hope that it may interest others of the same normal tastes . . . I am more interested in setting down a record of plain fact, than of [*sic*] producing "literature."[13]

The claim, in short, is that of the dispassionate observer, the chronicler or reporter, rather than that of either judge or man of letters. The assertion that reality is best served by "plain fact" is, of course, no more original than its obverse: the claim to find in "imaginative" literature a truth that transcends anything realizable by mere historians or Gradgrindian social scientists grubbing away for facts, facts, facts in their moldering archives. Yet, as with Bird's promised "truthful impression," the modern reader still must try to disentangle the plain facts presented about China from the mediation of their self-proclaimed disinterested observer.

In other words, we must pay Franck's warnings the attention they deserve, while going behind them as well. Here, I should make it clear, I am reading Franck as a historian, taking his writings as artifacts of the period that, properly interrogated, shed light on various aspects of those years after the Great War, and by no means only in China. "Travel writing," Sara Mills sensibly observes, "cannot be read as a simple account of a journey, a country and a narrator, but must be seen in the light of discourses circulating at the time."[14] It is easy enough to fit Franck into a generalized discourse of Western imperialism, and more specifically an American one, since he came from one of the two nations (Japan, of course, was the other) that emerged stronger rather than weaker from the war. So, for instance, he uses the term "white supremacy" without apology, and is strongly critical of Russian refugees in Shenyang (Mukden), Haerbin (Harbin), and Shanghai, whose distressing character flaws do so much to bring white prestige into disrepute.[15] While some others were beginning to question it, he remained a firm supporter of extraterritorial privilege (as did, in their own ways, people as disparate as the radical Agnes Smedley and the guardians of the foreign settlements in treaty ports such as Shanghai or Tianjin).[16] Like many other Americans, he repeats the technically true but highly misleading claim that America holds no concessions[17] (though he claims no moral high ground for his fellow countrymen on that account).

While America's relative position in the world emerged stronger from the war, strength is not the same thing as self-confidence. Perhaps it was no coincidence that Franck's youthful trip around the world came shortly after an Asian nation had defeated a European nation in battle, sending a shock through the West. Two decades later, while the challenges of the 1920s were felt most acutely by the European empires, they affected the American empire, formal and informal, as well (by 1919 Manuel Quezon was beginning his quest for Philippine independence), and against that background must be read Franck's worries about the behavior of Russian refugees, or the fears that extraterritoriality might be abandoned.

But there is more than imperialism and its anxieties at work here. Elsewhere, I have suggested that among those discourses circulating in the twenties was that of authenticity,[18] and Franck was by no means alone in his undertaking to discover "real China" by getting off the beaten track and examining the lives of ordinary people. Behind this project there lurk several different, if related, motives, not all of them peculiar to such travelers. One, of course, has to do with the relative ease with which distant lands could be visited as communications improved; by the 1920s, for instance, cruise ships were putting into Shanghai and Hong Kong as well as Yokohama and Kobe. The arrival of their passengers, streaming down the gangplanks of the *Berengaria* or the *Empress of Canada* onto the Shanghai Bund, ready for a day's shopping along Nanking Road or the Avenue Joffre, made it imperative for real travelers to distinguish themselves from mere tourists, as they had earlier done in Europe.[19] They must assure their readers they know the difference between real China and treaty port China. "Shanghai and Tientsin are white men's cities," wrote Bertrand Russell at the time, upset by their inauthenticity, and the sight of them "makes one wonder what the purpose of traveling is."[20] Touring the several foreign concessions of Tianjin by tram or automobile gave an impression of "a comfortable Western community in an Oriental land," Franck found, but told you nothing of the real country or even the real city. Later on, entering Shanghai "by the back door" after his stay in the north, he found the city "at first glimpse about as interesting as Omaha or Memphis," with its dismal railway yards, dingy station, trolley poles and honking automobiles that cluttered roads looking like the "back streets of any second-class American city."[21]

Nor did the Paris of the East, with its Western architecture, its Western clubs, schools, and churches, improve much upon acquaintance. Such sentiments were by no means new, of course; several decades earlier, travelers like Isabella Bird ("coasts usually disappoint," she wrote) and Elizabeth Kendall were anxious to escape treaty port China by forging ahead into the interior.[22] The cultural hybridity of cities like Shanghai or Hankou, whose foreign inhabitants imported all the conveniences of home (and added to them whole staffs of Chinese servants) threatened to blur the clear distinction between the West and the rest of the world, leaving travelers with the prospect of little more to discover than what Helen Carr describes as the fragmented and "shabby remnants of the tapestry of otherness their predecessors had woven."[23] Though Franck does not talk about the search for real China, or claim that he has found it, the subtext underlies everything he wrote, emerging, for example, in his unflattering references to self-styled China experts, or his claims to a natural affinity with the common man.

There is more to the quest for authenticity, however, than a simple desire to distinguish oneself from the tourist horde or treaty port expatriates. It also has a domestic, or metropolitan, aspect, and Franck's observations must be situated not only in the context of a changing China, but a changing America as well. As historians have recently begun to remind us, the America from which Franck came was passing through its own age of anxiety in the twenties, confronting a modernity marked by industrialism, urbanization, and a huge new immigrant population.[24] A country in danger of losing the very characteristics that once set it apart as the New World, it now was lurching along an unmarked road into a clouded future. The years saw many — particularly "old stock" Americans, to use the term common at the time — searching the past for those qualities that could be defined as peculiarly American. The building of the Rockefeller-financed Colonial Williamsburg in Virginia, or Henry Ford's Greenfield Village in Michigan (with its replica of Philadelphia's Independence Hall) stand as examples, as does the profitable Colonial revivalism of the parson-turned-entrepreneur, Wallace Nutting. Less happily, these years also brought a resurgence of the old nativism, seen among the respectable in the race writings of men like Lothrop Stoddard and Madison Grant, and among the less respectable, in the short-lived but significant rebirth of the Ku Klux Klan, directed particularly against the recently arrived immigrants. It is against this background that one should read Franck's seeming espousal of some of the common American prejudices of his day, as in his adversions against the Jews, particularly the Russian Jews, who managed both to dominate the new Soviet Union and to practice their grasping professions as exiles in North China; against credulous and superstitious Catholics, affecting their hocus-pocus and mumbo-jumbo; against lazy American Negroes, and so forth.[25]

Related to this quest for authenticity was a growing interest in regionalism, whose protagonists hoped to define a real America distinct both from the fawning Eurocentric elite culture of the northeast (these were not good years for the reputation of Henry James!) and from the ethnic melting pots and cultural experimentation of cities like New York and Chicago. I am not suggesting, of course, that the same impulses that gave rise to Colonial Williamsburg or the regional movements directly influenced Franck's writing, or explained its popularity. Still, there was a resonance between the nostalgia for a real America, and the belief that somewhere, if one only knew how to find it, a real China lay waiting to be discovered. Regionalism and the search for the authentic, in both its domestic and foreign incarnations, traveled easily with nervousness and nostalgia, seeming to offer the hope that mass society and mass marketing would not presently obliterate all the local differences America had known earlier, or, for that matter, that a country like China had shown before the rise of the treaty ports. For all the broad similarities among northern and southern Chinese, in one of his more optimistic moments Franck concluded that there still remained innumerable differences in the quality of daily life, "in contrast to the deadly standardized sameness of our own land of quantity production and nation-wide advertising, where one must shake the head hard to remember, as he walks along the same identical street, past the same identical shops, dodging the same identical automobiles, whether he is in Portland, Maine, or in San Diego." In his less optimistic moments, however, he could still observe that "[t]he sameness of Chinese towns is as depressing as are the minds of their inhabitants," though here, of course, it was not mass marketing that was to blame, but unthinking adherence to an ancient tradition.[26]

Mary Louise Pratt and Sara Mills point to a broad division in the style of narration in travel writing: the largely impersonal "manners and customs" writer, whose narrator faces into the background, and the "sentimental" figure, where the narrator takes center stage.[27] Put another way, the division is between those interested in explicating foreign lands and customs to an audience back home, and those more interested in the internal journey, the impressions and reflections called up by the experience of travel itself. No doubt Franck would have classed himself among the "manners and customs" writers, yet in fact he fits neatly into neither category. Nor does he fit easily into the new model of the ironic, anti-heroic writer of the interwar years, of whom Peter Fleming, surprised to find himself suddenly considered an expert on Chinese communism after an abortive attempt to visit the Jiangxi Soviet, is perhaps the best example. Irony is there in full measure in Franck, but it is an externalized irony, directed against the subjects of his investigations (the less attractive Westerners as well as Chinese) rather than against himself. We never find him, as we do with Fleming, Harold Speakman, or Isherwood and Auden, for instance, making fun of his own imaginings and preconceptions before he had seen the country. Rather he is closer to his fellow Americans, like Edgar Snow, or Agnes Smedley, or Graham Peck, whose judgments, bitterly critical of those aspects of China they dislike, are accompanied by hardly a hint of introspection or self-doubt, and perhaps veer closer to sarcasm than to irony.[28]

At best, his descriptions of street scenes or landscapes convey a real sense of place of the sort unlikely to come from any guidebook. Yet much as he avoids introspection, and much as he claims the status of disinterested observer, time after time Franck's narrator nevertheless climbs onto the podium. Though promising no overarching solution to China's problems (Christianity, socialism, modern medicine or business methods, for instance) he shows no reluctance to preach about the practical steps the Chinese might take to improve their lot. Coming from the America of Taylorism and Hooverism, with its almost mystical faith in the efficacy of rationality and engineering, he finds himself frequently throwing up his hands in the discovery that "[n]o other nation has the genius of the Chinese for doing some things in the worst way."[29] He takes every opportunity to nose out corruption and superstition, the latter manifest in an idolatrous reverence for the ways of the ancients, evident for example in the never-ending graves that occupy vast amounts of otherwise useful farm land (John Dewey, a few years earlier, had made the same observation).[30] Like his nineteenth-century predecessors, he is convinced that the heavy hand of Confucianism has long since stifled virtually all capacity for original thought, likening China's arrested civilization, in one striking metaphor, to a frozen waterfall (though he admits to possible signs of a slight thaw).[31] Religion draws some of his harshest judgments; Chinese monks are almost invariably lazy hypocrites, slaking their gustatory and sexual appetites on the sly, at the expense of credulous believers. The Mongols are even worse, with their saffron-robed lamas all over the place. "Cleanliness certainly has no relation whatever to godliness in this unedifying religion of creaking prayer-wheels and barbaric hubbub,"[32] and compared to them, even Chinese Buddhism comes off well.

There is little to be found in Franck of the new tolerance, even admiration, for China that is so marked a theme of travel writing about the country in the postwar years (as in Bertrand Russell's discovery that the Chinese "have a civilization superior to ours in all that makes for human happiness").[33] Franck's role may be one of reporter and observer, but it is also one of judge, and the rule book setting forth the standards of judgment is very much one written in the West. To put it another way, his stance is that of a reliable, if not perhaps entirely omniscient narrator, leaving us little room to mistrust his judgments, or to sense that there might be interpretations different from his own. Though he can write almost lyrically of what he sees, there is little sense of wonder, or discovery of the unexpected. Sometimes, too, he is disappointed, having expected the Yangtze gorges to be grander, or Xi'an to be more than the "abridged edition of Peking" that he finds there.[34]

It is almost tempting to say that the narrator of these particular travelers' tales leaves the country, two years after first crossing the frontier, without having seen or learned anything that would challenge earlier conceptions or change his mind. That indeed was the burden of a long and unfavorable review of *Southern China* in a Boston literary journal.[35] No pilgrimage unfolds, there is no voyage of discovery, no inner journey that leaves the protagonist wiser about himself than he was before. The very organization of the books strengthens their didactic nature. By and large *Northern China* and *Southern China* are geographically rather than chronologically constructed, sometimes seeming to have almost more in common with a guidebook, like the little red Baedeker-style *Guide to China* issued in the early twenties by the Japanese Government Railways, with its itineraries laid out ("Mukden to Peking," "Tsinan to Tsingtau," and so forth) for the convenience of the traveler.[36] His trip to Taiwan, for example — interesting particularly because it was a destination well off the itinerary of most travelers — is unmentioned in *Southern China*, even though it took place in the course of his travels there. Instead it found its way into his Japanese book because it was, after all, still part of Tokyo's empire. Such an arrangement serves the purpose of clarity, Franck says. But it also helps to emphasize his role as dispassionate adviser, keeping his readers focused on China rather than on the person of the narrator-visitor.

Still, by the time he wrote *Southern China*, some of the harsher views of the earlier book had been tempered, and it was perhaps this aspect that led a critic in the *Saturday Review of Literature* to remark that "[o]ne of the delights of his books is its more or less unconscious revelation of what might be termed the education of Harry Franck, the change that came over him," meaning an "apparently ever-increasing admiration and affection for the common people of the country."[37] Yet even when he gives himself the freedom to write of what he genuinely enjoys seeing, or to find some admirable qualities in those whom he observes, he is as likely as not to catch himself up short, as if his imagination must be kept from running away, checked by reminders of the ever-present realities of dirt, noise, overcrowding, and complete lack of any Chinese common sense. Thus when he praises the safety of Beijing, where — unlike American cities — women can go about safely while wearing jewels at any hour of the day or night, he immediately ascribes the reason to Chinese cowardice, to their unwillingness to "screw up their courage to an act of violence," almost as if their lack of criminality derives from their less admirable characteristics.[38]

If Franck's China seems very much the China he expects to see, it is at any rate no longer the China he had first sighted as a young man, when his ship, coming into Hong Kong, was approached by junks "manned by evil-faced, unshaven Monguls [*sic*]".[39] It is a country where the political and military turmoil of the day, much as it might dominate

UNIVERSITY OF WINCHESTER
LIBRARY

the headlines, is a largely superficial phenomenon, of little concern to the vast majority of those who toil in the fields, often unaware even that the Qing dynasty was overthrown a decade earlier.[40] It is a land still locked in its own ways, despite the best efforts of Western and Western-trained do-gooders to bring it the gospel of progress. For it is a country that expects little from those professing to lead it into a bright future, whether they be reforming warlords like Feng Yuxiang and Yan Xishan, or the Nationalists of the south — "[t]he stoutest reformer would be likely to lose heart before the unrivaled passive resistance of the Chinese against even their own best welfare; it needs unbroken generations of radicals to get permanent results."[41] For generations the land has been prey to corrupt and self-serving governments, and in Franck's China, the most corrupt and self-serving of all is that to be found, not among the *dujuns* of the north or the Yangtze valley, but in Sun Yat-sen's Guangzhou, overrun with a military rabble, and imposing fees on every conceivable service, commodity, and property to support itself. "A popular catchword has it that 'any people deserves the government it gets' but surely the Chinese, industrious, patient, cheerful under the most provoking circumstances, in many ways lovable, for all their often unpleasant and sometimes exasperating traits, merit better than they have today."[42]

If it is true, as the old cliché has it, that travelers often find simply what they expect, then we need to ask a further question: what is it that they do not find, what are those aspects of the countries they visit that are obvious to us, with all our powers of historical hindsight, but are hidden to them? Seven months after the Francks sailed home to America from Hong Kong, the killing of a dozen demonstrators by a British-led police force on May 30, 1925, in Shanghai's Nanking Road, led to a nationwide outburst, with strikes, demonstrations, and fierce denunciations of imperialism. Back home at the time, Franck contributed a long piece on Shanghai to the *New York Times*, though once again he refused to make any predictions about the future, confining himself largely to a description of the city. A flyer from a speaker's bureau, however — undated but presumably from 1925 or 1926 — listed "The Struggle for Power in Asia" as one of the topics he was willing to address, suggesting that with China taking up more and more of the front pages, he was now ready to step into the role he had earlier abjured of diplomatic and political prophet.[43]

Did he, by then, regret that he had not spent more time on such phenomena as the Young China he had scorned? Certainly, as the pace of the Chinese revolution picked up, fed by a revivified Guomindang and a rapidly growing Communist Party, as well as by the Soviet agent Borodin's "missionaries of revolution" (as Martin Wilbur calls them), the Western press looked round to see what it had missed. Though there is no way of knowing what Franck covered on the lecture circuit, his books would have been little help in explaining the storm that burst over China between 1925 and 1928. Of course it would be both unfair and pointless to criticize Franck for not being what he made no claim to be — a prophet, a guide through the swamp of warlord politics — but his insistence that the vast majority of Chinese were living in an unchanging world, beyond the sounds of the military and political battles of the day, helped little in explaining the China of revolution.

Granted, it is the easy privilege of later generations to look back and pick out what their precursors missed. In any case, the question is not that of a particular observer's accuracy or inaccuracy, and indeed my understanding in 2007 about the way China's history was being shaped at the time of Franck's visit may well come to seem fantastic to the observer of 2076, little better than a map showing dragons or sea monsters. Yet authenticity is often placed in a conceptual frame constructed by the beholder, and the desire of Franck and others to go behind the facade of superficial Westernization into the "real China" runs the risk that they will impose blinders on themselves. Another danger lurks in the hoary Western vision of China as a land with a long past but no real history, no change and development, so that all that is necessary is observation of the here and now, and "history" becomes no more than a diversion from present reality.

The quest for authenticity may also reflect a fear of the passing of the kind of China against which travelers like Franck (despite his disclaimers) sought to define themselves, and from which they drew their particular authority. If authentic China disappears, to be replaced by hybridized Shanghai, looking like Memphis or Omaha, does the possibility of the traveler's authenticity also disappear? "Possibly the most significant thing on the [Yangtze] river journey is the model town of a Chinese owning big modern cotton-mills there," he writes, presumably meaning the enterprises of the industrialist Zhang Jian at Nantong, near Shanghai, "but the mere traveler does not come to China primarily to see how well it has copied Western methods and misfortunes."[44]

There can be various reasons, of course, why travelers do not report all they see (even in books as long as Franck's). Some aspects they may consider unimportant, or uninteresting to their audiences (as in the case of Nantong); or they may look right past them because they contradict accepted ideas. That (and perhaps a distrust of both missionary and Young China optimism) may explain why Franck never visited any of the universities, secular or Christian, of Beijing, Shanghai, or Guangzhou, or why he never seems to have sought out any of the authorities of Nationalist Guangzhou during his stay there. Yet to say, like Russell and others, that Shanghai is not real China in the twenties, makes no more sense than saying that today's Shanghai, with its thousand skyscrapers, its up-market stores, restaurants, theaters and museums, is not real China either. What such statements really mean is that the actuality of Shanghai does not reflect the China of our imagination, is not the China we want to see, the China we know, deep within us, to be real. That China, our real China, must not be allowed its Shanghais. Though traveling with no guidebook, Franck and others like him resemble those Victorians described by John Pemble, visiting the Mediterranean, Murray or Baedeker in hand, authenticating their experience by looking at approved monuments, and thus finding "a landscape that took its color from their own emotions; an oracle that took its wisdom from their own expectations."[45]

## IV

Why bother to read Franck, then? A hostile critic might say that he certainly made good on his promise not to write "literature," and certainly there is no point expecting accounts like those of Waugh, Greene, Byron, Fleming, or some of the other luminaries of the years between the wars. His was, as the critic Joseph Warren Beach said of his earlier books, a leading example of the "naive style," determined only "to give us information historical, topographical, statistical, economic, and social. . . ." Such writing appeals to the large class of uninstructed readers who demanded little more than taking away the writer's meaning "in a gross and approximate way," unconcerned with either precision or elegance. Nor is there any point in looking for more, Beach admits, for Franck is entirely innocent of such intentions (of Theodore Dreiser, on the other hand, another proponent of the naive style, more should be expected).[46]

Perhaps so, but at its best Franck's writing can be almost lyrical, reflecting a strong sense of place. In any case, its shortcomings are not reason enough for historians, at least, to dismiss him, for they cannot be too choosy about the literary or artistic merits of their sources, which they read primarily to illuminate the times they study, often discovering that the light they shed is more interesting and more valuable than the subjects those sources ostensibly address.

Harry Franck's writings — like any artifacts — can, if properly read, enlarge our knowledge of those years between the wars. They can tell us, if only by indirection perhaps, of a particular American view of China and by extension, of a particular American view of what later generations came to call the Third World. Not that his was necessarily a majority view, for his often pessimistic conclusions, particularly about Western and Western-inspired Chinese reformers, left little room for his own country's *mission civilisatrice*, either sacred or secular. This surely put him at odds with many of his countrymen, and in 1927, two years after *Southern China* appeared, the conversion of Chiang Kai-shek to Protestantism, and his marriage to Soong Mei-ling, the Methodist graduate of Wellesley College, gave heart to those Americans who wanted to make out a progressive, democratic, perhaps even Christian China, struggling to be born.

What does he tell us of the land itself? Though much of the country through which his journeys took him might already be familiar to readers of Isabella Bird, Elizabeth Kendall, and others, his trip to Taiwan took him to a place that really was off the beaten track (Taiwan, he suggested, gave some idea of what a China ruled by Japan would be like, as French Indochina suggested a China under European domination).[47] Tempted though we may be to dismiss his criticisms of the early Republic simply as manifestations of Western arrogance, we are brought up short not only by Franck's often equally acerbic judgments on his own country and countrymen, but also by the realization that his views of China's failings often reflect those of the spokesmen of the May Fourth generation — Chen Duxiu or Lu Xun, for example. Not that Harry Franck gives any indication of having heard of the May Fourth leaders, and he has little good to say about Young China. Still, if such aspects as the continued practice of footbinding, or the unthinking reverence for old ways — "Confucius and Sons," *Kongjia dian*, as Hu Shi dismissively called it — really were detrimental to Chinese society, how much difference should the provenance of the critic make to us? For all his occasional preachiness and his common-sense prescriptions, he certainly did not hold up America as an example for China to follow.

Finally, if good travel writing, as has been said, not only seeks to illuminate the foreign, but also invites readers to consider their own domestic situations, Franck, for all the admitted *longueurs* in his prose, can also reveal something about the anxieties of his own America. His emphasis on the timelessness of his real China (once one got away from the corrupting modernism of the treaty ports) reflects the domestic search for the real America, a territory more likely to be found in the hinterland of Iowa or Wisconsin than in Boston or Philadelphia. His advice that real China should be left in peace to get on with its own life, rather than be captured by would-be reformers, domestic or foreign, reflects an American impatience with clever new theories (socialism, or literary and artistic modernism, for example), as often as not of foreign provenance, that threatened to corrupt the soul of real America. I do not mean to suggest that Franck was prescribing remedies for America's shortcomings; but was he, consciously or otherwise, reading into the foreign lands through which he traveled his own concerns for the changes abroad in his native country? And did his audience sense it as well? Perhaps so, and perhaps that is what upset a critic like Joseph Beach, with his dismissal of Franck's "naive style" and his "uninstructed readers."

Be that as it may, it is Franck's reflection of the spirit of the age (or at least one of its spirits), that makes his writings valuable as a source for the historian. They are historical artifacts, and like all such artifacts — literary, artistic, cultural in the broadest sense — they are absolutely truthful. The difficult question for the historian is to decide what they are absolutely truthful about, and what questions they can properly be asked if they are to return truthful answers.

# 11

## Journeys to War:
### W. H. Auden, Christopher Isherwood and William Empson in China

*Hugh Haughton*

## I

"Where does the journey look which the watcher upon the quay . . . so bitterly envies?" These are the opening words of "The Voyage," the poem which launches *Journey to a War*, W. H. Auden and Christopher Isherwood's account of their 1938 journey to China during the Sino-Japanese war. The poem, a partial response to Baudelaire's "Le Voyage," raises some of the fundamental questions of travel literature, setting up an opposition between the "true" and "false" journey, asking whether travel is ultimately about a quest ✓ for "the Good Place," and invoking the "watcher on the quay" as a figure of the envious reader. The question "Where does the journey look?" displaces the more usual "Where is the journey going?". The sonnet "The Ship" re-frames it in political terms:

> It is our culture that with such calm progresses
> Over the barren plains of a sea; somewhere ahead
> The septic East, a war, new flowers and new dresses
>
> Somewhere a strange and shrewd To-morrow goes to bed
> Planning the test for men from Europe; no one guesses
> Who will be most ashamed, who richer, and who dead.[1]

The book is a record of two Englishmen heading to Asia for the first time, but also a study of "our culture" looking at a reality which bears closely upon itself (it is a "test" for them). The camp phrase "New flowers and new dresses" captures the exotic appeal of travel writing in "our culture," but "war" and the "septic East" challenge it. This is not the "exotic East" and the term "septic" makes the reader ponder the source of the wound. Auden has already said "the false journey" is "really an illness" (making the illness the traveler's), but later we read about literal infections in the wartime Chinese hospitals they visit and Isherwood's metaphorical account of bombers caught in searchlights over Hankou "as if a microscope had brought into focus the bacilli of a fatal disease" (71). The "fatal disease" here is the war China had been afflicted with since 1927 and would continue to be until after the defeat of Japan and Mao's victory in 1949. "Yes, we are going to suffer, now; the sky / Throbs like a feverish forehead," Auden writes later (272), and that "we" aligns the "men from Europe" and the Chinese in the same "feverish" "now," with Europe poised on the brink of the war that will start "Tomorrow."

Auden's question "Where does the journey look?" reflects on what Valentine Cunningham calls the "huge audience for travel books" in the 1930s.[2] Indeed Samuel Hynes identifies "the journey" as "the most insistent of 'thirties metaphors," arguing that "the travel books simply act out, in the real world, the basic trope of the generation" as "the perimeter of awareness and the community of disaster expanded — to Africa, to Mexico, to China, to the whole troubled world."[3] Auden and Isherwood's *Journey to a War* was also part of the vogue for politically inflected travel discussed in Bernard Schweizer's *Radicals on the Road: The Politics of English Travel Writing in the 1930s* (2001). Martha Gellhorn wrote that she had no idea, back in the 1930s, "you could be what I became, an unscathed tourist of wars" and *Journey*, like Orwell's *Homage to Catalonia* and Evelyn Waugh's *Waugh in Abyssinia*, is a version of that distinct sub-species of travel literature, a war book.[4] Indeed Samuel Hynes calls *Journey* "the war-book of the period just before the war became the Second World War."[5] The bond between war reporter, travel writer and journalist in Orwell, Greene and Waugh makes *Journey to a War* a sign of the times, and, like Evelyn Waugh's *Scoop*, an example of the new genre of literary "war tourism."

*Journey to a War* had a mixed press. Evelyn Waugh, the author of a contemporary novel about war correspondents entitled *Scoop* (1937), writing from the Right concluded that while Auden, the "official young rebel" laureate had become "a public bore," Isherwood "had no news sense" and "nowhere in China did he seem to find the particular kind of stimulus that his writing requires."[6] On the other side of the political fence, Randall Swinger in *The Daily Worker* thought the authors "too pre-occupied by their own psychological plight to be anything but helplessly lost in the struggle of modern China." Saying we learn nothing but "accurate superficialities about the course of the war," he concludes that "the authors are playing: playing at being war correspondents, at being Englishmen, at being poets."[7] This element of "play," however, is a form of critique, and Auden's "In Time of War" is equally remote from accepted ideas of poetic travelogue and indeed war poetry as Isherwood's prose. Though Auden says "history opposes its grief to our buoyant song," the buoyant poetry of the sonnets, framed by the "subtle and chaotic impressions" recorded in the prose and the flat photographs, offers a questioning and compellingly estranged account of their journey to a war.

Paul Fussell, in his pioneering study of travel writing *Abroad*, thought it and *Letters from Iceland* (1936) marked "the decadent stage" of the "between-the-wars travel book."[8] He found both narratives "disturbingly discontinuous, interrupted by jokiness . . . and self-consciousness about the *travel book* genre itself." Valentine Cunningham, in similar spirit, dismissed them as "opportunistic rag-bags."[9] More recently Douglas Kerr, Tim Youngs and Maureen Moynagh have offered positive accounts of *Journey to a War*, but the book rarely figures in discussions of war or travel literature or even in accounts of Auden and Isherwood.[10] This is in part because of its joint ownership ("the hind and the front legs" of a pantomime monster, according to Waugh), in part because of its experimental form, in part because it is so different from both writers' other work.[11] Tim Youngs notes that "while other art of the period is admired for its experimentation with shape, Auden's travel writing is strangely damned for it" and observes that *Journey to a War* raises "deep questions about war, travel and travel writing, and China in relation to the West."[12] The story the foreword tells about the book's inception casts an interesting light on this:

> Early in the summer of 1937 we were commissioned by Messrs. Faber and Faber of London and by Random House of New York to write a travel book about the East. The choice of itinerary was left to our discretion. The outbreak of the Sino-Japanese War in August decided us to go to China. We left England in January 1938, returning at the end of July. (13)

"A travel book about the East" is a kind of Orientalist blank cheque, offering the young writers *carte blanche* as to where they would locate "the East." It was the outbreak of the War, the sort of contingency that deters most tourists, which "decided" them to go to China. "The East" was replaced by "A War." Isherwood wrote later that "China had become one of the world's decisive battlegrounds. And unlike Spain, it was not already crowded with star literary reporters." Indeed he reported Auden saying, "We'll have a war of our very own."[13] The book offered not only a journalistic account of China during the crisis period after the Japanese invasion, but a premonitory mapping of the European war (Isherwood was working on the text in London during the Munich crisis).[14] Though China had been involved in civil war between the Nationalist Government and the Red Army since 1927, this mutated into a war of resistance in Summer 1937 when the Nationalist leader Chiang Kai-shek determined to wage all-out war against the invading Japanese.[15] Lloyd Eastman calculates that "some fifteen to twenty million Chinese died as a direct or indirect result" and calls "the war with Japan . . . the most momentous event in the Republican era in China," leading ultimately to the Communist victory of 1949.[16] At the heart of their travel book stands Auden's sonnet sequence "In Time of War," where he writes that "maps can really point to places / Where life is evil now: / Nanking; Dachau" (274), setting the horrific "rape" of Nanjing in Autumn 1937 in the scales with the concentration camp in Nazi Germany. *Journey to a War* is a travel book that reminds European readers that any quest for "the Good Place" needs to know about places "where life is evil now," not just about "new flowers and new dresses."

## II

*Journey* looks very different from Auden's previous collaborative travel book, *Letters from Iceland* typified by the hi-jinks of Auden's "Letter to Lord Byron," extracts from guide-books and diaries, collages of quotations, in-jokes, and letters in which Auden and MacNeice perform their roles as travelers to a coterie of friends. At the heart of *Journey to a War* is Isherwood's travel diary, but it is introduced by Auden's "The Voyage" and five sonnets, and followed by thirty-two pages of "Picture Commentary" and the climactic "In Time of War: A Sonnet Sequence," with its extraordinary combination of idiosyncratic culture theory and the numinous vision of Rilke's *Sonnets for Orpheus* (which it invokes). The poems hardly refer directly to the journey, or indeed to China, but their symbolic logic is informed by Isherwood's account. The book ends with an admittedly "preachy" verse "Commentary" written in the discursive mode later developed in *New Year Letter,* set as "Night falls on China" while the authors cast their "European shadows on Shanghai." Though oratorical, it moves between East and West, with a global reach denied to most war poetry of the time: "For this material contest that has made Hongkew / A terror and a silence, and Chapei a howling desert, / Is but the local variant of" what Auden calls "the general war / Between the dead and the unborn."[17]

The relationship between specific reporting and the general map is always being called into question through the dual authorship and multiple form of *Journey to a War*. Towards the end Auden speaks of "When all the apparatus of report / Confirms the triumph of our enemies" (XXIII, 281), and one of the challenges of the book is to set different kinds of reporting apparatus against each other: a travel diary, a series of captioned photographs and a sonnet sequence followed by verse commentary. In *Letters from Iceland* Auden set poems by MacNeice and himself "for comparative reading" and said of the work of poet, novelist, and film director "These are our versions — each man to his medium."[18] *Journey to a War* likewise offers the reader different media "for comparative reading."[19] Where Isherwood's prose is personal, circumstantial and documentary, recording the details of their three-month journey through Southern China as "amateur war correspondents" in often comic terms, Auden's gnomic verse casts the war into an abstract allegorical idiom with almost no specific geographical, historical or personal indicators. The protagonists are a non-specified "they," "he" and "we," and operate in a largely anonymous topographical world defined in terms of "the city," "fountains," "rivers" and "mountains" and a political one dominated by "the Empire," "the tyrant's citadel," "savants," a "general" and "great buildings" which "jostle in the sun for domination." The Chinese war of Isherwood's narrative only surfaces explicitly halfway through Auden's sequence, where it figures within a much larger historical allegory, compounded of Darwin, Freud, Marx and Augustine, forming part of what John Fuller calls a "seriously secular theodicy."[20] All travel writing tends towards the condition of allegory, Auden's self-consciously so. Indeed his sequence begins with a version of the Fall and man's expulsion from Eden, and ends with a vision of mankind living "in freedom by necessity, / A mountain people dwelling among mountains." The poet writes of "to-night in China" (XXIII), invokes "the Eighteen Provinces" that have "constructed the earth" (XIII), names "Nanking" as a place "where life is evil now" (XVI) and speaks of "Shanghai in flames" (XX), but the reader is always conscious of China as part of a larger ethical psycho-drama of "the Present's unopened / Sorrow" (XX).

# III

Isherwood's Travel Diary initially projects a self-parodic account of the writers as amateur war-correspondents, complete with visiting cards labeled "Au Dung and Y Hsiao Wu," presenting the two of them as "eager to miss none of the sensational sights which had been promised us" (27):

> Here we were . . . steaming away from the dinner-tables, the American movies, the statue of Queen Victoria on the guarded British island, steaming west into dangerous, unpredictable wartime China. Now *it* — whatever it was — was going to start. This wasn't a dream, or a boys' game of Indians. We were adult, if amateur, war-correspondents entering upon the scene of our duties. But, for the moment, I could experience only an irresponsible, schoolboyish feeling of excitement. We scanned the river-banks eagerly, half-expecting to see them bristle with enemy bayonets.
>       "Look! A Japanese gunboat!" (28–9)

The ironic tone breaks momentarily as he describes the Japanese being "self-quarantined" in "their steel island," "disowned by the calm healthy river and the pure sanity of the sky," and the narrative's constant shifting of tone and viewpoint keeps the reader on their toes. Faced by professional war correspondents later, they apologetically describe themselves as "mere trippers, who had come to China to write a book" (53), but if the book they write is not a "serious" war correspondent's memoir, its frivolity is a form of critique.[21]

From their first approach to Canton (Guangzhou), where they are confronted by the unfamiliar mix of European and Asian cultures, the prose registers a dizzying mobility. The scenery, for example, reminds them of the Severn Valley, with the country house like a "mortgaged English estate" and junks like "Elizabethan galleons" "apparently sailing backwards." They then note a "little green gunboat" as "uniquely Chinese," "less like a war-ship than some exotic water-beetle," but it is near a British steamer where "a man in white ducks" is practicing golf, leading them to imagine a "comic drawing of a conscientious Japanese observer looking down" from a bomber upon "the wilderness of natural flags." By the British consulate, they see football-playing U.S. and British servicemen as "hairy, meat-pink men with powerful buttocks," and speculate that they must seem like grotesque giants to "the slender, wasp-waisted Cantonese spectators, with their drooping, flowerlike stance and shy brilliant smiles" (31). Taking tea at the embassy during an air raid, Isherwood grapples with his acute sense of cultural contradiction as he stares at the "dish of scones" and "framed photograph of an Oxford college" while listening to the "whine of the power-bomber, the distant thump of explosions" (32). "Understand," he tells himself, "that those noises, these objects are part of a single, integrated scene. Wake up." At that moment, he says, "I really did wake up. At that moment, suddenly, I arrived in China" (32). By the next page, however, he is comparing their view over the Kwantung (Guangdong) plain with its "miniature mountains" and "hat-like peaks" to the "landscape of *Alice Through the Looking Glass*" (33). Auden had said "It is the strangeness that he tries to see," and nonsense is an embodiment of the strangeness produced in the observers by the clash of cultures. Though Isherwood speaks of an "integrated scene," his technique emphasizes disintegration, as in the dissonance between "the far-off explosions of the morning air-raid and the strains of our host's harmonium" (35).

The cultural and aesthetic dissonances Isherwood records in the early stages of the journey deepen as they move inland. After a long, boring train journey, when they pass "peasants on the stations" who "wore huge turbans, like figures in a Rembrandt biblical painting" and soldiers toiling past, "in their heavy equipment, patiently clutching paper umbrellas," they arrive at Wuchang in a blizzard. On the ferry to Hankou they are jammed up against "Coolies" "with the averted, snot-smeared, animal faces of the very humble, the dwellers in Society's smallest crevices, the Insulted and Injured," while "Auden's paper umbrella had broken in the storm" and was "wrapped round his head like a grotesque kind of hat." Soon after at Hankou, "the real capital of wartime China," the problem of History and authority is brought into brilliant focus:

> All kinds of people live in this town — Chiang Kai-chek, Agnes Smedley, Chou En-lai; generals, ambassadors, journalists, foreign naval officers, soldiers of fortune, airmen, missionaries, spies. Hidden here are all the clues which would enable an expert, if he could only find them, to predict the events of the next fifty years. History, grown weary of Shanghai, bored with Barcelona, has fixed her capricious interest upon Hankow. But where is she staying? Everybody boasts that he has met her, but nobody can exactly say. Shall we find her at the big hotel, drinking whisky with the journalists in the bar? Is she guest of the Generalissimo, or the Soviet Ambassador? Does she prefer the headquarters of the Eighth Route Army, or the German military advisers? Is she content with a rickshaw coolie's hut? (50–1)

With its wittily camp allegorizations it is hard not to detect Auden's hand in this, and Douglas Kerr reminds us that the distinction between prose and poetry is not necessarily that between the two authors.[22] Once again, it undermines the authority of the writer, reminding us not only of the variety of the dramatis personae and multiple viewpoints, but the mirage of "History" as unified authoritative narrative. Clearly, in this complex and crowded international scene, a historian might be able to see the clues to future history, but the writer knows he cannot. He can record clues, but not decipher them, sense the presence of History, but not identify her.

It is after their interview with the leaders — "the Generalissimo" Chiang Kai-shek and his wife "Madame," Mr Donald (the Generalissimo's influential adviser) and T. T.

Li, "the official mouth-piece of the Government" (54) — that the Journal describes an air raid over Hankou, and the view shifts from the political theatre of politicians, generals, missionaries and ambassadors to that of war. Warned earlier about the dangers of the trip ahead, Isherwood had said that "the air-raids would help to pass the time, and a night in the paddy-fields would provide excellent copy," reminding the reader of the strange parasitism of the war writer. This comes into vivid focus where they first witness an air raid, encountering at first hand the horrific form of warfare which would dominate the Second World War:

> A pause. Then, far off, the hollow, approaching roar of bombers, boring their way invisible through the dark. The dull, punching thud of bombs falling, near the air-field, out in the suburbs. The search-lights criss-crossed, plotting points, like dividers; and suddenly there they were, six of them, flying close together and high up. It was as if a microscope had brought dramatically into focus the bacilli of a fatal disease. They passed, bright, tiny, and deadly, infecting the night. The searchlights followed them right across the sky; guns smashed out; tracer-bullets bounced up towards them, falling hopelessly short, like slow-motion rockets . . . It was as tremendous as Beethoven, but *wrong* — a cosmic offence, an insult to the whole of Nature and the entire earth. I don't know if I was frightened. Something inside me was flapping about like a fish. (70–1)

High-precision war reporting ("the search-lights criss-crossed, plotting points, like dividers") combines here with the novelist's record of his own reactions ("something inside me was flapping about like a fish") and the metaphoric projection of war as "bacilli of a fatal disease." The sense of aesthetic pleasure ("it was as tremendous as Beethoven") jostles here with a sense of ethical and ecological shock ("an offence to the whole of Nature"). After a later raid on the Japanese emperor's birthday, Isherwood describes the civilian casualties with comparable precision:

> They were terribly mutilated and very dirty, for the force of the explosion had tattooed their flesh with gravel and sand. Beside one corpse was a brand-new, undamaged straw hat. All the bodies looked very small, very poor, and very dead, but, as we stood beside one old woman, whose brains were soaking obscenely through a little towel, I saw the blood-caked mouth open and shut, and the hand beneath the sack-covering clench and unclench. Such were the Emperor's birthday presents. (175)

This is war reporting of a high order, with the Sassoon-like reference to "the Emperor's birthday presents" registering the horrific discrepancy of worlds. Almost immediately, he reverts to accounts of parties with "the Navy and our friends from the Consulate," a row with Germans in which he finds himself uneasily defending "the British Empire," and their arrival at the bizarrely Europeanized "Journey's End," governed by the grotesque Mr Charleton, a sort of transplanted Mr Norris, with a "drilled troop of house-boys in khaki shorts" (178). Such unnerving cuts and clashes between scenes and styles are

integral to the narrative, as it moves between recording Isherwood's awareness of the
horrors of war and the absurdities of their privileged social world.

Isherwood's quick-footed, often comic account of their journey to the front and on
to Shanghai, ends with the poets safe in the privileged international compound, where
"the semi-skyscrapers of the Bund present, impressively, the façade of a great city"
dumped upon an "unhealthy mud bank" (237–8). Again, it is the clash of worlds he
records as he notes that "The International Settlement and the French Concession form
an island, an oasis in the midst of the stark, frightful wilderness which was once the
Chinese city." On one side of Suzhou Creek are "streets and houses, swarming with
life; on the other is a cratered and littered moon-landscape, intersected by empty, clean-
swept roads." Occasional Japanese sentries stand guard, while "every Chinese or foreign
property has been looted." "Like formidable, excluded watchdogs," he writes, "the real
masters of Shanghai inhabit the dark, deserted Japanese Concession, or roam the lunar
wilderness of Chapei, looking hungrily in upon the lighted populous international town"
(240–1).

There follows an unreal scene where they discuss their trip with some extremely
polite Japanese men, a scene of Isherwood farce which comes as near as he allows
himself to political propaganda. "You have been traveling in China?" they are asked,
"How interesting . . . I hope you had no inconvenience?" "Only from your aeroplanes,"
Isherwood replies. Their politeness still unruffled, the Japanese announce "we really love
the Chinese," and, "[T]hat is the nice thing about this war. We in Japan feel absolutely no
bitterness towards the Chinese people" (244). This triggers a rare moment of bitterness
from the travelers:

> It was hardly surprising, we retorted, with some heat, that the Japanese didn't
> feel bitter. Why should they? Had they ever had their towns burnt and their
> women raped? Had they ever been bombed? Our four gentlemen had no
> answer ready. They merely blinked. They didn't appear in the least offended,
> however. Then one of them said: "That is certainly a most interesting point
> of view." (245)

After some further account of the privileged life of the expatriate community in Shanghai
where "there are garden-parties and night-clubs," Isherwood reports a Japanese man
defending "the wholesale bombing of Canton on the ground that it is more humane
than a military occupation of the city." Faced with such contradictions, and recoiling
from his own complicity in the situation, "the well-meaning tourist, the liberal and
humanitarian intellectual can only wring his hands over all this and exclaim 'Oh dear,
things are so awful here — so complicated' " (253). This brings home to the reader
the compromised and ultimately impotent stance of the "men from Europe" come to
get "copy" from the war. If their journey to the elusive "front" seems anti-climactic
and inconclusive, that is surely the point. Isherwood said later that he had been "all
too conscious of being Little Me in China," with "his riding-boots and his beret and
his turtleneck sweater" being "symptoms of an amateur's stage-fright," but observed
that the reader could "pick up a surprisingly varied assortment of information from him

about the country and the period." [23] The diary is indeed packed with extraordinarily complex impressions of China in crisis that, while avoiding the idiom of the "serious" and "committed" 1930s political commentator, registers complex political realities on the pulses. William Empson, meeting the duo in Hong Kong, said that "Isherwood was the one who was worrying about politics" and the worry shines through the camp "Little Me in China" playfulness of the travel journal as it does in his masterpiece *Goodbye to Berlin* of the following year.[24]

## IV

Recounting one of their many train journeys, Isherwood reported that "Auden, with his monumental calm, had completely undressed." Auden's poetry reflects on their wartime trip with a "monumental calm" of its own. The title "In Time of War" suggests Haydn's great *Missa in Tempore Belli*, and the riddling sequence replays their journey to the front in a gnomically sublime key which is an unlikely blend of Dryden and Rilke. Its resistance to direct interpretation gives it some of its peculiar force. Like Yeats' sequence in *The Tower*, the sonnets form a meditation in time of war and gain their full historical weight when read in relation to what precedes them, the opening sequence about travel, Isherwood's mobile self-ironizing war journal and the visual record of Auden's set of photographs. The style of the poetry is both playful and marmoreal, a strange historical baroque that is the antithesis of the chatty "Letter to Lord Byron" but registers the problematic decorum of this Asian travel book. When taken out of its original context, in Auden's later collections where it is printed in thoroughly revised form as "Sonnets from China" or in the later edition of *Journey to a War* where the revised text is reprinted without the photographs, the sequence loses much of its power.[25] Like so much of Auden's best work of the 1930s, including the documentary poetry of "Night-Mail," the verse drama, and travel books, it is occasional and collaborative, mixing poetry with other media. When juxtaposed, as originally designed against Isherwood's prose and the "Photographic Commentary," the sequence generates an electric charge it does not have on its own.

There are over sixty photos, beginning with formal mug shots of "The Chiangs" and other leading Chinese, including Chou En-lai (Zhou Enlai) as representative "communist" and Du Yueh-seng (Du Yuesheng) as "capitalist," C. C. Yeh as "Intellectual" against two anonymous "Coolies." They move on through a series of portraits of Chinese soldiers and officials to foreign doctors and missionaries, Ambassadors and Advisers, then to pictures of the "war zone" with captions such as "In the Trenches," "Enemy planes overhead," and pictures of war victims, refugees and bombed cities under such captions as "The Innocent," "The Guilty" and "Houses," this last being a photo of Chapei (Zhabei) in ruins after the siege of Shanghai. Reading through the series of images, you graduate from quasi-official portraits of officials, including foreign press and photo journalists such as Peter Fleming as "Special Correspondent" and Robert Capa as "Press Photographer," to bleak images of wartime devastation filled with the anonymous victims of "In Hospital" and "Refugees in camp." The final images are of pictures of ordinary life amid the ruins captioned "La Condition Humaine," stills from a contemporary war film called *Fight to the Last* ("a mere mimicry of the West," in Isherwood's words) and over the caption "Unknown Soldier" a picture of a young Chinese boy in uniform staring thoughtfully away to the side of the frame.[26] Above their sometimes quasi-anthropological, sometimes ironic captions, the photos not only document the people caught up in the conflict as agents and patients, generals and soldiers, insiders and outsiders, but problematize the whole enterprise. The one image of either traveler is of a touristically debonair-looking Auden beside a Chinese soldier in the trenches. Like the images of Fleming and Capa (who we hear "found the Chinese face unsatisfactory for the camera, in comparison with the Spanish," 165) they document not only the war but the war reporters.

"In Time of War" follows that last photo of the "Unknown Soldier," relating Auden's sequence to two of the major legacies of the First World War, the war poem and the tomb of the unknown soldier. The juxtaposition of the different "apparatus of report" helps contextualize the metaphysical scenario played out in the first half of Auden's sequence, and then, when mid-way the poetry shifts from its general account of human history to the war in China, to test its almost algebraic generalizations about the human condition against Isherwood's prose and the photos.[27] The lynchpin sonnet XVI opens "Here war is simple like a monument: / A telephone is speaking to a man; / Flags on a map assert that troops were sent; / A boy brings milk in bowls" (274), but its effect is the opposite of simple. The poem draws on the many encounters with generals and leaders recorded in the narrative, in particular that when A. W. Kao, standing in for General Ku, explains the "strategic situation with a simple map":

> Everything was lucid and tidy and false — the flanks like neat little cubes, the pincer-movements working with mathematical precision, the reinforcements never failing to arrive punctual to the minute. But war, as Auden said later, is not like that. War is bombing an already disused arsenal, missing it, and killing a few old women. War is lying in a stable with a gangrenous leg . . . War is untidy, inefficient, obscure, and largely a matter of chance. (202)

The "here" of the poem is abstract like "A telephone is speaking to a man," but it is corroborated by Isherwood's account of the lecture in Tunki. The poem opens out, to speak of "living men in terror of their lives / Who thirst at nine who were to thirst at noon, / And can be lost and are, and miss their wives, / And, unlike an idea, can die too soon" (274). The gap between the "plan" and "a man," the rhyme between "wives" and "lives," the narrowing shape of the sonnet where "now" rhymes with "Dachau," map the war in quite different terms to Isherwood's, using the Shakespearean sonnet to epic effect. Its juxtaposition of "Nanking, Dachau" in the rhyme with "now," sets the Nazi concentration camp of Dachau against the notorious "Rape of Nanking" by the Japanese in December 1937, when, as *The Cambridge History of China* records, "during seven weeks of savagery, at least 42,000 Chinese were murdered in cold blood, many of them buried alive or set afire with kerosene" and "about 20,000 women were raped."[28] Behind the poetic shorthand of the "simple monument" and "map" are complex forms of documentation, including the photos of Chinese soldiers.

"Far from the heart of culture he was used / Abandoned by his general and his lice" (XVIII) is the closest Auden gets to writing a conventional war poem. It too can be set against Isherwood's prose and the photos of "The Innocent" and "The Guilty," where we see an equivalent of the poem's anonymous "he," dead under a "padded quilt" and "turned to dust in China." Of the dead soldier Auden says "He will not be introduced / when this campaign is tidied into books" but he gestures, through the poem, to what neither poem nor book can properly record, the individual. Saying "His name is lost for ever like his looks" counters the phony rhetoric of military epitaphs such as "Their names will live for ever," with "his looks" rooting "his name" in an actual person. Adding meaning "like a comma," as Auden says the soldier does, may seem a minimal function, but the comma that follows helps expand the sentence (and the Spenserean sonnet rhyme-scheme) to include an image of restored humanity on a loved earth on which "where are waters, / Mountains and houses, may be also men." If the poetry draws strength from the photos and the prose, it also works through the force of its own medium.

The same is true of Sonnet XIX which describes a party where "Across the lawns and cultured flowers drifted / The conversation of the highly trained." It offers, with its polite "exchange of views" what "seemed a picture of the private life" (277). This is a summary account of the official engagements and diplomatic entertainments often comically chronicled in the diary, but brought to a different pitch. The sonnet, with Auden's characteristic ability to establish unlikely bridges, sets that conversation against the "far-off" armies, waiting "for a verbal error / With all the instruments for causing pain," insisting that "on the issue of their charm depended / A land laid waste, with all its young men slain, / The women weeping, and the towns in terror." The relation of trivial-seeming "charm" and "error" to "A land laid waste" and "towns in terror" is shocking, playing out in a different key Isherwood's sense of the "beautifully contrived charade" of the Ambassador's "official garden party" in the International Settlement at Shanghai, not far from the "lunar wilderness of Chapei" (241). Auden's eerily anonymous, almost euphemistic re-descriptions (such as "all the instruments for causing pain" rather than "guns" or "bombs" or "arms"), and his non-specific "towns in terror" work on their own terms as shorthand for the conditions of modern war, but the reader can read them against Isherwood's specific reports.

Where Isherwood's narrative ends abruptly and inconclusively in a grimace of self-critique, Auden's sequence ends with an astonishing image of human lostness that recalls the original account of the secular fall with which it opens, while insisting on ethical freedom. This allegorical coda offers a final ironic reflection on the metaphor of the journey: "Wandering lost upon the mountains of our choice, / Again and again we sigh for an ancient South, / For the warm nude ages of instinctive poise, / For the taste of joy in the innocent mouth" (XXVII). Envying "streams and houses that are sure," the poet says "we are articled to error," abandoning the pernicious doctrine of human perfectibility and the General Will associated with Marxism. The poem concludes with an image that reflects our nostalgic dream of "The Good Place" while insisting on our intellectual freedom: we "[w]ere never nude and calm like a great door, / And never will be perfect like the fountains; / We live in freedom by necessity, / A mountain people dwelling among mountains" (XXVII). This is an incongruously luminous destination to the sequence. Auden's lines call up Isherwood's description of Auden's account of war as "a handful of lost and terrified men in the mountains, shooting at each other in the undergrowth." Now, however, it is translated into different terms that insist on the intellectual and moral "freedom" which ultimately locks us all into a shared predicament.

## V

It is ironic that *Journey to a War* offers pen-portraits of two of the most influential travel writers on China of the period, the American leftist Agnes Smedley and Peter Fleming, Special Correspondent of *The Times*. Peter Fleming had already written *One's Company* (1934), an account of a journey across the Trans-Siberian Railway and through Southern China, and *News from Tartary* (1936), a chronicle of his trip from Beijing to India during the Civil War. Fleming figures in the guise of the English traveler as hero in *Journey to a War,* where, faced with the amateur Auden and Isherwood, he is every inch the professional. Isherwood notes his dress was "almost absurdly correct," as if he had "stepped straight from a London tailor's window, advertising Gent's Tropical Exploration Kit" (207). They were initially "defensive" towards him, due to "professional jealousy" and "anti-Etonianism," while he suspected they were "hundred percent ideologists." As they scramble towards a mountain pass, Isherwood reports "the Fleming legend accompanying us like a distorted shadow" (214), and when they eventually part, quotes Auden saying "Well, we've been on a journey with Fleming in China, and now we are real travelers for ever and ever. We need never go further than Brighton again" (232). The camp blend of Oscar Wilde and J. M. Barrie captures the sense of impersonation they feel in the presence of the "real traveler" but also draws attention to the contrast between his kind of travel book and theirs.

The same could be said of Agnes Smedley, the other travel author they encounter, the author of *China's Red Army Marches* and *China Fights Back: An American Women with the Eighth Route Army*, an account of the Sino-Japanese War published by the Left Book Club in 1938. She writes as explicit propagandist, being "deeply irrevocably convinced that the principles embodied in the heart of the Eighth Route Army are the principles that will guide and save China" and inspire "the liberation of all subjected Asiatic nations" (116). With its devotion to the heroism of the Red Army, Smedley's prose offers a dramatic contrast to the non-aligned style of *Journey to a War.*

*Journey to a War* is highly self-conscious about its own tactics, as it steers its way between other kinds of travel text. These include the heroic propaganda reporting of Smedley, the adventure story of Fleming, and classic Orientalist narratives. On the one hand Isherwood tells A. W. Kao that "atrocity stories" would "make little impression in the West," distancing himself from the style of *China Fights Back*. On the other hand he describes himself and Auden reciting "passages from an imaginary travel-book called 'With Fleming to the Front' " (214), parodying the author of *News from Tartary*. In fact, as they take the steamer to Shanghai, Isherwood speaks of the "traveler's dream" of the Orient with terminal irony. "A cabin port-hole is a picture-frame," he says, "No sooner had we arrived on board than the brass-encircled view became romantic and false." He goes on:

> The brown river in the rain, the boatmen in their dark bat-wing capes, the tree-crowded pagodas on the foreshore, the mountains scarved in mist — these were no longer features of the beautiful, prosaic country we had just left behind us; they were the scenery of the traveler's dream; they were the mysterious, *l'Extrême Orient*. Memory in the years to come would prefer this simple theatrical picture to all the subtle and chaotic impressions of the past months. This, I thought — despite all we have seen, heard, experienced — is how I shall finally remember China. (234)

Faber had originally commissioned a "travel book about the East," and Isherwood's words mark the gap between the "dream" of the "mysterious" Orient and the journey recorded in the text. This is the "false journey" that their joint text tries to resist. The Travel Diary prefers to register "subtle and chaotic impressions" rather than the imaginary "China" of the Western "dream" or the rhetoric of "Chinese propaganda." Kerr argues that Isherwood's text "thematizes a kind of failure" and that China "precipitates a kind of crisis of representation for the genre, mode and authority of Isherwood's writing, a crisis that writing is too scrupulous not to admit, and from which it salvages its distinct tone of comedy."[29] One can argue, however, that, as in *Goodbye to Berlin*, this is inherent in Isherwood's whole stance towards their wartime travel book which ultimately locates neither "History" nor "China."

## VI

Auden was not the only English poet to report back from China at this time. William Empson spent two years in the country from August 1937 to August 1939, returning to England on the outbreak of the Second World War. Though he wrote nothing on the scale of *Journey to a War* he wrote two important poems, the balladic "China," a riddling account of the relation between China and Japan, and an epistolary-style longer poem "Autumn on Nan-Yueh" about his experience with the "exiled universities of Peking." Both of these were published in *The Gathering Storm* (1940), a couple of years after *Journey to a War*. Empson had bumped into his fellow English travelers in Hong Kong, and noted that while "Isherwood was the one who was worrying about politics," Auden had "the glamour of Oscar Wilde."[30]

It now seems extraordinary that two of the most talented English poets in the 1930s should have been in China during the Sino-Japanese war, and reported back on it in verse and prose. Auden's "In Time of War" is the most sustained war poem of the 1930s, while Empson's "Autumn on Nan-Yueh" is a witty political meditation on the intellectual life of refugees in time of war and on the aesthetics and politics of escape.

Empson had already visited China in 1933 and worked in Japan, so though he did not cash in on the vogue for travel writing, he had much greater knowledge of the country than his fellow writers. He traveled widely in China, making a ninety-day journey to Li Jiang on muleback, as well as working and living with the exiled Chinese universities for two years in Nanyue, Mengzi, and the walled city of Kunming. Empson's letters, essays, notes and broadcasts on China have not been collected, but include travel notes, a draft essay on life in Yunnan, a wartime propagandist article on "A Chinese University" (1940) and a BBC broadcast "China on the March" (1942). In a personal letter to his mother, Empson distanced himself with characteristic directness from both the Left-Wing commentators and devotees of the Orient, but showed a remarkable solidarity with Chinese intellectuals on the ground: "I cannot pretend all these passions about backing freedom against fascism, and all that, which make most of my friends think it dignified to be in China . . . I am proud to say that all these beastly little Lovers of the Far East have slunk off leaving only one man namely me." "Autumn on Nan-Yueh" affirms that "Politics are what verse should / Not fly from" but confesses a dislike for "The revolutionary romp" and steers as clear of leftwing posturing as Auden and Isherwood. Empson said "I hope the gaiety of the thing comes through; I felt I was in good company."[31]

"Autumn on Nan-Yueh," a long 234-line poem composed in exile on the "holy mountain," is all about flight. "If flight's as general as this," it begins, turning the crisis of the Chinese universities of Beijing fleeing the Japanese into a trigger for a high-flying meditation on "flight" in general. Empson began work on his post-war critical masterpiece, *The Structure of Complex Words,* during the months at Nanyue, and the poem is an essay on that complex word. The epigraph from Yeats' "Michael Robartes and the Dancer," speaks of "all in flight" and Empson's poem hinges on the two main senses of the word, the "aeronautical" one of "flying" and the contrasted one of "fleeing" or escape. Escaping capture, escaping bombing, preserving the Chinese universities in exile, gives "Escape" a good name: "So dreams it may be right to flee, / And as to fleeing, that we may."

Like Auden's "In Time of War," Empson's reflections on wartime China are strangely abstract, turning the "holy mountain" into a place to meditate on the role of the intellectual. "What / in God's name are you doing here?," he asks himself at one point, answering in the name of "A vague desire to be about / Where important things occur." That said, he dissociates himself from the "Pandarus school of trout / That hangs round battles just to purr," thinking of Pandarus in Shakespeare's *Troilus and Cressida* but presumably referring to the war journalists of the 1930s whose job it was to make copy out of conflict. The poem's China is primarily the shared intellectual predicament of those on the mountain, seen from the viewpoint of an expatriate English critic rather than a "traveler." We catch a few glimpses of the mountain "Sacred to Buddha, and a god / Itself," with its "topmost abbot" that has "passed Greats" and the disabled pilgrims "Brought there in baskets or in crates." We also catch a sense of the presence of the military threat — the place, we gather, is "fit for bombs" because it has "Ministers upon the spot / (Driven a long way from the War) / And training camps" — as well as of drunkenness and sociability ("The chaps use drinks for getting near"). As to Empson's own feelings about the place, it is only at the end, where he has to "fly again" as the universities leave for elsewhere, that we get a glimmer of his personal sense of regret at leaving, as the verse captures his elegiac sense of privilege at being part of this extraordinary Chinese refugee culture:

> We have had the autumn here. But oh
> That lovely balcony is lost
> Just as the mountains take the snow.
> The soldiers will come here and train.
> The streams will chatter as they flow.

That one exclamatory poetic "oh" speaks volumes. The "flow of personal chat" ends on a lyric view from the "lovely balcony" which approximates to the effect of Arthur Waley's or Pound's translations from the Chinese. The glimpse of lost mountains, balcony, and streams, is still caught up, however, in the human experience of others. We hear of the soldiers coming to Nanyue to train, but also that "The streams will chatter as they flow," referring to the mountain streams in winter but also the "streams" of chattering soldiers and refugees, part of the larger "flow" of speech and travel in wartime China, with which he is aligned.

"I said I wouldn't fly again / For quite a bit," he says towards the end, and "Autumn on Nan-Yueh" turned out to be one of Empson's last poetic flights. So if Empson began as a Cambridge poet, we could say that he ended, in some sense, as a Chinese one. The experience of teaching in Japan and China was to prove integral to the peculiar anthropological complexity of much of his later criticism, including *The Structure of Complex Words* begun at Nanyue, and his most developed critique of Christianity, *Milton's God*. "Autumn on Nan Yueh" offers a unique record of the poet's participation in an extraordinary moment of Chinese intellectual history, a companion piece to Victor Purcell's portrait of him in his contemporary travel book, *Chinese Evergreen* (1938), and the much later account of the exiled universities by Rosalie Chou — the writer Han Suyin — in the third volume of her autobiography, *Birdless Summer* (1968). It remains unique in the expatriate literature on China, in part because it is so unimpressed by its unique grounding in the imagined community of Chinese exiles.

# VII

The trip to China proved to be a watershed for Auden and Isherwood as well as Empson. Isherwood wrote up their separate diaries in Brussels and London, on returning from China, and Auden composed the bulk of "In Time of War" at the same time. Though *Journey to a War* tends to be viewed apart, it needs to be seen in terms of other work completed in this period. This was the moment when Isherwood recast *The Lost* as *Goodbye to Berlin*, and when Auden wrote some of his most compelling poems of the 1930s: these include "Musée des Beaux Arts," the sonnets "The Poet" and "The Novelist," and "Edward Lear" and "Rimbaud," his poems about nineteenth-century poet travelers.[32] "In Time of War" reminds us that Auden should be classified, alongside Brecht, as a great civilian war poet of the period while Isherwood's travel journal looks forward to the disaster-haunted documentary mode of *Goodbye to Berlin*, which was published in the immediate aftermath of completing the China book in 1939. Their collaborative Chinese text set both poet and novelist on new courses.

For Auden and Isherwood, as for Empson, the experience of wartime China helped precipitate a political crisis in relation to the Left. Isherwood wrote that "After China, it was only a matter of time before I should stop repeating slogans, borrowing opinions and start to think for myself." It was "the post-Munich hangover," he says, that triggered his "meditative fit" while the boat trip to the U.S.A. with Auden in 1939 "provided the opportunity." "A voyage, in this respect," he said, "resembles an illness . . . we can pause and take stock of our position."[33] On Isherwood's account, this transatlantic voyage involved one of the most momentous stock-takings in contemporary literature. "One morning on deck, it seems to me, I turned to Auden and said: 'You know, I just don't believe in any of it any more — the united front, the party line, the antifascist struggle. I suppose they're okay, but something's wrong with me. I simply can't swallow another mouthful.' And Auden answered: 'No, neither can I.' " Auden's agreement, he says, took him completely by surprise. "Now, in a few sentences, with exquisite relief, we confessed our mutual disgust at the parts we had been playing and resolved to abandon them, then and there. We had forgotten our real vocation. We would be artists again, with our own values, our own integrity, and not amateur socialist agitators, parlor reds."[34] After Spain, after China, after Munich — place-names that name the historical crises at this time — the two writers were heading not only for a new life in America, but new intellectual destinations. In a sense their direction now was a Journey from a War, but their Journey to a War in China lay behind it.

# 12

## Agnes Smedley:
### The Fellow-Traveler's Tales

*Douglas Kerr*

A fellow-traveler is someone who travels along with another. In the 1930s, as the equivalent of the Russian word *popútchik*, the English phrase "fellow-traveler" acquired a more specialized meaning, indicating one who sympathizes with the Communist movement without actually being a party member. It seems an apt sign under which to think about the writings of Agnes Smedley about wartime China in the 1930s and 1940s. Travel writing, perhaps fortunately, rarely has unmixed motives, and the motives of Smedley's Chinese travel writing express themselves in the genres of journalism, autobiography, historiography, war reporting, propaganda, ethnography, lyric and, as we shall see, in mythography. But always it is politically committed writing, its author passionately engaged with the ideological and military struggle out of which would be born, in her own lifetime, the People's Republic. This essay is concerned with the picture of China, the meaning of China, and the truth about China, produced in Agnes Smedley's writing about the country.

The question of the truth of Agnes Smedley's life and writing is a contentious one. She was a lifelong radical, and she associated with people whose activities were clandestine, sometimes illegal, and even viewed as treasonable, in America, Europe and China. She was suspected of espionage; in 1949 she was named in a U. S. Army report on a pro-Soviet wartime spy ring in Japan and China, and at the time of her death in London in 1950, she was scheduled to be subpoenaed by the House Un-American Activities Committee on her return to the United States.[1] Her most recent biographer establishes that this was not merely Cold War hysteria, and that she really had undertaken spying and covert action on behalf of the Chinese Communists, the Soviet Union, and (indirectly) the German imperial government.[2] But if these clandestine activities were necessarily undertaken in the dark, her sympathies were no secret, and are inscribed all over her writing about China. She may have been a spy in secret, but she was a partisan in the open, and all her Chinese writing was done in the service of the revolution, even though her understanding of the revolution's nature and needs shifted.

To further the cause, which she never doubted, it was a moral imperative, as well as a professional commission, to combat ignorance and lies about China by reporting the truth to people overseas who had no other means of knowing it, and if necessary to heighten, dramatize, or even create the truth. Sometimes the truth needed help. And if Agnes Smedley was a kind of Bunyanesque Valiant-for-Truth, writing was her weapon of war. And yet for her, as for the radical puritan Bunyan, writing was also suspect. It had a poor record, giving itself promiscuously to lies and vain display; at best, it stood between the experience and the people to whom it was to be conveyed. Already in her autobiographical novel *Daughter of Earth*, written before her arrival in China, there are signs of a distrust of the verbal medium itself. "I do not write mere words," her narrator says at one point. "I write of human flesh and blood."[3] Such a commitment to a demotic plain style for the immediate transmission of personal witness, and the corresponding rejection of vain display and mediated representation, can be located in a dissident and revolutionary English tradition, though in Agnes Smedley's writing it also comes with a specifically American and Emersonian inflection.

The disclaiming of rhetoric is a characteristic of radical writing. It lies behind the equally paradoxical claim of Wilfred Owen, in the draft Preface to his book of polemical war poems, "Above all, I am not concerned with poetry." Owen declared that "the true poets must be truthful"; the rest was literature.[4] Possessed by the urgency of what they had to say, both Owen and Smedley were impatient with the language that sometimes seemed inadequate to the task. This exasperation with the limitations of language might be converted into a formal resource (as sometimes in Owen, and in the modernism of T. S. Eliot's Sweeney and his complaint, "I gotta use words when I talk to you").[5] In Smedley it is a sign of her romanticism, and it leads her in one direction to try to push past language, to communicate reality directly — to "write of human flesh and blood" — and in the other direction towards allegory, an ideal writing in which there is no gap between words and the truth they embody. Like Owen before her, Smedley developed a highly crafted rhetoric while claiming to give a naïve unvarnished report of war.

## Agnes Smedley's travels

Agnes Smedley arrived in China, as a correspondent for the liberal *Frankfurter Zeitung*, late in 1928. She was a newcomer to China but not to revolutionary activism. She had been writing for more than a decade about the plight of the poor in India, as part of her long-term involvement with the Indian nationalist movement in exile, first in the United States and later in Europe, and she was convinced that China was poised to become the principal theatre of a global war between oppressed peoples and their exploiters.

Her own background had given her first-hand experience of the struggle. Born into poverty on a tenant farm in Missouri, she grew up in very difficult family circumstances in rough settler towns in Colorado, when the American southwest was opening up to the railroad and the mining companies, and, she was to remember, "Rockefeller's Colorado Fuel & Iron Company owned everything but the air."[6] She worked as a teenage schoolteacher in New Mexico, and carried a gun, according to the account she gives in *Daughter of Earth*, before scraping together a college education in Arizona and California. It was as a student that she developed her commitment to both socialism and feminism and started to write. She moved East to New York in 1916, immersing herself in the world of political activism, journalism and intrigue, first working for Margaret Sanger's birth control movement, and later involving herself increasingly with the cause of Indian independence from Britain. She was arrested and imprisoned in 1918 as a result of her association with Indian political exiles, and the movement for Indian independence would consume much of the next ten years of her life, in the United States and then in Europe. Her espousal of this cause, which in many ways anticipates her later identification with the Chinese Revolution, grew out of her American loyalties, as she was quite shrewd enough to recognize.

> Together with my [Indian] comrades, I was speaking and writing, and I felt that I was molding the native earth of America. In working with them I realized how American I was, how native of my soil, and how I could instinctively appeal to principles, traditions and ideas of the American people, when they could make but an intellectual appeal. *Bahin* [sister], some of them called me, and it warmed my heart and aroused strength and determination within me. For in it was not only love, but comradeship. I loved them with the love I had been unable to give to my brothers, to my father, to my class (*DE*, 358–59).

She contracted a "revolutionary marriage" with Virendranath Chattopadhyaya — "to me he was not just an individual," she said, "but a political principle" (*BHC*, 23) — living with him in Berlin and continuing her studies, her activism and her writing. In Berlin she suffered a breakdown in health, and underwent a period of psychoanalysis which "continued torturously for two years" (*BHC*, 19). The autobiographical novel *Daughter of Earth* emerged from the crisis and introspection of this period, and the journey to China was partly — as every journey is, according to W. H. Auden's poem "The Voyage"[7] — an attempt to leave a former life behind, a bid for renewal.

She crossed the Soviet-Manchurian border into China at the end of December 1928; first impressions were not encouraging. "Our luggage stamped, we turned to face — the Middle Ages" (*BHC*, 27). It was an analogy common enough to be cliché, made interesting in Smedley's case because America had not had a Middle Ages; and yet before long she was just as likely to be reminded by China of the exigent and dangerous American West of her own upbringing. After Manchuria, she began to make her way south, visiting Beijing and Nanjing, and settling in May 1929 in Shanghai, then China's most populous city and the largest of the treaty ports. She was to spend longer in the raffish and cosmopolitan city than anywhere else in the country, though she wrote of it disparagingly, for she did not think much of any Chinese city, with the later exception of embattled Hankou. One reason for this predilection was that the Communists had been largely driven out of the Chinese cities and were now a rural movement. Smedley's vision of Chinese modernity was not one of urban sophistication, but of a redemptive puritan plainness to be discovered in the army, the peasants, and the revolution.[8] In Shanghai she associated first mostly with other foreigners, with German, Indian and American exiles, and with Chinese intellectuals, often overseas-educated. In December 1929 she first met the writer Lu Xun, and became involved with the new League of Left-Wing Writers. She was also busy helping Soong Ching-ling (Madame Sun Yat-sen) with correspondence and speech writing, especially for the League against Imperialism, and establishing herself as one of the best-informed Western press correspondents in the city.

In 1932 she was putting together the essays, stories and impressions that would be published as *Chinese Destinies* (1933), and beginning her work on the Jiangxi Soviet (the area under Communist control, which she had not visited), which became *China's Red Army Marches* (1934). Her friends now numbered the writers Harold Isaacs, Edgar Snow, and J. K. Fairbank, and her enemies included the British intelligence services, who knew of her history of anti-imperial activism and kept her under surveillance, and the Kuomintang thugs who made Shanghai such a perilous place for left-wing civilians. In 1936, feeling suffocated in Shanghai, Smedley moved to Xian and had the journalistic good fortune to be on the spot in December when the "Young Marshal," Zhang Xueliang, kidnapped Chiang Kai-shek and forced him to cease hostilities against the Communist forces and form a united front against further Japanese encroachments in China. Smedley's print and radio reporting of this momentous development made her famous. A more important consequence for her came in the form, at long last, of an official invitation to her to visit the new Communist headquarters at Yanan.[9]

The journey from Xian took her three weeks, and on arrival in the Communist stronghold she lost no time gathering information about the revolution and its personnel, and getting it out to publications in China and abroad. In a roomy cave carved into the mountain walls enclosing the Yanan citadel, she wrote up her lengthy interviews with Mao Zedong, Peng Dehuai, Zhu De, Zhou Enlai and other Communist leaders, and began the biography of the Red Army's peasant commander-in-chief, Zhu De, which would be published after her death as *The Great Road* (1956). In 1937 she applied to join the Chinese Communist Party, but was told she would be more useful as an outsider. In the months she spent in Yanan, what might be called her leisure activities included rat extermination, gardening, distributing anti-Fascist pamphlets from Spain, and teaching the Communist leadership dancing, an initiative not wholly popular with the revolutionary wives. The intrigues and quarrels which punctuated and eventually curtailed her stay are not included in her published accounts, and she left to return to Xian, after injuring her spine in a fall from a horse, in September 1937, a painful journey narrated at the beginning of *China Fights Back* (1938).

She was next invited by Zhu De to join the Eighth Route Army under his command in the field, and she stayed with them for three months, in an interval of peace between the Communists' pact with Chiang and the Marco Polo Bridge incident which led to the declaration of war against Japan. She was then sent to Hankou (part of the conurbation of Wuhan, on the Yangtze), which had become China's new capital after the fall of Nanjing. Increasingly under air attack, Hankou was becoming the focal point of the war and was shortly to strike the visiting Christopher Isherwood as containing "all the clues which would enable an expert, if he could only find them, to predict the events of the next fifty years."[10] Arriving in January 1938, Smedley put her considerable energies to work helping to organize the supply of Chinese Red Cross services to the Red Army. She had now become a correspondent for the *Manchester Guardian*, and her work was also appearing in *China Today*, the *Nation*, the *Modern Review* and elsewhere. She stayed for ten months in Hankou, slipping out a few days before the city fell to the Japanese in October. "The last days of Hangkou still remain in my mind as rare, unusual days from the psychological and human viewpoint," she was to recall; the atmosphere reminded her of Shaw's doomed *Heartbreak House*.[11] Now she travelled to join the newly formed Communist-led guerilla units of the New Fourth Army operating along the southern shores of the lower Yangtze, as a war correspondent and medical worker.

She remained with the Fourth Army in central China from November 1938 to April 1940, much of the time on the move and in grueling conditions, in "the longest sustained tour of a Chinese war zone by any foreign correspondent, man or woman."[12] These travels, if this is an adequate word, are chronicled in *Battle Hymn of China*, her best book, though it omits most of the complexities of her own political and personal life. Unlike her earlier books about China, this one begins with a sketch of her early life, as if to insist on a continuity between her American and European experience and her Chinese wanderings, while its title declares an affinity between this Chinese campaign and a definitive American struggle.[13] Meanwhile its dedication leaves no doubt about its own loyalties — "To the Soldiers of China: Poor, Glorious Pioneers in the World Struggle against Fascism." Besides her reputation overseas as an authoritative reporter of the situation in China, Smedley had also acquired some celebrity among the Chinese soldiers she wrote about, and her arrival in a unit was often greeted by a request to lecture to the troops on all sorts of matters including Chinese-American relations, the present military situation in China, and "suggestions for improvement" (*BHC*, 319).[14]

After a further breakdown in health, she reluctantly agreed to leave for Chongqing, the latest seat of the Republican government, and in August 1940 she reached Hong Kong, where she underwent surgery (on the gall-bladder) at Queen Mary Hospital. Colonial Hong Kong — where she was forbidden by the police from speaking, writing, or taking part in public life (*BHC*, 354) — joined the list of Chinese cities which felt corrupt and inauthentic to her after the rigorous simplicities and sacrifices of life at the front. In 1941 she returned to the United States, with the aim of recovering her health and helping to sway American public opinion behind the Chinese struggle. This was by no means the end of her adventures, but she was never to return to China. She died in England in the year after the declaration of the People's Republic. Her ashes were placed in the Cemetery for Revolutionaries in Babaoshan in Beijing.

## Propaganda and Truth

Agnes Smedley's writing about China at war, and especially her account of her months with the Eighth Route Army and later the New Fourth Army, has no equivalent in English literature. To approach it as a kind of travel writing is indeed willfully to miss much of the point, yet it raises in particularly interesting ways the perennial questions about representation, modality, and alterity raised by travel narratives of a less urgent motive. And the question of motive in her writing is certainly crucial, as she reports readily admitting when accused by her fellow American, the military observer Captain Evans Carlson, of not being impartial.

> Of course I am not impartial and make no such pretence. Yet I do not lie, do not distort, do not misrepresent. I merely tell what I see with my own eyes and experience day by day. This is the truth. Why am I in this army and not in another? With all my heart, with all that gives me consciousness, I am convinced of the high purpose, the integrity of this army. I know of the great heroism of the Chinese troops that fought from Shanghai to Nanking. But it is with the Eighth Route Army that I want to live and work. (*CFB*, 255)

What begins as a justification for her writing ends as a statement of political loyalty and something like vocation. Smedley's writing out of political commitment was perhaps more the norm than the exception among authors of her generation. What is remarkable here — it could be considered exalted, naïve, or disingenuous — is the denial of any conflict, the closing of any gap, between her political loyalties and a truthful report. A few years later George Orwell, looking back on the Spanish Civil War and contemplating the grotesquely biased reporting of that conflict, had started to believe that an objectively true history of even the facts of that war — or anything else — might henceforth be impossible (a fear to be projected into *Nineteen Eighty-Four*).[15] Smedley will admit no contradiction in her own writing, between her heroization of the Chinese revolution and especially its soldiers (and the demonization of their enemies), and the credit she claims as a faithful and authoritative reporter of actuality.[16] And this denial accounts for the characteristic co-presence in her work of a reiterated revolutionary and puritan commitment to the naked truth, and the deployment of what we can recognize as highly literary and traditional tropes, usually associated with the rhetoric of the heroic, in epic, ballad, and romance. Epic is truth, truth epic.

She was a writer among soldiers, constantly and uncomfortably aware of her own anomaly. She is an extra in the scene of revolution — another meaning for the phrase "fellow-traveler." Often she feels useless, or worse, an impediment. The feeling is acute in the wonderful opening section of *China Fights Back*, describing her frightful return journey from Yanan to Xian through the mountains. Cold, wet, hungry, weary, and in constant pain from her spinal injury, she registers the beauty of her surroundings guiltily. "I lay on the stretcher and looked at the endless mountain ranges in all directions, at the occasional flames of leaves turning red. The mountain range over which we passed was covered with low bushes and small trees, with a profusion of every kind of flower

— bluebells, white daisies, all kinds of yellow and purple wildflowers" (*CFB*, 25). Here was an occasion for what writers, and especially travel writers, are expected to do; but she veers away from the temptation to aestheticize the landscape, for she is only too aware of the hungry and exhausted men, the bearers and the bodyguards, without whose work she would literally not be able to move through it. "I am, and travel like, an aristocrat, in comparison with the simple men of the Eighth Route Army" (*CFB*, 31).[17] Aesthetics were beside the point, if not actually associated with reprehensible luxury, inequality and decadence. After finally reaching Xian, she records her disgust at hearing music from Beijing on the radio. "Or we can get the sickening Shanghai night-club music — about a man handing a woman an orchid. An orchid in the midst of death and destruction in Shanghai! The gentleman hands her an orchid! Not a bomb, but an orchid!" (*CFB*, 40). A time of bombs was no time for orchids.

She had no patience for beautiful writing; she was also wary of celebrity authors making copy out of their travels, like Auden and Isherwood, and later Hemingway.[18] Yet her own claim to be a simple reporter of facts — "I merely tell what I see with my own eyes and experience day by day" — does not stand up to the evidence of party-line orthodoxy in her work. In her early writing the Kuomintang is described as not much better than a criminal gang, but her hostility to Chiang Kai-shek and his party is suppressed during the years of their alliance with the Communists, only to be resumed after the break-up of the united front. Of greater interest is the way the realism, even naturalism, of her descriptions of Chinese life surrenders from time to time under political pressure to what looks like a quite different mode of writing.

Her first book of impressions of China, *Chinese Destinies*, could be described as a human geography, and is a kind of cinematographic montage of the country, consisting of vignettes of character and the narrative of the lives of usually ordinary Chinese people, caught up in the tumult of national events. Much that is both informative and moving in this volume derives from her scrupulous observation of the conditions of life among very poor peasants and soldiers. And yet her sense of a national teleology, signaled in the title, sometimes leads her to invest these lives with a historical portentousness that makes them exemplary, and even allegorical; the characters start to behave and speak operatically. Here is an example from the chapter "The Revolt of the Hunan Miners," which climaxes in the execution of two hundred enemies of the revolution. ("Few indeed! For the miners killed only the consciously guilty.")[19] Yu-kung, a young soldier ordered to give the signal on his bugle for the execution to begin, now recognizes among the dead his own father, a "yellow labour union leader." He speaks to a senior revolutionary.

"It was my father — he was also killed out there. I blew the bugle."
Sung paused and gazed down at the pale, boyish face turned up to him. The big hand of the older man rested on the black head of the youth tenderly, and in the eyes of the lad came an answering gleam of love and confidence.
Sung spoke: "You are not alone. We must all learn that we may have to sacrifice father, mother, sister, brother, in the revolution. But you are a Communist Youth — your life belongs to the Party. You have no family, no father and mother beyond the Party. Is that not right?"

> "Yes," Yu-kung's voice responded.
> "Now keep close to me," Sung told him. And Yu-kung stood by him through all the times that followed when the mass meeting was held and preparations made for the marching (*CD*, 122).

It is possible this is based on an actual anecdote reported to Smedley in Shanghai by one of her Communist informants, but the narrative itself is certainly fictive and the dialogue as manufactured as any battlefield exchange in Livy, whose methods it quite closely resembles. The passage is the more repellent when put alongside more directly observed sketches in the same book of the experience of peasants, students and intellectuals and women of all sorts. The point is that the propaganda motive here guides the pen and dehumanizes both the characters and the narrative which speaks for them. This scene of suffering becomes merely translucent, so that the political light can shine right through it. The gap of representation is closed, leaving no space for critical assent or dissent.[20] Smedley's Communist discourse comes close to Fascism at such moments — as it does elsewhere, in her rhetoric of blood and earth.

*China's Red Army Marches* (1936), Smedley's account of the Communist campaigns of 1928 to 1931 of which, again, she had no first-hand experience, contains quite a lot more of this sort of thing. In a method elaborated in *Chinese Destinies*, information is typically mediated through the experiences and memories of individual but representative fighters and peasants, miners and commissars. One chapter is entitled "Ballad of the Seven Bridges," and is indeed a narrative prose version of a ballad, a favorite form of revolutionary expression, which gives an extra license for a frankly epic incident.

> Then there was the peasant woman working with the Red Army Medical Corps who saw her own son wounded and dying within range of enemy bullets. Through his blue lips she heard him call her: "Mother! Mother!"
> Forgetful of the battle and of enemy bullets, the woman walked right into the open, bent down and half pulled, half lifted her son to safety. But when she looked into his face she saw that he was not her son at all, but Lin Piao, one of the bravest of the Red Army commanders.
> Something had happened to this peasant woman in those fierce moments, and the love she bore her own son swept beyond him and embraced Lin Piao and all the sons who fought in the Red Army. The men of the Red Army all began to resemble her son and to bear an echo of his voice in their speech. It was then that this peasant woman became one of the Red Army, and the fate of its men became her fate.[21]

There is nothing intrinsically wrong with magical representation, or indeed with propaganda, but what rings false about this kind of writing is its inappropriateness to a mode of representation that makes the truth-claims of documentary realism. But perhaps this points to a feature of social realist representation itself. Realism, like Marxism, grows out of science, and deals with the inference of general laws from the empirical observation of reality; both discourses are drawn to the objective *and* the prophetic, the documentary *and* the visionary. Naturalism in fiction is not a stranger to clumsy propaganda, banal prophecy, clunking symbolism. Such moments might be seen as symptomatic of a crisis within the history of realism itself, in its efforts to show how individual lives are connected to the large patterns of teleology. Smedley's reportorial instinct for unvarnished naturalism and her allegorical transfigurations are after all not in contradiction, but two sides of the same coin: her China is both earthly and visionary, documentary and myth.[22]

We might expect that this allegorizing tendency occurs when Smedley is reporting events she had not experienced first-hand, and there is no observer in the scene. But this is not the case, as we can see by tracing a motif — indeed a genealogy, or at least a family resemblance — in *Battle Hymn of China*. In Shanghai Smedley had known and worked with Lu Xun, and greatly admired him. While in Xian in 1936, she hears that he has died. "The news of my own father's death had reached me shortly before, and I had felt regret and sorrow; the death of Lu Hsün came to me not only as a personal sorrow, but as a national tragedy" (*BHC*, 99). Smedley was not alone in seeing Lu Xun as in some sense both a father and a symbol of the nation, but he has a curious post-mortem manifestation soon after, when she arrives at the headquarters of the First Red Army Corps at Tungli.

> This was the first time that I had seen the Red Army *en masse*, and I looked around curiously. I was profoundly impressed by their faces. Instead of the depressed, empty expression characteristic of so many soldiers, their faces had something of the vital awareness that had been so pronounced in the great Lu Hsün. (*BHC*, 109–10)

The role of father and national symbol seems to have been inherited by the Red Army itself. The process of transference is complete in the remarkable scene when for the first time she meets Zhu De, the commander-in-chief. "Indeed, he looked like the father of the Red Army. . . . I flung my arms around his neck and kissed him on both cheeks" (*BHC*, 118).

And it is not only the great writer and the great general who are epic figures; so too are the anonymous soldiers like those she will later watch hurrying silently along a mountain path at night, in the transfiguring light of destiny. As each soldier steps out of the shadows and passes swiftly before her, it is as if she is witnessing the course of history itself.

> The scene seemed unreal, yet as real as the stone cliffs. The iron Chinese people, destined to decide the fate of all Asia and, in countless ways the destiny of mankind, stepped up out of the darkness, passed, and then with swift and silent march, plunged into the darkness again. One big man passed by and I must have exclaimed at something. For he turned his face back toward me, laughing until he was lost in the darkness. (*CFB*, 141)

Homer's heroes consort with and are often related to the Olympian pantheon, ever-present in their affairs. Smedley's characters are on equally close terms with transcendental presences — history, revolution, the land — and sometimes elicit an equally high style. Their experiences, hardships and triumphs, meticulously reported, cast not merely a national shadow but a universal one. "To me the problems, strength and weaknesses of China seemed to be those of the whole world" (*BHC*, 349). China for Smedley was a revelation, a country in which the truth was manifest.

## Naturalization and Myth

There is one governing and organizing trope in Smedley's writing that brings together the local and the universal, the documentary and the mythic, while at the same time enabling the repressed aesthetic of China to pour back into her record. We can approach it by taking seriously the title she chose for her autobiographical novel, *Daughter of Earth*. It is to be found in a passage like the following, her description of awakening with the dawn on her first morning at Zhu De's headquarters in the mountains, to hear the distant strains of music, "something so sweet, so entrancing, that I lifted myself from my bed and strained my ears to hear." She goes outside.

> And there I found the orchestra. It was the music of dawn, of the coming of the day. A bird's trill sounded here, sounded there. . . . The faint echo of a dog's bark came, and the low, soft lowing of a cow came like the notes of a distant musical instrument. All the life of the earth was awakening. The forest and the life within the forest stirred. I stood in wonderment and listened to this music, so sweet, so unutterably sweet. Then, through this faint, discernible and yet almost indiscernible music came a new sound. The first bugle call of the day. It came, gentle, coaxing, and it seemed to be shaking the shoulders of the fighters gently, gently, saying, "Come now, get up, do get up, please get up! Comrade, do not be lazy, look, the day is here!" (*CFB*, 87–8)

Students of literature or music will recognize this as an example of *aubade*, an idealizing and highly conventional evocation of the sights and sounds of dawn, with a long romantic tradition behind it. But the passage, conventional as it is, also denies its artificiality (to do so is of course a convention of *aubade*). It is telling that what at first seemed like an orchestra turned out to be neither artistic nor composed, but nothing more or less than the sounds of the awakening earth itself. And Smedley can allow herself this literary flourish because the dawn of the day is also a call to the resumption of the life of the revolution. The bugle call redeems her nature-writing from frivolity and mere embellishment, while in the other direction its seamless integration into the scene of nature confers on the revolution the status and inevitability of a natural process. The Eighth Route Army is thoroughly naturalized. In the dawn and in the revolution, the East is Red.

Through its soldiers — most of them, she emphasizes, peasants — the Red Army is not just fighting for the land. It *is* the land. The trope of naturalization, so consistently employed, creates a myth (in Roland Barthes' sense) of the Communist revolution in which it is represented as a natural force, an expression of the earth itself.[23] This helps to explain why for Smedley the real China is to be found in the mountains and not the cities. Her own rural background, as a "daughter of earth," is her password into this company and her credentials as its historian, and earthy qualities or appearance mark the heroes apart from the rest. In the army itself "was a simple grandeur as fundamental and as undemonstrative as the earth," she reports. "They belonged to China, they *were* China" (*BHC*, 131). There is a closed circle of identity between the Party, the army, the folk and the earth. On the march, the sound of a soldier's flute reminds her that in the Chinese masses a stream of folk culture continues to run, "unspoiled by the imitation of Western 'civilization' as in Shanghai where many middle-class Chinese have no knowledge of nor respect for the native culture of the people" (*CFB*, 184). Zhu De, the peasant commander, is impeccably earthy, even chthonic, but the test can be applied to anyone: she takes to one general "because he looked like the knot of a tree" (*CFB*, 267); Captain Evans Carlson is treated at first with suspicion, but "when you went walking with him you found that he was as firm as the farmers of his native New England" (*BHC*, 142).

The army and the area it occupies is China, in Smedley's view, because it embodies both the past and the future of the country. The past contained in folk memory is expressed in its manners, its language, ballads and music. The future is inscribed in the earth itself as the soldiers pass, "for the Eighth Route Army literally covers the country with its slogans, written by hand — slogans that spring from the hearts and minds of the men in its ranks" (*CFB*, 206). So thorough-going is this trope of naturalization, that separation from the army can only be experienced as a kind of death. *China Fights Back* describes how Zhu De and the other commanders ask Smedley to leave the Eighth Route Army and go to Hankou. Her reply — "in words they did not understand" — is couched in the highly poetic language which her upbringing had taught her as the primary idiom of passion and truth. "Entreat me not to leave thee, or to return from following after thee; for whither thou goest I will go; and where thou lodgest I will lodge; thy people shall be my people and thy God my God" (*CFB*, 268). The Biblical words — from the Book of Ruth, Chapter 1, Verse 16 — are the plea of a sojourner begging to be no longer in transit, but accepted into the native community. It is a poignant moment. Her request is denied; she must resume her travels. "It seemed I was bidding farewell to the very earth" (*CFB*, 272). The next dawn, she sets out miserably. A few days later she is watching hungry refugees fighting to board the train to Hankou. In the carriage she encounters other passengers allegorical of republican China's woes — a rich landlord with his family and mountains of possessions, a cruel mother who strikes her child, a Chinese Christian woman preaching hellfire. She has returned to the other China, the fallen world.

I finish with one last anecdote, to illustrate the account I have given of Smedley's representations of China, but also to suggest that her material is not always obedient to the political will that structures it. *China Fights Back* is written in the form of journal entries, usually annotated with a place-name and a date. For most of November 1937 she had been on the march every day with the headquarters of the Eighth Route Army; her journal entry of November 21 is headlined "*A village of unknown name*," and begins like this.

> This is the first time I have slept through most of the night for many weeks. Once in the night I thought the day had come, and rose to see. The moon was nearly full and was shining on the earth covered with its white blanket of snow. It was a scene of indescribable loveliness. The marks of poverty in this poor village were obliterated and the buildings were patches of shining white roofs and of dark, sombre shadows that hid I do not know how many destinies. I returned to the cold *k'ang* to dream of the ruins of Pompeii. For hours it seemed to me I visited the streets and buildings of this ancient city. In the ruins I found pieces of old ivory of many shapes and sizes, and I found bronzeware of great beauty. I was gazing down into a dark pit filled with relics when, aroused by the bugle call, I awoke to a new day. (*CFB*, 184–5)

A veteran of psychoanalysis, Smedley set herself to interpret her dream, and concluded that she had been wandering through the "highways and byways" of her own existence as she slept. "It is hardly encouraging to know that your subconscious mind regards you as an old ruined city filled with ancient relics, and with but few things worth salvaging" (*CFB*, 185). Perhaps this is what the dream meant, and it is an interpretation consistent with Smedley's view that the future of the world was taking shape in China and her own culture with its European roots had had its day. But there may be other ways of reading the dream when we take it in its narrative context.

There are two dreamworks in the account, the first being the transfiguration of the village by moonlight, so vivid — like a dream — that it seems to be really day. The moonlight turns the prosaic village into a picture, aestheticizing it into indescribable loveliness, erasing the signs of its poverty and investing it with a romantic interiority and mystique.[24] Is the dream perhaps an admonition, warning the dreamer that there are more important, powerful and lasting things than aesthetic objects, which could not save the people of Pompeii and in any case distract us from the truth, as the moonlight tells a lie about the village? Maybe in the dream Smedley's puritan conscience was reminding her that to dwell on the beauties of China was to falsify the country, ignoring its suffering and struggle.

But it is also possible to read the moonlit scene as a prophetic vision, in which the secret ministry of the moon performs a transfiguration that the revolution too promised, a transformation of China into a place where nature and human habitation in harmony create beauty and peace and redeeming purity, and poverty and war have disappeared, and history has been accomplished and transcended. This utopian vision, the imagined end (in both senses) of China's revolution, could be taken as yet another instance of Smedley's desire for closure. But in this case the closure is soon opened up, by the unappeased unconscious, with a dream that supplies its troubling contradiction. Here a dark chasm, a traditional site of prophecy in romantic writing, discloses a different and far from euphoric vision of the future. It is the future not as idyll but as apocalypse, a sobering prospect of the death of a great civilization, its ruins and relics picked over by a visiting tourist in a dream. Where after all, in Auden's words, did the journey look, for China? How secure, in the end, were the great teleological certitudes of the revolution to which Agnes Smedley had committed her life and writing? Aroused from this dream by the bugle call, she would soon be on the march again. But the troubling dream was not forgotten, and its murky shapes remained part of her experience and memory of China, and of the record she left behind.

# Notes

**INTRODUCTION**

1. Archibald John Little, *Mount Omi and Beyond* (London: Heinemann, 1901), 103.
2. W. H. Auden and Christopher Isherwood, *Journey to a War* [1939], rev. ed. (London: Faber, 1973), 8.
3. Peter Fleming, *One's Company: A Journey to China* (London: Cape, 1934), i.
4. E. G. Kemp, *The Face of China* (London: Chatto and Windus, 1909), vii.
5. Bertrand Russell, *The Problem of China* (London: George Allen and Unwin, 1922), 17.
6. Ibid., 74–5.
7. See Colin Mackerras, *Western Images of China* (Hong Kong: Oxford University Press, 1989).
8. Jonathan D. Spence, *The Search for Modern China*, 2nd ed. (New York: Norton, 1999), 117.
9. George Earl Macartney, *An Embassy to China: Lord Macartney's Journal 1793–1794*, ed. J. L. Cranmer-Byng (London: Longmans, 1962), 238. Macartney died in 1806 and the last Manchu emperor abdicated in 1912.
10. At the time of the Japanese surrender in 1946 there were 1.25 million Japanese troops in China and a further 900,000 in Manchuria, and over 1.75 million Japanese civilians in the country. See Spence, 460.
11. Michel Butor, "Travel and Writing," *Temperamental Journeys: Essays on the Modern Literature of Travel*, ed. Michael Kowalewski (Athens, GA: University of Georgia Press, 1992), 60.
12. Helen Carr, "Modernism and travel (1880–1940)," in *The Cambridge Companion to Travel Writing*, eds. Peter Hulme and Tim Youngs (Cambridge: Cambridge University Press, 2002), 70–86; quotation 73.
13. Evelyn Waugh, "Preface" in *When the Going was Good* (Boston: Little, Brown and Company, 1947), ix–xii; quotation xi.

14. See James Duncan and Derek Gregory, "Introduction," in *Writes of Passage: Reading Travel Writing*, eds. James Duncan and Derek Gregory (London: Routledge, 1999), 1–13.

15. Michael Kowalewski, "Introduction: The Modern Literature of Travel," in *Temperamental Journeys: Essays on the Modern Literature of Travel*, ed. Michael Kowalewski (Athens, GA: University of Georgia Press, 1992), 1–16; quotation 8. See also Peter Hulme, "Travel writing has four near neighbours, in generic terms: the novel (literature), ethnography (anthropology), the document (history), and reportage (sociology)." Peter Hulme, "Introduction," in *Studies in Travel Writing* 1 (1997): 1–8; quotation 5. Peter Bishop, too, points to the hybrid nature of the travel genre, which is regularly "conceived to be either a poor cousin of scientific observation, or else to fall short of the creativeness of 'pure' fiction." Peter Bishop, *The Myth of Shangri-La: Tibet, Travel Writing and the Western Creation of Sacred Landscape* (Berkeley: University of California Press, 1989), 3.

16. Mary Baine Campbell, "Travel Writing and Its Theory," in *The Cambridge Companion to Travel Writing*, eds. Peter Hulme and Tim Youngs (Cambridge: Cambridge University Press, 2002), 261–78; quotation 265.

17. See, for this paragraph, Campbell, 266 and 263. Campbell also gives examples of these formal approaches to travel literature.

18. See Campbell, 271–3, who names James Clifford, George Marcus and Clifford Geertz (with his concept of "thick description") as major influences from anthropology. Campbell also shows how models of otherness, beginning with Frantz Fanon's psychology of alterity and ending with Jacques Lacan's model of object relations, have been taken up by postcolonial critics like Gayatri Spivak and Homi Bhabha, who feature prominently in travel writing theory.

19. Campbell, 262. See the following critical studies, which show this shift in emphasis to the postmodern paradigm: Caren Kaplan, *Questions of Travel: Postmodern Discourse of Displacement* (Durham and London: Duke University Press, 1996) and Alison Russell, *Crossing Boundaries: Postmodern Travel Literature* (New York: Palgrave, 2000). See also Kristi Siegel's "Introduction: Travel Writing and Travel Theory" for an overview of recent developments in travel writing studies, in *Issues in Travel Writing: Empire, Spectacle, and Displacement*, ed. Kristi Siegel (New York: Peter Lang, 2002), 1–9.

20. Duncan and Gregory, 3.

21. Duncan and Gregory, 3.

22. Michael Hanne, "Introduction," in *Literature and Travel*, ed. Michael Hanne, Rodopi Perspectives on Modern Literature Series 11 (Amsterdam: Rodopi, 1993), 3–7, quotation 5, emphasis added.

23. See Peter Hulme and Tim Youngs, "Introduction," in *The Cambridge Companion to Travel Writing* (Cambridge: Cambridge University Press, 2002), 1–13; 6. See also Zweder Von Martels, "Introduction: The Eye and the Mind's Eye," in *Travel Fact and Travel Fiction: Studies on Fiction, Literary Tradition, Scholarly Discovery and Observation in Travel Writing*, ed. Zweder Von Martels (Leiden: Brill, 1994), xi–xviii, particularly xvii.

24. Campbell, 261.

25. Paul Fussell, *Abroad* (New York and Oxford: Oxford University Press, 1980), 219–20.

CHAPTER 1

1. John Francis Davis, *Sketches of China: Partly During an Inland Journey of Four Months, Between Peking, Nanking, and Canton; With Notices and Observations Relative to the Present War*, Vol. 1 (London: Charles Knight and Co., Ludgate Street, 1841), 68.

2. Ibid., n.p.
3. John Francis Davis, *The Chinese: A General Description of the Empire and its Inhabitants: With the History of Foreign Intercourse Down to the Events which Produced the Dissolution of 1857* (London: J. Murray, 1857), n.p.
4. Nigel Leask, *British Romantic Writers and the East* (Cambridge: Cambridge University Press, 1992), 20.
5. Coleridge claimed to have composed "Kubla Khan" after falling asleep while reading a seventeenth-century travelogue that had assimilated materials from Marco Polo's writing. As Karen Fang has recently pointed out, the poem moreover "distills eighteenth-century conventions of Chinese beauty into its allegory of high romantic genius ("Empire, Coleridge, and Charles Lamb's Consumer Imagination," *SEL: Studies in English Literature, 1500–1900* 43.4 [2003]: 824).
6. Jane Austen, *The Complete Novels* (Oxford: Oxford University Press, 1994), 568, 570.
7. Austen, 570.
8. See Andrew Blake, "Foreign Devils and Moral Panics: Britain, Asia and the Opium Trade," in *The Expansion of England: Race, Ethnicity and Cultural History*, ed. Bill Schwarz (London: Routledge, 1996), 232.
9. Davis, *Sketches*, 1:2.
10. Ibid., 2: 158–9.
11. Nigel Leask, *Curiosity and the Aesthetics of Travel-Writing, 1770–1840: "From an antique land"* (Oxford: Oxford University Press, 2004), *passim*.
12. Davis, Preface to *Sketches* [n.p.].
13. Compare also Nicholas Clifford on later travel writing in *"A Truthful Impression of the Country": British and American Travel Writing in China, 1880–1949* (Ann Arbor, MI: University of Michigan Press, 2001), 47.
14. Clifford refers to Henry James's interest in the chiaroscuro of Italy and then proceeds to look at later travellers looking for the authentic (94); Susan Schoenbauer Thurin concentrates on female travellers, most notably Isabella Bird Bishop and Constance Gordon Cumming, two of the most prolific Victorian women writers of travel accounts (*Victorian Travelers and the Opening of China, 1842–1907* [Athens: Ohio University Press, 1999]). Much has been written on their, primarily commercial, rivalry. See also Lila Marz Harper, *Solitary Travelers: Nineteenth-Century Women's Travel Narratives and the Scientific Vocation* (Madison, NJ: Fairleigh Dickinson University Press, 2001), 22; Susan Morgan, *Place Matters: Gendered Geography in Victorian Women's Travel Books about Southeast Asia* (New Brunswick: Rutgers University Press, 1996), *passim*.
15. Thurin, 96.
16. Davis, *Sketches*, 1:39.
17. Ibid., 1:129, 1:47–8.
18. Ibid., 1:82.
19. Ibid., 1:128.
20. Ibid., 1:77.
21. Ibid., 1:77–8.
22. Ibid., 13:17.
23. Ibid., 1:196.
24. Charles Dickens, *Little Dorrit* (Oxford: Oxford University Press, 1989), 18, 20.
25. Ibid., 152.

26. Compare Jeremy Tambling, "Opium, Wholesale, Resale, and for Export: On Dickens and China, Part I," *Dickens Quarterly* 21.1 (2004): 28–43; Wenying Xu, "The Opium Trade and *Little Dorrit*: A Case of Reading Silences," *Victorian Literature and Culture* 25.1 (1997): 53–6.

27. Thurin, 60.

28. The "dead silence" on the slave trade in *Mansfield Park* has been seen as evidence of a preoccupation with differentiated spaces of alterity and imperial cultural productions ever since Edward Said's influential analysis re-inscribed the novel within geopolitical discourses of its time. See Edward Said, *Culture and Imperialism* (London: Chatto and Windus, 1993), 73. For detailed discussions of the problematic see Susan Fraiman, "Jane Austen and Edward Said: Gender, Culture, and Imperialism," *Critical Inquiry* 21.4 (1995): 805–21; Franco Moretti, *Atlas of the European Novel* (London: Verso, 1999), 27. Compare also Tamara S. Wagner, *Longing: Narratives of Nostalgia in the British Novel, 1740–1890* (Lewisburg, PA: Bucknell University Press, 2004), Chapter 2 and parts of Chapter 3.

29. Published much later in the century, Trollope's 1876 *The Way We Live Now* (London: Penguin, 1994) sports an exclusive focus on commerce, in which the Chinese emperor is hosted by an upstart man of commerce. While the banquet in honour of the emperor is a feasting of commercial new men, it is the stereotypically inscrutable "oriental" who figures as a silent spectator of all that is wrong with the way British commercial society lives now.

30. Compare Andrew Blake on opium visions from De Quincey's "Malay dream" to *Dorian Gray* (especially 253–4.)

31. Leask, *Curiosity*, 1. Leask speaks of countries located in "torrid zones" that shared "the fate of being considered 'antique lands' by Europeans" despite their cartographic and cultural distance.

32. Davis, *Sketches*, 1:156, 1:284, 2:72–3.

33. Ibid., 2:83–4.

34. Ibid., 2:18–9.

35. Clifford, 23, 27.

36. John Stuart Mill, *On Liberty*, ed. David Spitz (New York: Norton, 1975), 67.

37. Davis, *Sketches*, 1:146–7.

38. Ibid., 1:7.

39. Ibid.

40. Ibid., 1:64.

41. Ibid., 2:34, 1:54.

42. Ibid., 1:7.

43. Compare Tamara S. Wagner, *Occidentalism in Novels of Malaysia and Singapore, 1819–2004: Colonial and Postcolonial Financial Straits* (Lewiston, NY: Mellen, 2005).

44. Thurin, 146, 18–9. As Thurin briefly touches upon the significance of Chinese occidentalism in her important study of British travel writing, she even goes so far as to speak of a reverse of Mary Pratt's seminal discussion of the imperialist or orientalist "gaze": "The Chinese racializing of the foreign visitor demonstrates the reverse of Pratt's findings on the 'gaze'. . . . The 'foreign devil' meeting the 'celestial' and the 'barbarian' meeting the 'barbarous' represents a unique combat between counter-stereotypes, a simultaneous orientalizing and occidentalizing" (20).

45. The *OED* gives the following entry for "Rufus": "A. adj. = RUFOUS a. 1884 Harper's Mag. Mar. 622/1 The red-tailed hawk, so named from the deep rufus color of its tail feathers.

1887 PHILLIPS Brit. Discomyc. 261 Cups . . . externally rufus-brown . . . ; hymenium concave, pale rufus. B. n. (Also with capital initial.) 1. U.S. slang. A countryman. 2. colloq. A nickname for a red-haired person." Dickens significantly termed one of the Victorian novel's most detestable, and also most notoriously red-haired, villains "this detestable Rufus" in *David Copperfield* (Chapter 26). I am grateful to Mitsuharu Matsuoka for pointing this out.

46. Couze Venn, *Occidentalism: Modernity and Subjectivity* (London: Sage, 2000), 1, 80. Looking specifically at the writing of modernism in early twentieth-century China, Shu-mei Shih takes a slightly different approach by arguing that "[r]ather than any 'representational containment' of the Western Other, Occidentalism promoted the Other as having universal value over the now particularised Chinese culture" (*The Lure of the Modern: Writing Modernism in Semicolonial China, 1917–1937* [Berkeley: University of California Press, 2001], 14).

47. Chen Xiaomei, *Occidentalism: A Theory of Counter-Discourse in Post-Mao China* (Oxford: Oxford University Press, 1995), 4–5. Ismail Talib has similarly called it "orientalism's other as an existing reverse process" ("After the (Unwritten) 'Postcolonial' in Southeast Asia: What Happens Next?" *The Silent Word: Textual Meaning and the Unwritten*, eds. Robert Young, et al. [Singapore: Singapore University Press, 1998], 63). At the centre of occidentalism's recent proliferation in literary and cultural theory is really foremost the oscillation of its meaning between a study of "the West" and a revisionist strategy. The *OED* lists only one meaning of "occidentalist" as "one who favours or advocates Western customs, modes of thought" or "studies the languages and institutions of Western nations." Dictionary definitions aside, it has become undeniably common to use "occidentalism" to describe a primarily hostile reaction to "the West." More recently, Ian Buruma and Avishai Margalit have altogether dismissed occidentalism as a "hateful caricature" of "Western" modernity and proceeded to argue that "[n]o Occidentalist, even the most fervent holy warrior, can ever be entirely free of the Occident." (*Occidentalism: The West in the Eyes of its Enemies* [New York: Penguin, 2004], 6, 144.) Compare Wagner, *Occidentalism*, 25–30.

48. Judith Snodgrass, *Orientalism, Occidentalism, and the Columbian Exposition: Presenting Japanese Buddhism to the West* (Chapel Hill: University of North Carolina Press, 2003), 11.

49. Snodgrass, 11.

50. Davis, *Sketches*, 2:161.

51. Ibid., 1:32–3.

52. Ibid., 1:34–5.

53. Leask, *Curiosity*, 4.

54. Davis, *Sketches*, 2:149.

55. Ibid., 1:191.

CHAPTER **2**

1. W. H. Medhurst, *A Glance at the Interior of China Obtained During a Journey to the Silk and Green Tea Countries* (London: John Snow, 1850). An edition of *A Glance at the Interior* published by the Shanghai Mission Press with more limited circulation had appeared the previous year.

2. Medhurst, *Glance*, 1.

3. Medhurst to Reverend Tidman, September 6, 1855, *CWM LMS* (Central China Correspondence: School of Oriental and African Studies Archive), Box 2 Folder 1 Jacket A.

4. The Missionary Society was founded in the late eighteenth century as part of the revival of Protestant Evangelism by a group of Anglican and Presbyterian clergy and laymen. By 1818, when it was renamed the London Missionary Society, it was broadly non-denominational though generally Congregationalist in outlook. Mission work began in the South Seas, expanded to North America and South Africa and Asia. The first LMS missionary to work with the Chinese, Robert Morrison, arrived in Penang in 1805. For more on Morrison, see Lindsay Ride, *Robert Morrison: The Scholar and the Man* (Hong Kong: Hong Kong University Press, 1957). For a general history of the London Missionary Society's activities in the nineteenth century, see Richard Lovett, *The History of the London Missionary Society 1795–1895* (London: Henry Frowd, 1899). For a recent critical study of the LMS, though not one that includes China, see Anna Johnston, *Missionary Writing and Empire* (Cambridge: Cambridge University Press, 2003). For accounts of another LMS missionary in China, see Norman J. Giradot, *The Victorian Translation of China: James Legge's Oriental Pilgrimage* (Berkeley, CA: University of California Press, 2002) and Lauren F. Pfister, *Striving for 'the Whole Duty of Man': James Legge and the Scottish Protestant Encounter with China*, Scottish Studies International (Frankfurt: Peter Lang, 2004). For another recent assessment of nineteenth-century mission work in China not exclusively focused on the LMS, see Ryan Dunch, "Beyond Cultural Imperialism: Cultural Theory, Christian Missions, and Global Modernity," *History and Theory* 41 (Oct 2002): 301–25.

5. W. H. Medhurst, *China Its State and Prospects, with especial reference to the spread of the gospel; containing allusions to the antiquity, extent, population, civilization, literature and religion of the Chinese* (London: John Snow, 1838), 96. Emphasis original.

6. For more on sixteenth and seventeenth-century Jesuit writers, see, among many others, Jonathan Spence, *The Memory Palace of Matteo Ricci* (New York: Penguin, 1985) and David Mungello, *Curious Land: Jesuit Accommodation and the Origins of Sinology* (Honolulu: University of Hawaii Press, 1989).

7. See A. J. Broomhall, *Hudson Taylor and China's Open Century*, 7 vols. (Sevenoaks, Kent: Hodder and Stoughton and the Overseas Missionary Fellowship, 1981).

8. Travel narratives by Medhurst's immediate contemporaries at the LMS Shanghai mission include: William C. Milne, *Life in China* (London: Routledge, 1858); Jane R. Edkins, *Chinese Scenes and People* (London: James Nisbet, 1863); Alexander Williamson, *Journeys in North China, Manchuria, and Eastern Mongolia, with some account of Corea* (London: Smith, Elder and Co., 1870); and Isabelle Williamson, *Old Highways in China* (London: The Religious Tract Society, 1884).

9. Medhurst, *Glance*, 38.

10. See, for example, John King Fairbank, *Trade and Diplomacy on the China Coast: The Opening of the Treaty Ports 1842–1854*, 2nd ed. (Stanford, CA: Stanford University Press, 1969), 294–5.

11. These include English-Japanese, English-Hokkien (Fujianese), English-Chinese, and English-Formosan dictionaries, pamphlets on the proper translation of the word God into Chinese, translations of the Historical Classic and Thousand Character Classic, geographical descriptions of Shanghai, the Malayan Archipelago, and elsewhere, and various phrase books including the posthumous *Chinese Dialogues* (Shanghai: n.p., 1861) which gave

foreigners a set of questions and responses which are both specific and miscellaneous. The Chinese respondent is by turns solicitous — "You will find this broth very nice. Use a soup spoon, and you will more easily spoon it up" — and silent, as the foreigner's questions grow more pointed. Later sections become sets of questions with no answers: "What work do you do?/ What is your idea in coming? Why did you not come yesterday?/ Why did you not come earlier?/ Why do you not do as I say?" (24) or commands barely disguised as questions: 'Have you seen my little knife?/ Hand me your little knife that I may see whether it is mine or not?" (26), and always leading: "Are you acquainted with any persons who drown girls?" (39). As a model for engaging with natives, it is confident where *A Glance at the Interior* is cautious, a token of its later publication date.

12. For an insightful discussion of Medhurst's innovations in tract-writing, see Jane Kate Leonard, "W. H. Medhurst: Rewriting the Missionary Message" in Suzanne Barnett and John Fairbank, eds., *Christianity in China: Early Protestant Missionary Writings* (Cambridge, MA: Harvard University Press, 1985): 47–59. She concludes: "Medhurst's emphasis on secular learning had a profound and lasting effect on the Protestant missionary movement in China. He turned it away from narrowly defined religious concerns to a broadened commitment to education, both Western and Chinese. This reorientation affected the missionaries themselves. It created a class of missionary-scholars like Medhurst who ultimately played a vital role as cultural mediators in the treaty ports after the Opium War. He was a leader both in transmitting the history and values of the West to the Chinese and in interpreting China with depth and sensitivity to the West." (59)

13. The term is Andrew Walls'. See *The Missionary Movement in Christian History: Studies in the Transmission of Faith* (Maryknoll, NY: Orbis Books; Edinburgh: T&T Clark, 1996) as well as *The Cross-Cultural Process in Christian History: Studies in the Transmission and Appropriation of Faith* (Maryknoll, NY: Orbis Books; Edinburgh: T&T Clark, 2002).

14. See, for example, the works of Robert Fortune, in particular *Three Years Wandering in the Northern Provinces of China, Including a Visit to the Tea, Silk and Cotton Countries* (London: John Murray, 1847); Karl Gützlaff, *Journal of Three Voyages Along the Coast of China in 1831, 1832, and 1833* (London: F. Westley and A. H. Davis, 1834); and Evariste Regis Huc, *Travels in Tartary, Thibet, and China in the Years 1844, 1845, and 1846*, trans. William Hazlitt (London: T. Nelson, 1856).

15. This is surprising, however, given recent scholarly interest in missionary enterprises during the age of empire. See Gauri Viswanathan, *Outside the Fold: Conversion, Modernity, and Belief* (Princeton, NJ: Princeton University Press, 1998); Anna Johnston, *Missionary Writing and Empire, 1800–1860* (Cambridge: Cambridge University Press, 2003); and Eric Reinders, *Borrowed Gods and Foreign Bodies* (Berkeley, CA: University of California Press, 2004).

16. Fortune, *Three Years Wandering*, 4.

17. See Jonathan Crary, *Techniques of the Observer: On Vision and Modernity in the Nineteenth Century* (Cambridge, MA: MIT Press, 1990); Jennifer Green-Lewis, *Framing the Victorians: Photography and the Culture of Realism* (Ithaca, NY: Cornell University Press, 1996); and James Ryan, *Picturing Empire: Photography and the Visualization of the British Empire* (Chicago: The University of Chicago Press, 1997). For a general overview of the field, see Vanessa R. Schwartz and Jeannene M. Przyblyski, eds., *The Nineteenth-Century Visual Culture Reader* (New York: Routledge, 2004).

18. See Elizabeth H. Chang, " 'Eyes of the Proper Almond Shape': Blue and White China in the British Imaginary 1823–1883," *19th-Century Studies* 19 (2005): 17–34.

19. These include James Weldon Johnson's *Autobiography of an Ex-Coloured Man* (1912), Nella Larsen's *Passing* (1928), and John Howard Griffin's *Black Like Me* (1961). For scholarly work on passing narratives, see, among others, Elaine K. Ginsberg, ed. *Passing and the Fictions of Identity* (Durham, NC: Duke University Press, 1996) and Gayle Wald, *Crossing the Line: Racial Passing in Twentieth-Century U.S. Literature and Culture* (Durham, NC: Duke University Press, 2000). See also Gail Ching-Liang Low, *White Skins Black Masks: Representation and Colonialism* (London: Routledge, 1996) for a reading of passing practice as "cross-cultural disguise."

20. See, for example, Amy Robinson, "It Takes One to Know One: Passing and Communities of Common Interest," *Critical Inquiry* 20 (Summer 1994): 715–36.

21. Michaels, challenging the idea that race can be understood as an exclusively cultural construct, writes: "the very idea of passing — whether it takes the form of looking like you belong to a different race or of acting like you belong to a different race — requires an understanding of race as something separate from the way you look and the way you act" ("The No-Drop Rule," *Critical Inquiry* 20 [Summer 1994] 758–69, 768). See also Ron Mallon's cogent analysis of the challenges to Michael's position in his "Passing, Traveling, and Reality: Social Constructionism and the Metaphysics of Race," *Noûs* 38, 4 (2004): 644–73.

22. This is not to set aside the powerful body of work on Christian visual rhetoric. See, among many others, David Morgan, *The Sacred Gaze: Religious Visual Culture in Theory and Practice* (Berkeley, CA: University of California Press, 2005), ed. Robert S. Nelson, *Visuality Before and Beyond the Renaissance; Seeing as Others Saw* (Cambridge: Cambridge University Press, 2000), and Mark Taylor, *Disfiguring: Art, Architecture, Religion* (Chicago: University of Chicago Press, 1992). I argue because of the unique status of China as a site of visual difference, as well as the Protestant missionary's especially contested attitude to Chinese "idolatry," questions of vision here are marked rather differently than elsewhere.

23. This is a renovation that he imagines must concurrently take place at the linguistic level. As he writes to the LMS Directors while working in the Ultra-Ganges Mission: "The chief difficulty with the Chinese seems to be, to make them at all sensible of their guilt, and danger, principally because sin in their estimation is a very different thing from what it is in ours, the word *sin* in their language being synonymous with crime, and those things only being accounted sinful which are cognizable and punishable by human laws" (Medhurst to LMS Directors, June 30, 1832, *Oriental and Indian Collections* [British Library], MSS Eur C794). These questions of uneven linguistic correspondence would form a central part of Medhurst's career, particularly as he embarked on his translations of the Old and New Testaments, and I do not want to underestimate their importance. But a full study of the intersections between textual and visual modes of translation exceeds the bounds of this essay.

24. Fortune, *Three Years Wandering*, 253.

25. Medhurst, *Glance*, 10–11.

26. *Glance*, 8.

27. Ibid., 23.

28. Ibid., 128.

29. Ibid., 145.

30. Ibid., 47.

31. Ibid., 104–5.

32. Ibid., 122.
33. Ibid., 33.
34. Ibid. 99.
35. Ibid.
36. Ibid., 22.
37. Ibid., 17.
38. Ibid.
39. Ibid., 21.
40. Ibid., 146.
41. Ibid., 99–100.
42. Medhurst, *China*, 482.
43. Medhurst, *Glance*, 170–1.
44. Ibid., 171.
45. Ibid., 177.
46. For more on the tea industry, see Robert Gardella, *Harvesting Mountains: Fujian and the China Tea Trade, 1737–1935* (Berkeley, CA: University of California Press, 1994).
47. Medhurst, *Glance,* 167.
48. Ibid., 190–1.
49. Ibid., 192.

CHAPTER 3

1. Elgin, *Letters and Journals of James, Eighth Earl of Elgin*, ed. Theodore Walrond (London: John Murray, 1872), 325; hereafter *L&J*, with reference to page number in the text.
2. "The Second Opium War" is perhaps more historically accurate than "the *Arrow* War," as it is clearly conscious of the historical continuity between these two major Sino-British military conflicts in the mid-nineteenth century. The First Opium War (1840–42) ended with the ceding of Hong Kong to British rule and created immediate conditions of possibility for the *Arrow* incident. See also note 4 below.
3. J. R. Seeley, *The Expansion of England* [1884], ed. (John Gross Chicago: The University of Chicago Press, 1971), 13.
4. Sir Harry Parkes, the British Consul in Guangzhou at the time, had, of course, a different version of the incident, and his narrative of the incident may be of some historical interest: "Lorcha is the name given to a class of vessels of partly English and partly Chinese rig, that is greatly in request in these waters on account of the facility with which these craft are worked by native crews. . . . The *Arrow* was one of them, and had a regular register which was in my hands at the time that her crew was seized by the Chinese officers. The seizure took place in open day in a crowded anchorage, and was conducted with unusual display and circumstance. Four mandarins and nearly forty men boarded the lorcha, hauled down her flag, and bound and carried off her crew to a war junk lying close by. . . . I addressed the Imperial Commissioner a temperate letter, begging him to restore the men to their vessel in a public manner. . . . The Commissioner, however, . . . refused all satisfaction on the ground, as he alleged that the lorcha was not an English vessel, and that her crew, being Chinese, were amenable only to his jurisdiction; and having once made this statement he ceased to take any notice of applications addressed him by Sir John Bowring and myself, and would depute no officer to discuss the matter with me." Stanley Lane-Poole, *The Life*

*of Sir Harry Parkes, Sometime Her Majesty's Minister to China and Japan,* vol. 1 ([1894] Wilmington: Scholarly Resources Inc. 1973), 228–9. For a more recent study of the *Arrow* incident and the Second Opium War, see J. Y. Wong, *Deadly Dreams: Opium, Imperialism and the Arrow War (1856–1860) in China* (Cambridge: Cambridge University Press, 1998).

5. Karl Marx, "Parliamentary Debates on the Chinese Hostilities," in Karl Marx and Frederick Engels, *Collected Works,* vol. 15 (London: Lawrence & Wishart, 1986), 209.

6. The editor's head-note to Bowring's speech "The Influence of Knowledge on Domestic and Social Happiness" introduces him thus: "Dr. Bowring has been a great traveler. He has resided successively in Spain, Portugal, Russia, Finland, Sweden, Germany, and Holland. Of late years, he has been chiefly engaged in foreign missions of importance, in relation to trade and commerce. In 1828, he visited the Low Countries, to examine the manner in which their public accounts were kept; and in 1830, he made a mission of the same kind to France, in company with the late Lord Congleton, then Sir Henry Parnell. In 1831, he was nominated with Lord Clarendon, then the Hon. Mr. Villiers the Ambassador at Madrid, to examine with two French Commissioners, into the tariffs of France and Great Britain, with a view to the extension of trade between the two countries. In 1834, he was charged with a mission, of the same kind, to Belgium; in 1835, with one to Switzerland; and in 1836, with one to Northern and Central Italy. The last mission to which Dr. Bowring was engaged, was that to Egypt, Syria, and the East, which is yet likely to lead to the most advantageous results." John Bowring, *The Influence of Knowledge on Domestic and Social Happiness* (London: John Chapman, [?1840]), 2.

7. Bowring to Clarendon, September 9, 1856, quoted in G. F. Bartle, "Sir John Bowring and the Arrow War in China," *Bulletin of the John Rylands Library* 43.2 (March 1961): 299.

8. For a vivid account of the Parliamentary debates on the *Arrow* incident, see Marx, "Parliamentary Debates on the Chinese Hostilities."

9. For a study of Palmerston's liberalism, see E. D. Steele, *Palmerston and Liberalism: 1855–1865* (Cambridge: Cambridge University Press, 1991).

10. Hannah Arendt's reflections on the origin and formation of imperial foreign policy are worth quoting here: "Imperialism was born when the ruling class in capitalist production came up against national limitations to its economic expansion. The bourgeoisie turned to politics out of economic necessity; for if it did not want to give up the capitalist system whose inherent law is constant economic growth, it had to impose this law upon its home governments and to proclaim expansion to be an ultimate political goal of foreign policy." Arendt, *The Origins of Totalitarianism* (San Diego, New York, London: Harcourt Brace Jovanovich, 1973), 126.

11. Harriet Martineau, *A British Friendship and Memoir of the Earl of Elgin and Kincardine* (Windermere: J. Garnett, 1866), 28.

12. W. P. M. Kennedy, *Lord Elgin* (London and Toronto: Oxford University Press, 1926), 227.

13. "Of all possible subjects," W. H. Auden says, "travel is the most difficult for an artist, as it is the easiest for a journalist" (Auden, *The Dyer's Hand and Other Essays* [London: Faber and Faber, 1962], 310). One perhaps can understand why as a subject travel is most difficult for an artist, but it should not be easiest for a journalist. In practice, it is almost impossible to determine "travel writing" in generic terms. It identifies neither a specific mode of expression, as it is the aggregate of many different forms — diaries, journals, letters, essays, nor a discursive field of topics that might bring this variety of writings

together. Travel writing cannot be a mere set of reports or observations. It is the traveler who decides on what to see and how to write about it. A travel writer is a writer before he is a traveler, and he decides on what to see and what to write about before travel starts. As Sontag observes, "Before there was travel — in my life, at least — there were travel books. Books that told you the world was very large but quite encompassable. Full of destinations." Susan Sontag, "Homage to Halliburton," in *Where the Stress Falls: Essays* (New York: Farrar, Straus and Giroux, 2001), 255.

14. Parkes, for example, "thought 'the Earl' supercilious and essentially weak: he disliked and deprecated his cautious perfunctory policy, and augured no good from his return [Elgin's second mission]." See Lane-Poole, *The Life of Sir Harry Parkes*, vol. 1, 339.

15. The other is the Wallace family. See Sydney Checkland, *The Elgins, 1766–1917: A Tale of Aristocrats, Proconsuls and Their Wives* (Aberdeen: Aberdeen University Press, 1988), 1.

16. See Walrond, "Memoir of James, Eighth Earl of Elgin," in *L&J*, 3. The quotation is from *Hamlet*, III, 1.

17. See Walrond, "Memoir of James, Eighth Earl of Elgin," in *L&J*, 6–7.

18. See Kennedy, *Lord Elgin*, 34–5.

19. Kennedy, *Lord Elgin*, 31.

20. J. L. Morison, *British Supremacy and Canadian Self-Government, 1839–1854* (Glasgow: James MacLehose and Sons, 1919), 217.

21. Kennedy, *Lord Elgin*, 256–7.

22. Elgin, "The Address of the Earl of Elgin (Ambassador Plenipotentiary to the Courts of Pekin and Japan) to the Merchants, Prior to the Execution of Recent Treaties with the Emperors of China and Japan," included as an appendix in François Froger, *A Journal of the First French Embassy to China, 1698–1700* (London: Thomas Cautley Newby, 1859), 207; original small capital letters.

23. Elgin, "The Address of the Earl of Elgin," 206; original italics.

24. See Checkland, *The Elgins, 1766–1917*, 163.

25. Byron, *The Curse of Minerva*, 1:208. While the sculptures were being removed from the Parthenon in 1810, Byron was in Athens and saw shiploads of the marbles being carried away. Parts of *The Curse of Minerva* were drafted near the site. Prior to *The Curse of Minerva*, Byron had already attacked this act of barbarity in an earlier poem *English Bards and Scotch Reviewers*. For Keats' celebration of the marbles, see his sonnets "On Seeing the Elgin Marbles" and "To B. R. Haydon, with a Sonnet Written on Seeing the Elgin Marbles." In a related essay, I have discussed in some detail the romantic aesthetic in the context of global imperialism. See Q. S. Tong, "The Aesthetic of Imperial Ruins: The Elgins and John Bowring," *boundary 2: an international journal of literature and culture* 33, no. 1 (Spring 2006): 124–50.

26. John Newsinger, "Elgin in China," *New Left Review* 15 (May–June 2002): 139.

27. Fuimus, "Letter to His Excellency the Right Honorable Lord Elgin, on Responsible Government, together with His Lordship's celebrated speech, delivered in the House of Commons, as Lord Bruce, in 1841, deprecating, in the strongest terms, all appointments to office by a tottering ministry, not enjoying the confidence of the people" (Montreal: Printed by Donoghue and Mantz, 142, Notre Dame Street, January 1847), 12, 17.

28. John Bowring, *The Political and Commercial Importance of Peace: A Lecture Delivered in the Hall of Commerce London* (London: Peace Society [?1846]), 23–4; original italics.

29. See Bernard Semmel's *The Rise of Free Trade Imperialism: Classical Political Economy, the Empire of Free Trade and Imperialism, 1750–1850* (Cambridge: Cambridge University

Press, 1970), which, though published more than three decades ago, remains an important study of the relations between free trade and imperialism.

30. Seeley, *The Expansion of England*, 89–90; italics original.

31. See W. H. Dawson, *Richard Cobden and Foreign Policy: A Critical Exposition, with Special Reference to Our Day and Its Problems* (New York: Frank-Maurice, 1927), 193.

32. Richard Cobden to John Bowring, August 28, 1859 (n.p.: Special Collections, The University of Hong Kong Library).

33. See Keith Windschuttle, "Liberalism and Imperialism," in *The Betrayal of Liberalism: How the Disciples of Freedom and Equality Helped Foster the Illiberal Politics of Coercion and Control*, eds. H. Kramer and R. Kimball (Chicago: Ivan R. Dee, 1999), 81.

34. See Maurice Cowling, *Mill and Liberalism* (Cambridge: Cambridge University Press, 1990), il.

35. For a recent critique of the relationship between liberalism and imperialism, see Uday Singh Mehta, *Liberalism and Empire: A Study in Nineteenth-Century British Liberal Thought* (Chicago: University of Chicago Press, 1999).

36. C. K. Ogden, *Jeremy Bentham, 1832–2032: Being the Bentham Centenary Lecture, delivered in University College, London, on June 6th, 1932* (Bristol: Thoemmes Press, 1993), 21.

37. Elie Halévy, *The Growth of Philosophic Radicalism*, trans. Mary Morris (London: Faber, 1949), 510.

38. Marx and Engels, *Manifesto of the Communist Party,* in *Collected Works*, vol. 6, 487–8; my italics.

39. Checkland, *The Elgins, 1766–1917*, 164.

40. J. L. Morison, *The Eighth Earl of Elgin: A Chapter in Nineteenth-Century Imperial History* (London: Hodder and Stoughton, 1928), 310.

41. Morison, *The Eighth Earl of Elgin*, 312.

CHAPTER **4**

1. John Thomson, *Straits of Malacca, Indo-China, and China, or, Ten Years Travels, Adventures, and Residence Abroad* (New York: Harper and Brothers, 1875), v. For background information on Thomson, see Stephen White, *John Thomson: A Window to the Orient* (London: Thames and Hudson, 1985).

2. John Thomson, *Illustrations of China and Its People: A Series of 200 Photographs, with Letterpress Descriptive of the Places and People Represented*, 4 vols. (London: Sampson Low, Marston, Low and Searle, 1973), I, "Introduction." (These volumes are unpaginated; reference will be to volume number and to the title of the photograph the text accompanies.)

3. Thomson, *Straits*, 9.

4. White, *John Thomson,* 9–19.

5. Thomson, *Illustrations*, "Introduction".

6. Thomson explicitly states this to be his aim in *Illustrations*, "Introduction," *Straits*, 8, and in "Notes of a Journey to Southern Formosa," *Journal of the Royal Geographical Society* 43 (1873): 97.

7. Thomson, *Straits*, v–vi. Light imagery such as this is recurrent in Thomson.

8. John Thomson, "Geographical Photography," *Scottish Geographical Magazine* 23, no. 1 (1907): 14.

9. Thomson, *Straits*, 216.
10. The description of Eastern realms as barren, uninteresting, and without history before Western penetration is an almost standard feature of Thomson's accounts. See Thomson, *Illustrations*, texts accompanying "Hongkong," "Canton," and "Foochaw Arsenal"; Thomson, *Straits*, 2 (on Dutch rule in Java and Malaya), 93 (Singapore), 345 (Japan).
11. James R. Ryan, *Picturing Empire: Photography and the Visualization of the British Empire* (Chicago: University of Chicago Press, 1997), 67, and generally 61–8.
12. Thomson, *Illustrations*, "Introduction."
13. Ibid.
14. G. [*sic*] Thomson, "Notes of Cambodia and Its Races," *Transactions of the Ethnological Society of London* n.s. 6 (1869), 246–52. White identifies the piece as Thomson's work, and the illustrations, though engravings rather than photographs, are clearly based on Thomson's photographs. Crawfurd's series of articles began in Volume 3 of the journal (1865), with contributions on language as a test of race and on racial mixtures; continued in Volume 4 (1866) with "On the Physical and Mental Characteristics of the Negro," and in Volume 5 (1867) with a companion piece on Europeans and Asiatics; and, in the same volume as Thomson, Crawfurd's two pieces cover racial classification according to form of the skull and according to skin, hair, and eyes. In another contribution to the same volume, "On the Plurality of the Races of Man," Crawfurd supports the theory of polygenesis.
15. Wallace contributed an article to the Ethnological Society of London in 1865, describing the Malay peninsula's racial composition in terms of a contest between Malays and Papuans. See his "On the Varieties of Men in the Malay Archipelago", in *Transactions of the Ethnological Society of London* (henceforth *TESL*) 3 (1865): 196–215. His theories are more fully developed in *The Malay Archipelago: The Land of the Orang-Utan, and the Bird of Paradise: A Narrative of Travel, with Studies of Man and Nature* (New York: Harper and Brothers, 1869); Wallace summarizes his account of the races of the region in the final chapter, "On the Races of Man," 584–99. See also his *Studies in Science and Society*, 2 vols. (London: Macmillan, 1900), I, Chapters 19–21. For background information on Wallace's place in the ethnography of the 1860s, see George Stocking, *Victorian Anthropology* (New York: Free Press, 1987), 96–102. On the period discussion about races in the Pacific, see Douglas A. Lorimer, "Theoretical Racism in Late-Victorian Anthropology, 1870–1900," *Victorian Studies* 31, no. 3 (1988): 413–5.
16. See Walter Fergus and G. F. Radwell (presented by Francis Galton), "On a Series of Measurements for Statistical Purposes recently made at Marlborough College," Francis Galton, "Notes on the Marlborough School Statistics," and Colonel A. Lane Fox (later Pitt-Rivers), "Principles of Classification," all in *Journal of the Anthropological Institute* (henceforth *JAI*) 4 (1875): 126–30, 130–5, and 293–308. For the next installment of Galton's work, see *JAI* 5 (1876): 174–80. For background on Galton, see Stocking, *Victorian Anthropology*, 92–6. On Pitt-Rivers's museum, see David K. van Keuren, "Museums and Ideology: Augustus Pitt-Rivers, Anthropological Museums and Social Change in Victorian Britain," *Victorian Studies* 28, no. 1 (1984): 171–89.
17. The project was initially developed under the aegis of the British Association for the Advancement of Science, who published the first edition in 1874, and later editions were re-edited by the Anthropological Institute. For Pitt-Rivers's involvement, see F. W. Radler, "Report on Anthropology at the Meeting of the British Association," *JAI* 3 (1874): 333. Pitt-Rivers's contributions, mostly on aspects of material culture, are initialed A. L. F. (Augustus Lane Fox), even in later editions.

UNIVERSITY OF WINCHESTER
LIBRARY

18. Tylor also notes, however, that most "race-portraits" of the period were scientifically inadequate, and that the value of proper photographic techniques would be in part "to check the rash generalization as to race so common in ethnological systems." He goes on nevertheless to enumerate generalizations of his own. See E. B. Tylor, "Dammann's Race-Photographs," *Nature* 15 (January 6, 1876): 185–6.

19. W. L. Distant, "Eastern Coolie Labour," *JAI* 3 (1874): 139–44; quotation 139.

20. G. W. Leitner, "The Siah Posh Kafirs," *JAI* 3 (1874): 341–60, esp. 341–4.

21. C. H. Read, preface to *Notes and Queries on Anthropology*, eds., C. H. Read and John George Garson, 3rd ed. (London: Anthropological Institute, 1899).

22. Henry Balfour, "Presidential Address," *JAI* 34 (1908): 13.

23. British Museum (C. H. Read, ed.), *Handbook to the Ethnographical Collections* (London: British Museum, 1910), 43.

24. On Huxley's system see Elizabeth Edwards, "Photographic 'Types': The Pursuit of a Method," *Visual Anthropology* 3, no. 2–3 (1990): 241–7; quotation on 245. Edwards notes that, significantly, almost only subjects photographed in strict accordance to Huxley's guidelines were prisoners, people under absolute British authority.

25. The photograph is labeled "Nicobar Islanders," and appears as a frontispiece, not accompanying any article. W. L. Distant, in an explanatory note to the photograph, credits it to Ralph Meldola, 1875. His justification for printing it parallels Thomson's own regular first-contact-with-camera assertions: "They are, I believe, the first that have ever been taken of these little known people." See *JAI* 7 (1877): 209 and frontispiece. The development of the halftone process in the 1880s provided the technological breakthrough that facilitated the journalistic uses of photography, but photographs were not a regular feature of print journalism until the last decade of the century. On these developments, see Beaumont Newhall, *History of Photography* (New York: MOMA, 1982): 249–57.

26. See E. F. Im Thurn, "Anthropological Uses of the Camera," *JAI* 22 (1893): 191–4 and Plate XI.

27. Thomson, "Geographical Photography," 17.

28. For a convenient summary of these developments, see Douglas Lorimer, "Theoretical Racism in Late-Victorian Anthropology, 1870–1900," *Victorian Studies* 31, no. 3 (1988): esp. 421–5.

29. Ryan, *Picturing* Empire, 163.

30. See, for instance, on Cambodians, Thomson, *Straits* 100, "Notes on Cambodia," 251–2; on Laotians, Thomson, *Straits* 116; on the Hak-kas of Guangdong province, Thomson, *Straits* 259; on racial variation along the Han River, Thomson, *Straits* 284, and on suggestions of Indian racial admixture in Nankow, Thomson, *Straits* 534.

31. Thomson, *Straits*, 325; see generally 315–38; "Notes of a Journey," 101–6; and Thomson, *Illustrations*, "Natives of Formosa." In the latter, Thomson speculates on the absence of Negroes in the islands, suggesting that in an earlier migratory period they had "given place to the stronger and fairer race."

32. Thomson, *Illustrations*, I, "Macao." See also Thomson, *Straits* 20, 277 (on Portuguese), 243, 497 (on decadent Tartars).

33. Thomson, *Straits*, 20 (here referring to the Portuguese of Penang). For a strong environmentalist argument in the same period, see Winwood Reade, *Savage Africa: Being the Narrative of a Tour in Equatorial, Southwestern, and Northwestern Africa* (London: Smith, Elder, 1863), 509–28. Reade makes a similar intervention in the debate at the

Anthropological Society of London over James Hunt's notorious paper, "On the Negro's Place in Nature"; see *Journal of the Anthropological Society of London* 2 (1864): xviii. Richard Burton also argued for environmental degradation, at least in the Mideast; see W. H. Wilkins, ed., *The Jew, the Gypsy, and El Islam* (London: Hutchinson, 1898), esp. 316–20. For a more balanced, Darwinian account, see T. H. Huxley, "On the Methods and Results of Ethnology" (1865), in *Man's Place in Nature and Other Anthropological Essays* (New York: Greenwood, 1968), 244–6, 249–52.

34. Thomson, *Straits*, 277. For the strongest views on the disastrous consequences of racial mixture, the polygeneticist London Anthropological Society provides especially rich material. See for instance the anonymous review of the anonymous 1864 pamphlet "Miscegenation" in *Anthropological Review* 2 (1864): 116–21.

35. *Illustrations*, I, "Macao." On race and class, see Douglas A. Lorimer, *Colour, Class and the Victorians: English Attitudes to the Negro in the Mid-Nineteenth Century* (New York: Leicester University Press, 1978), esp. Chapter 5.

36. On the innovatory character of Thomson's move to the street, see White, 21, 38, 41.

37. Quoted in White, 38.

38. Thomson, *Straits*, 309.

39. For a comparable contemporary view, see H. P. Robinson, *Pictorial Effect in Photography* (London: Piper and Carter, 1869), esp. 21–3. For a slightly later view of photography that even more closely parallels Thomson's simultaneous concern with anthropological science and artistic photography, see P. H. Emerson, *Naturalistic Photography for Students of the Art* (London: Sampson Low, Marston, Searle and Rivington, 1889), esp. 29–33.

40. The same argument was used by Dr. Barnardo when he was charged with creating fraudulent photographic portrayals of street urchins. See Valerie Lloyd, *The Camera and Dr. Barnardo* (Hartford: Barnardo School of Printing, [1974]), 12.

41. Quoted in White, 40.

42. Thomson quoting Ruskin quoted in White, 40. Robinson also uses Ruskin as a touchstone on unity of the subject. See Robinson, *Pictorial Effect*, 18, 21.

43. Thomson, *Straits*, 94.

44. Thomson, *Straits*, 189.

45. Such a practice also had a technical side: more restricted depth of focus allowed Thomson to use a faster shutter speed. The technique is even more prominent in his London than in his Chinese photographs.

46. In this practice Thomson could well have been following the example of Richard Beard, whose daguerreotypes for Mayhew's *London Labour and the London Poor* similarly always associated laborers with the tools of their trade. The parallel is particularly significant since Thomson, in his later work in the East End, openly acknowledges Mayhew's importance as a model for his work. See Thomson's preface to John Thomson and Adolphe Smith, *Street Life of London* (1875–76; collected in book form in 1877).

47. Ryan, *Picturing Empire*, 163.

48. Thomson, *Illustrations*, I, text to "Hongkong Sedan Chair." This is another of Thomson's recurrent motifs; see, for example, the texts for "Foochaw Coolie" and "Shanghai wheelbarrow" in *Illustrations*, and the discussion of contented shanty-town residents in Thomson, *Straits*, 263.

49. Thomson, *Straits*, 176.

50. Thomson, *Straits*, 511, 512.

51. Thomson, *Illustrations*, I, "Physic Street."
52. Thomson, *Illustrations*, III, "Street Groups, Kiu-Liang"; see also the text of untitled Plate XXIX, describing "a costermonger of the lowest order."
53. Thomson, *Straits*, 498.
54. Thomson, *Illustrations*, I, "Canton Junk."
55. Thomson, *Illustrations*, II, "Beggars." In English texts, this is an implicit sub-theme in Mayhew's discussion of beggars, but an even more open parallel can be found in Mayhew's brother Augustus's "documentary" novel *Paved with Gold, or, The Romance and Reality of London Streets* (1857–58). The most familiar incarnation, of course, is Dickens's Fagin.
56. See Thomson, preface to *Street Life*; for a fuller discussion of Thomson's London images, see my "Photography and the Image of the London Poor" in Debra N. Mancoff and D. J. Trela, *Victorian Urban Settings: Essays on the Nineteenth-Century City and Its Contexts* (New York: Garland Publishing, 1996), 179–94, or *Fixed Positions: Working-Class Subjects and Photographic Hegemony in Victorian Britain* (Ph.D. dissertation, Indiana University, 1994), Chapter 5. See also Ryan, *Picturing Empire*, 173–80.
57. Thomson, *Street Life*, 2. The imagery of "stamped" personalities is another recurrent one in Thomson's work. Thomson's contributions to the text are usually distinguishable from his co-author Adolphe Smith's by identifying initials, but even when not identified by initial are readily identifiable by stylistic traits. See Prasch, *Fixed Positions*, 193 n. 5.
58. Thomson, *Street Life*, 12.
59. Thomson, *Street Life*, 95.
60. Thomson, *Straits*, 463.

CHAPTER 5

1. Mrs. J. F. Bishop [Isabella L. Bird], *The Yangtze Valley and Beyond: An Account of Journeys in China, Chiefly in the Province of Sze Chuan and among the Man-tze of the Somo Territory* (London: John Murray, 1899), 300.
2. "Chinese Cookery," *Temple Bar* 93 (1891): 112.
3. See Jay Denby, *Letters of a Shanghai Griffin to His Father and Other Exaggerations* (Shanghai: The China Printing Company, 1910), 124–9. A "griffin" was a young civil servant newcomer to the East. It can be difficult to distinguish between literature produced by visitors to China, like Bird, and Britons resident in China, like Archibald Little and his wife Alicia Bewicke, who also traveled and produced narratives about the country. While not seeing these groups as necessarily equivalent, this essay treats their narratives collectively as phenomena of travel writing in the broader sense of the genre.
4. Bird would later repeat this idea in *Chinese Pictures: Notes on Photographs Made in China* (London: Cassell and Company, 1900), where she annotates a picture of a child eating rice with chopsticks, stating, "As a rule the Chinese are good cooks, and the food is wholesome, steaming being the favourite method."
5. "Bird's Nest Soup," *The Cornhill Magazine* 8 (January 1887): 80. Also reprinted in *The Eclectic Magazine of Foreign Literature, Science, and Art* 45 (1887), 371–7.
6. Because articles in the periodical press were often anonymous, it is difficult to gauge how direct the authors' experiences of China and the Chinese would have been, but it is clear that the work of travel writers and specifically naturalists was key to the topics and ideas they present in these pieces.

7. "The Edible Birds' Nests of the Eastern Islands," *The Penny Magazine of the Society for the Diffusion of Useful Knowledge* 10 (1841): 368. See also John Crawfurd, *History of the Indian Archipelago: Containing an Account of the Manners, Arts, Languages, Religions, Institutions, and Commerce of Its Inhabitants* (Edinburgh: Archibald Constable and Co., 1820), 3: 437.

8. The later history of the trade in birds' nests would bear out this pattern, as the domains for collecting the nests in Southeast Asia, such as the Malay peninsula and Borneo, came under European control, as did the shipping trade in the region. Cf. Dai Yifeng, "Food Culture and Overseas Trade: The Trepang Trade between China and Southeast Asia during the Qing Dynasty," in *The Globalization of Chinese Food*, eds. David Y. H. Wu and Sidney C. H. Cheung (London: Curzon, 2002), 21–42, whose author argues that the trade in sea-cucumbers largely remained in Chinese hands during this period.

9. See George Wingrove Cooke, *China and Lower Bengal: Being "The Times" Correspondence from China in the Years 1857–58* (London: Routledge, Warne, and Routledge, 1861), 235–44. The original piece on "A Chinese Dinner" appeared in the *Times* on February 2, 1858. For a biographical synopsis of Cooke, see *Nineteenth-Century Travels, Explorations and Empires: Writing from the Era of Imperial Consolidation 1835–1910*, Vol. 4: *The Far East*, ed. Susan Schoenbauer Thurin (London: Pickering and Chatto, 2003), 1–2.

10. John Dudgeon, "Diet, Dress, and Dwellings of the Chinese in Relation to Health," in *The Health Exhibition Literature* (London: Executive Council of the International Health Exhibition, and for the Council of the Society of Arts/William Clowes and Sons, 1884), 19:317. Dudgeon was also the author of the travelogue *Notes by the Way: Taken during a Journey by the So-called Overland Route to China* (London: Williams and Strahan, 1866).

11. See David Burton, *The Raj at Table: A Culinary History of the British in India* (London: Faber and Faber, 1993), 1–11.

12. See Jules Verne, *The Troubles of a Chinaman*, in *The Leisure Hour* (1880), 55–8.

13. See Archibald John Little, *Through the Yang-tse Gorges, or Trade and Travel in Western China* (London: Sampson, Low, Marston, Searle, and Rivington, 1888), 305.

14. Arthur H. Smith, *Chinese Characteristics* (London: Keegan Paul, Trench, Trübner, and Co. Ltd., 1892), 2. An identical edition appeared in 1890 in Shanghai, published by the *North China Herald*.

15. See Lydia H. Liu's introduction to her edition of *Chinese Characteristics* (Norwalk, CT: EastBridge, 2003), i. See also Charles W. Hayford, "Chinese and American Characteristics: Arthur H. Smith and His China Book," in *Christianity in China: Early Protestant Missionary Writings*, eds. Suzanne Wilson Barnett and John King Fairbank (Cambridge, MA: Harvard University Press, 1985), 153. For further biographical details, see Kathleen L. Lodwick, "Smith, Arthur Henderson," *American National Biography Online* database, accessed April 3, 2006.

16. See "Chinese Cookery," reprinted from *The Pall Mall Gazette* in *Littell's Living Age*, 5th series, 144.1857 (January 17, 1880): 190.

17. C. F. Gordon Cumming, *Wanderings in China*, 2 vols. (Edinburgh and London: William Blackwood and Sons, 1886), I:219. In contrast to India, where women dominated culinary discussions, in China, given the paucity of British women residents, most descriptions were by men. Descriptions by women tend to come from those involved in missionary work or expeditions.

18. Charles Darwin, *The Descent of Man and Selection in Relation to Sex* (Princeton, NJ: Princeton University Press, 1981), 12.
19. Henry Spencer Ashbee, *The Metropolis of the Manchus* (London: n.p., 1882), 31.
20. James Dyer Ball, *Things Chinese: Being Notes on Various Subjects Connected with China* (London: Sampson Low, Marston, and Company, Limited, 1892), 154.

CHAPTER **6**

1. Robinson has spoken of the problem of lumping together a variety of women under the rubric "woman traveller," and making general observations. Jane Robinson, introduction to *Unsuitable for Ladies: An Anthology of Women Travellers*, selected by Jane Robinson (Oxford: Oxford University Press, 1994), xii; xvii. My use of the phrase women travelers is neither deprecating — i.e. women who were "curious and plucky enough to think of leaving home but hardly *serious* travellers" (ibid., xvii) — nor does it erase differences between the individual travelogues and travelers.
2. Michel Foucault, *The Archaeology of Knowledge* (London: Tavistock, 1974), 8.
3. Ellen Newbold LaMotte, *Peking Dust* (New York: The Century Co., 1919), viii.
4. Ibid., viii.
5. Mrs. [Emily Lucy French] Daly de Burgh, *An Irishwoman in China* (London: T. Werner Laurie, [1915]), 143.
6. Dorothy Middleton, *Victorian Lady Travelers, With a New Introduction* (Chicago: Academy Chicago Publishers, 1982 [1965], rpt. 1993), 22.
7. Critical studies of the role of Victorian women are numerous. See, for example, Nina Auerbach, *Woman and the Demon: The Life of a Victorian Myth* (Cambridge, MA: Harvard University Press, 1982); Jenni Calder, *Women and Marriage in Victorian Fiction* (London : Thames and Hudson, 1976); Gail Cunningham, *The New Woman and the Victorian Novel;* Foster, *Victorian Women's Fiction: Marriage, Freedom, and the Individual* (London: Croom Helm, 1985); Patricia Stubbs, *Women and Fiction: Feminism and the Novel, 1880–1920* (London: Methuen, 1981). Vicinus writes explicitly: "The most popular alternative to vacuity for the middle classes was charity." Martha Vicinus, "Introduction: The Perfect Victorian Lady," in *Suffer and Be Still: Women in the Victorian Age*, ed. Martha Vicinus (Bloomington: Indiana University Press, 1972), vii–xv; xi.
8. Isabella Bird Bishop, *The Yangtze Valley and Beyond: An Account of China, Chiefly in the Province of Sze Chuan and among the Man-Tze of the Somo Territory* [1899], in ibid., *Collected Travel Writings*, 12 vols. (Bristol: Ganesha Publishing, 1997), 11: 192.
9. Henrietta died in 1880 and John, after only five years of marriage, in 1886. Middleton, 39–40.
10. See Alexandra Allen, *Traveling Ladies* (London: Jupiter, 1980), 247–8; 264. Tinling writes of another Henrietta Bird Hospital in Amritsar. Marion Tinling, *Women into the Unknown: A Sourcebook on Women Explorers and Travelers* (New York: Greenwood Press, 1989), 51.
11. Isabella Bird Bishop, *The Golden Chersonese and the Way Thither* [1883], in ibid., *Collected Travel Writings*. op. cit., vol. 6: 87.
12. Ibid., vol. 6: 88.
13. Ibid., vol. 6: 89.
14. Ibid., vol. 6: 91.

15. E. G. [Elizabeth Georgina] Kemp, *Chinese Mettle* (London: Hodder and Stoughton, 1921), 29.
16. C. F. [Constance Frederica] Gordon Cumming, *Wanderings in China*, 2 vols. (Edinburgh and London: William Blackwood, 1886), I: 168.
17. Ibid., I: 169; I: 167.
18. Ibid., I: 169.
19. Michel Foucault, *The Order of Things: An Archaeology of the Human Sciences* (New York: Vintage, 1994), xv.
20. Mary Gaunt, *A Broken Journey: Wanderings from the Hoang-Ho to the Island of Saghalien and the Upper Reaches of the Amur River* (London: T. Werner Laurie, [1919]), 75.
21. Ibid., 82.
22. [Mary Wortley Montagu], *The Selected Letters of Lady Mary Wortley Montagu*, ed. Robert Halsband (Harmondsworth: Penguin, 1970), 91.
23. Ibid., 91.
24. Cicely Palser Havely, "Bird, Isabella (1831–1904)," *Literature of Travel and Exploration: An Encyclopedia*, 3 vols., ed. Jennifer Speake (New York and London: Fitzroy Dearborn, 2003), I: 102–4; 103.
25. Bird, *Yangtze*, 11: 210.
26. Susan Schoenbauer Thurin, *Victorian Travelers and the Opening of China, 1842–1907* (Athens: Ohio University Press, 1999), 138.
27. Mary Gaunt, *A Woman in China* (London: T. Werner Laurie, 1914), 384.
28. Grace Thompson Seton, *Chinese Lanterns* (New York: Dodd, Mead and Company, 1924), ix.
29. Seton, 191–2. Seton has several interesting encounters with Chinese people, which unfortunately cannot be discussed in this essay. Her role as president of the Connecticut Women's Suffrage League causes Seton to discuss the American women's vote with the Chinese president Li Yuan-Hung, and her experiences in organizing and commanding a woman's mobile relief unit in France during the First World War provide interesting material for discussions with Soong Ching-ling, Dr Sun Yat-sen's wife, also a forethinker in women's rights. For Seton's biography see Lucinda H. MacKethan, "The Setons at Home: Organizing a Family Biography" at http://www.nhc.rtp.nc.us:8080/biography/mackethan. htm (accessed March 21, 2005). "[R]aising the status of women," says Soong Ching-ling to Seton during their first meeting in Shanghai in February 1923, and "enlarging the opportunities for their education and participation in the general work of the country" is the challenge at hand, and she summarizes, hitting a keynote with the suffragist Seton, "a happier womanhood in China is bound up with a successful Republic in China" (Seton, 174).
30. Mrs. Archibald [Alicia] Little, *Intimate China: The Chinese As I Have Seen Them* (London: Hutchinson, 1899), 134–44.
31. Ibid., 145.
32. Ibid., 163.
33. See ibid., 136. "[I]t is very easy to alter the shape of the feet by binding them ever a little tighter, as many a European lady has done with her waist."
34. See Mary Louise Pratt, *Imperial Eyes: Travel Writing and Transculturation* (London and New York: Routledge, 1991).
35. Elizabeth Crump Enders, *Swinging Lanterns* (New York and London: D. Appleton and Co., 1923), 333.

36. Hans-Georg Gadamer, *Truth and Method*, trans. rev. Joel Weinsheimer and Donald G. Marshall, 2nd, revised edition, (New York: Continuum, 1997), 270. My following analysis of travelogues through a hermeneutical theoretical framework is indebted to an article by Zhang Longxi, in which he first invokes Gadamer's as an appropriate model for the self's encounter with otherness. Zhang Longxi, "The Myth of the Other: China in the Eyes of the West," *Critical Enquiry* 15 (Autumn 1988): 108–31; reference to Gadamer, 128–31.

37. Gaunt, *Woman*, 141.

38. Ibid., 141.

39. See Gadamer, 306: "[U]nderstanding is always the fusion of these horizons supposedly existing by themselves."

40. Ibid., 269. Nicholas Clifford employs a similar critical framework in his study of British and American travel writing about China. He understands the travelogue as a dialogic "interplay between the subjective and objective, between observer and observed, between things seen and heard and the ways they were recorded." It is on the second of these pairs, the dialogue between observer and observed, that my essay focuses. See Nicholas Clifford, *'A Truthful Impression of a Country': British and American Travel Writing in China, 1880–1949* (Ann Arbor, MI: University of Michigan Press, 2001), 15.

41. Gaunt, *Woman*, 148.

42. See Gaunt, *Woman*, 25; 370.

43. See Foucault, *Order*, xv.

44. Gaunt, *Woman*, 147.

45. Gaunt, *Woman*, 141 and Gadamer, 388.

46. Cumming arrived in Shanghai from Korea on Christmas Day 1878, but decided to continue by boat straight to Hong Kong. She went, also by boat, to Guangzhou, returned to Hong Kong, and continued by sea up the Chinese coast, going ashore to visit Shantou, Xiamen, Fuzhou, Ningbo, Shanghai, Yantai, and Tianjin.

47. Cumming, II: 159; II: 153; II: 155.

48. Ibid., II: 161–2.

49. Ibid., II: 160.

50. Ibid., II: 160.

51. Ibid., II: 160–1.

52. See the critical assessment of Cumming by Thurin, 84; 93; quotation: Cumming, II: 162. Cumming's text is characterized by attention to more touristic issues, such as accommodation and shopping, which, arguably, indicates a changing sense of the readership for China travel.

53. The reviewer in *The Academy* praises Scidmore's description of the British Legation as one of the finest ever produced. Rev. of *China: the Long-Lived Empire*, by Eliza Ruhamah Scidmore, *The Academy* 59 (July–December 1900): 68–70; particularly 69.

54. Scidmore, "Peking," 864.

55. Both quotations, ibid., 864.

56. Eliza Ruhamah Scidmore, "Rev. of *China: the Long-Lived Empire*," *The Literary World* 10 (August 1, 1900): 147–8; 148.

57. Alicia Little, *Round About My Peking Garden* (London: T. Fisher Unwin, 1905). Emily Daly also lived through the "increasing unrest in China, which terminated in the fantastic madness of the Boxer outbreak" (Daly, 174), but, fearing for her safety, fled with her children and amah first to Japan, and via Vancouver to her native Ireland (ibid., 174–206), only to return to China in March 1901. In constant contact with her husband, who stayed

behind, she reports on the Rebellion from a distance. The most detailed account of the siege of Peking is the account of the American missionary woman Mary Porter Gamewell, who lived and worked in China between 1871 and 1900. Rather unfortunately, she was first caught in the middle of the Sichuan Chongqing riots of July 1886, where Christian missions were forced to close down and, second, an eyewitness of the siege of Beijing, as related in *Mary Porter Gamewell and Her Story of the Siege of Peking*, [ed.] A. H. Tuttle (New York: Eaton and Mains, 1907).

58. Little, *Garden*, 11.
59. Little, *Garden*, 27.
60. Ibid., 31.
61. Alicia Little, *Guide to Peking* (Tientsin: Tientsin Press, 1904), 78.
62. Gaunt, *Woman,* 64 and 70.
63. Ibid., 64.
64. Ibid., 57–8.
65. Ibid., 58–9.
66. Ibid., 59; LaMotte, 167.
67. See Foster, *Across New Worlds*, 170.
68. LaMotte, 49. LaMotte also accuses the Western powers of corruption and, in turn, corrupting the Chinese to keep the country in a state of weakness, which makes it easier to control (LaMotte, 74–5). In 1917, on her visit to Beijing, LaMotte sarcastically comments on what would later become known as the Lao-Tsi-Kai incident when France illegally expanded her territory and imprisoned Chinese soldiers when, at the same time, the Allies were engaged in a "civilising" mission in war-ridden Europe against the barbaric Germans (ibid., 112).
69. Immanuel Kant, *The Critique of Judgement*, trans. with analytical indexes James Creed Meredith (Oxford: Clarendon, 1952), 104–5.
70. See, for example, Sara Suleri, *The Rhetoric of English India* (Chicago: The University of Chicago Press, 1992), 24–48.
71. Alicia Little, "In the Wild West of China," *The Nineteenth Century* 39 (Jan/ June 1896): 58–64; 63.
72. Ibid., 63.
73. See Pratt, 201ff. See Sara Mills for an analysis of the often subversive and paradoxical position of Victorian women's travel writing within the predominant colonial discourse. Sara Mills, *Discourses of Difference: An Analysis of Women's Travel Writing and Colonialism* (London and New York: Routledge, 1991). Little and Kemp, however, provide a much less subversive reiteration of colonial strategies, as explored here.
74. E. G. Kemp, *The Face of China: Travels in East, North, Central and Western China. With Some Account of the New Schools, Universities, Missions, and the Old Religious Sacred Places of Confucianism, Buddhism, and Taoism* (London: Chatto and Windus, 1909), 192.
75. Pratt, 202.
76. Kemp, *Face of China*, 192, emphasis added.
77. Pratt, 204.
78. Kemp, *Face of China*, 193.
79. Little, "Journey," 483.
80. Elizabeth Kendall, *A Wayfarer in China: Impressions of a Trip Across West China and Mongolia* (London: Constable, 1913), 27–8.

81. Kendall, 27.
82. Ibid., 25.
83. Gaunt, *Woman*, 215.
84. Ibid., 212.
85. Yi-Fu Tuan, *Passing Strange and Wonderful: Aesthetics, Nature, and Culture* (Washington, DC: Island Press, 1993), 132. Yi-Fu Tuan's comparative analysis of the Western and the Chinese experiences of art and nature informs the rest of my essay, even if his understanding of Chinese landscape painting as a reflection of the underlying cosmological forces has been revised by art historians. See Tuan, 132ff. For this "older" understanding of Chinese painting see Michael Sullivan, *The Birth of Landscape Painting in China* (Berkeley and Los Angeles: University of California Press, 1962).
86. Gaunt, *Woman*, 218–9.
87. Ibid., 212.
88. Ibid., 219.
89. This process is in art history known as "painting as praxis," and derives from the Qing painter Shitao's reflections on and practice of painting. I am grateful to Yeewan Koon, the University of Hong Kong, for pointing me towards Jonathan Hay's important book, *Shitao: Painting and Modernity in Early Qing China* (Cambridge: Cambridge University Press, 2001), particularly Chapter 9. Shitao's painting philosophy — a viewer being taught to see, and in this communication process with his teacher also undergoing self-analysis, which leads to an enhanced sense of subjectivity — introduces the birth of the subject. Shitao is thus often considered one of the first "modern" painters, who substitutes the older idea of the landscape's embodiment of the cosmos-at-work (see above) with a self-centred cosmology.
90. Hay, 239.
91. Gaunt, *Woman*, 225.
92. Hay, 239; 248.
93. See Hay, 241.
94. Gaunt, *Woman*, 225.
95. See Hay, 247.
96. Gaunt, *Woman*, 226.
97. Foucault, *The Order of Things*, xx. My brackets.
98. Quoted in ibid., xv.

CHAPTER 7

1. A few titles in the enormous literature on altruism include James R. Ozinga, *Altruism* (Westport, CT and London: Praeger, 1999); Shaun Nichols, *Sentimental Rules* (Oxford: Oxford University Press, 2004); Robert F. Haggard, *The Persistence of Victorian Liberalism: The Politics of Social Reform in Britain, 1870-1900* (Westport, CT: Greenwood Press, 2001).
2. Mary Louise Pratt, *Imperial Eyes: Travel Writing and Transculturation* (London and New York: Routledge, 1992).
3. The Gertrude Bell Archieve: *The Letters*, May 5 1903. http://www.gerty.ncl.ac.uk/letters/1610.htm.
4. For a fuller discussion of the Littles' work in China, see my *Victorian Travelers and the Opening of China, 1842–1907* (Athens: Ohio University Press, 1999).

5. Little, *Intimate China* (London: Hutchinson and Co., 1899), 5. Further references to this work are cited in the text as IC.

6. Little, *The Land of the Blue Gown* (London: T. Fisher Unwin, 1902), 43. Further references to this work are cited in the text as BG.

7. Charles Dickens, *Great Expectations*. With an Introduction by David Trotter. Ed. with Notes by Charlotte Mitchell (London: Penguin, 1996), 40.

8. I am grateful to the John Murray publishing house for permission to peruse Bird's letters.

9. In *The Yangtze Valley and Beyond*, Isabella Bird gives an acerbic account of the seeming fruitlessness of the religious work of this frugal missionary. See *The Yangtze Valley and Beyond* (London: John Murray, 1899; reprint, Boston: Beacon Press, 1987), 319.

10. Fan Hong, *Footbinding, Feminism and Freedom: The Liberation of Women's Bodies in Modern China* (London: Frank Cass, 1997) provides a succinct summary of the social significance of the bound foot and a long list of Chinese philosophers and writers who criticized it (50).

11. See Kuang-sheng Liao, *Anti-foreignism and Modernization in China 1860–1980* (Hong Kong: Chinese University Press and New York: St. Martin's Press, 1984), 40–52 and Dorothy Ko, *Cinderella's Sisters: A Revisionist History of Footbinding* (Berkeley: University of California Press, 2005), 14–8 on the role of missionaries, foreign-born activists, and the Chinese themselves in ending footbinding.

12. Little considered her interview with Li Hung-chang (Li Hongzhang), then Viceroy of Guangzhou, a sort of journalistic coup. She devotes eight pages to it (BG 311–9).

13. "Kung Hui-chung" has proved difficult to identify and it is possible he is a misapprehension of Little's.

14. Tim Futing Liao, "Women in the Taiping Movement in Nineteenth-Century China" in *Women and Social Protest*, eds. Guida West and Rhoda Lois Blumberg (New York and Oxford: Oxford University Press, 1990), 120–33. Liao notes that the Red Lantern Girls and Blue Lantern Widows in the Boxer era had unbound feet and were the "first truly liberated women in China" (132). See also Fan Hong, *Footbinding, Feminism and Freedom: The Liberation of Women's Bodies in Modern China*.

### CHAPTER 8

1. Quoted by Mary H. Wilgus, "Sir Claude MacDonald, the Open Door, and British Informal Empire," in *China, 1895–1900* (New York: Garland, 1987), 5.

2. Harry G. Gelber, *Opium, Soldiers and Evangelicals: Britain's 1840–42 War with China and Its Aftermath* (New York: Palgrave Macmillan, 2004), 12.

3. Susan Morgan, *Place Matters: Gendered Geography in Victorian Women's Travel Writings about Southeast Asia* (New Brunswick, NJ: Rutgers University Press, 1996), 145.

4. Quoted by James L. Hevia, *English Lessons: The Pedagogy of Imperialism in Nineteenth-Century China* (Durham, NC: Duke University Press, 2003), 13.

5. Eiko Woodhouse, *The Chinese Hsinhai Revolution: G. E. Morrison and Anglo-Japanese Relations, 1897–1920* (London: Routledge, 2004), 9.

6. Thomas Richards, *The Imperial Archive: Knowledge and the Fantasy of Empire* (London: Verso, 1993), 1.

7. Hevia, 13.

8. Nicholas J. Clifford, *"A Truthful Impression of the Country": British and American Travel Writing in China, 1880–1949* (Ann Arbor: University of Michigan Press, 2001).

9. Susan Schoenbauer Thurin, *Victorian Travelers and the Opening of China, 1842–1907* (Athens: Ohio University Press, 1999), 17.

10. Isabella Bird Bishop, preface to *The Yangtze Valley and Beyond: An Account of Journeys in China, Chiefly in the Province of Sze Chuan and Among the Man-Tze of the Somo Territory.* 1899. *Rpt.* (Boston: Beacon Press, 1987), vii, viii.

11. Gelber, 1.

12. Ibid., 52.

13. Ian Hernon, *The Savage Empire: Forgotten Wars of the 19th Century* (Thrupp, Gloucestershire: Sutton Publishing, 2000), 69.

14. Gelber, 52.

15. Glenn Melancon, *Britain's China Policy and the Opium Crisis: Balancing Drugs, Violence and National Honour, 1833–1840* (Aldershot, Hampshire: Ashgate, 2003), 2, 6, 137–9.

16. Gelber, 157.

17. Ibid., 159.

18. Ranbir Vohra, *China's Path to Modernization: A Historical Review from 1800 to the Present* (Upper Saddle River, NJ: Prentice Hall, 2000), 44–5.

19. Quoted by Wilgus, 17.

20. Ibid.

21. Vohra, 56, 60.

22. Vohra, 80.

23. Yueh-Hung Chen, "Anglo-American Policy toward China." M.A. thesis (Kent State University, 1958), 29.

24. E. W. Edwards, *British Diplomacy and Finance in China, 1895–1914* (Oxford: Clarendon Press, 1987), 19.

25. L. K. Young, *British Policy in China, 1895–1902* (Oxford: Clarendon Press, 1970), 79.

26. Bishop, *The Yangtze Valley*, 11.

27. Thurin, 137.

28. Bishop, *The Yangtze Valley*, 520.

29. Ibid., 3.

30. Ibid., 7.

31. Ibid., 10.

32. Ibid., 10

33. Archibald Colquhoun, *Overland to China* (London: Harper, 1900), 314.

34. Young, 82.

35. Bishop, *The Yangtze Valley*, 11.

36. Ibid., 11.

37. Ibid., 520.

38. Ibid., 528; my italics.

39. Ibid., 527.

40. Ibid., 54.

41. Ibid., 81.

42. Ibid., 87.

43. Ibid., 176.

44. Ibid., 63.

45. Ibid., 62.

46. Ibid., 95.

47. Ibid., 11.

48. Ibid., 11.
49. Lila Marz Harper, *Solitary Travelers: Nineteenth-Century Women's Travel Narratives and the Scientific Vocation* (Cranbury, NJ: Associated University Presses, 2001), 133.
50. Bishop, *The Yangtze Valley*, 534.
51. John Thomson, *Thomson's China: Travels and Adventures of a Nineteenth Century Photographer*, ed. Judith Balmer (Hong Kong: Oxford University Press, 1993), xiii.
52. John Thomson, *Illustrations of China and Its People, A Series of Two Hundred Photographs with Letterpress Descriptive of the Places and People Represented*, 4 vols. Reprinted as *China and its People in Early Photographs*, ed. Janet Lehr (New York: Dover Publications, 1982).
53. John Thomson, *Through China with a Camera* (Westminster: A. Constable and Co., 1898).
54. Pat Barr, *A Curious Life for a Lady: The Story of Isabella Bird, A Remarkable Victorian Traveller* (Garden City, NY: Doubleday and Company, 1970), 271.
55. Nancy Armstrong, *Fiction in the Age of Photography: The Legacy of British Realism* (Cambridge: Harvard University Press, 1999), 106.
56. Isabella Bird Bishop, *Chinese Pictures: Notes on Photographs Made in China* (New York: Charles L. Bowman, 1900), 28.
57. Bishop, *The Yangtze Valley,* 534.

## CHAPTER 9

1. For a critique of the writing of colonial administrators and their representations in fictional discourse, see David Bivona, *British Imperial Literature, 1870–1940: Writing and the Administration of Empire* (Cambridge: Cambridge University Press, 1998).
2. Lugard is best known for his *Political Memoranda* (1919) which was first issued in 1905 as a manual of instructions for his political officials in Northern Nigeria, and *The Dual Mandate* (1922) in which he codified his theory of Indirect Rule. Both works went through a number of editions during Lugard's lifetime and their dissemination helped to consolidate his reputation as Britain's African and pan-imperial expert.
3. Flora to Edward Lugard, July 29, 1907. *Lugard Papers* (MSS. Brit. Emp.), S. 66, 37.
4. "HongKong's New Governor: Scenes of his arrival," *The Hongkong Telegraph*, July 29, 1907.
5. The newspaper refers to Lugard's earlier career as a military campaigner in west Africa before he obtained civilian appointment as the governor of Northern Nigeria prior to his Hong Kong posting.
6. In Hong Kong, Lugard is continuing his transition to civilian life after a career spent largely in campaigns against slavers, and the pacification of indigenous communities resistant to British commercial enterprises and territorial advance in west Africa. The hitherto unexamined relation between Lugard's Hong Kong and African careers is the subject of my "Imperial Globalization and Colonial Transactions: 'African Lugard' and the University of Hong Kong," *Critical Zone 2* (Hong Kong and Nanjing: Hong Kong University Press, 2007). In his letters to his brother, Lugard refers recurrently to his uneasy relationship with his deputy, the colonial secretary, Francis Henry May who, unlike Lugard, had spent most of his career in Hong Kong. He sees May as the leader of colonial — and colonialist — trading interests who not only opposed the university project out of concern about its financial encumbrance, but were also actively hostile to possible competition from Chinese university graduates. The views of the traders were voiced quite openly in

English-language newspapers. See, for example, a series of editorials in *The Hongkong Telegraph* on February 17, March 5, June 5, July 3, 1909, querying the viability of the university as a financial proposition and the possible success of the appeal for funds.

7.  Two further examples, outside of the context of travel: Lugard in a letter to Sir Edward Grey: "Truly I often wonder whether the dream of the Yellow Peril is not likely to come true some day, and the Chinaman by sheer ability and industry will dominate the commerce of the world" (undated, 1909, cited in Margery Perham, *The Life of Frederick Dealtry Lugard Later Lord Lugard of Abinger*, vol. 2 [London: Collins, 1960], 373). Also Flora to Edward: "I think he [Lugard] . . . has found the Chinese very superior to any non-European race with which he has hitherto had to deal" (January 14, 1912, *Lugard Papers*, 37).

8.  Frederick Lugard to Edward Lugard, January 10, 1908, cited in Perham, vol. 2, 372.

9.  Beatrice Webb was a member of the Royal Commission on the Poor Law between 1905 and 1909, and she and Sidney were the authors of the Commission's Minority Report which advocated state intervention in tackling the underlying causes of poverty. They were prolific writers, and published volumes on trade unionism, local government, education, and their own experience and lifework as activists.

10.  The Webbs' Asian journal remained unpublished until the centenary year of the London School of Economics in 1992. All quotations are from *The Webbs in Asia: The 1911–1912 Travel Diary*, ed. George Feaver (London: Macmillan, 1992) to which page references refer.

11.  This observation is in the journal entry for November 6, 1911. The Webbs first arrived at Mukden on October 25.

12.  It is useful to remember that the Webbs' reputation was severely dented by their enthusiastic support of Stalinist Russia in *Soviet Communism: A New Civilization* (London: Victor Gollancz, 1937).

13.  Charles Eliot, *Letters from the Far East* (London: Edward Arnold, 1907). Page references following quotations are from this text.

14.  It is necessary to register the fact that while he was commissioner for the East African Protectorate in 1900–04, Eliot put in place a policy of white supremacy and granted large land concessions to white settlers. See Charles Eliot, *The East Africa Protectorate* (London: Edward Arnold, 1905).

15.  P. J. Cain and A. G. Hopkins, *British Imperialism, 1688–2000* (1993), 2nd ed. (London: Longman, 2002).

CHAPTER **10**

1.  "Harry A. Franck: Wandering in China and Japan," publicity brochure in possession of the University of Iowa. http://sdrcdata.lib.uiowa.edu/libsdrc/details.jsp?id=/franck/2 (accessed March 23, 2005).

2.  John Cutler, review of *Wandering in Northern China*, in the *Boston Evening Transcript*, November 3, 1923, book section, 3; Clarissa Rinaker, review of *Northern China*, in the *Nation*, December 26, 1923, 744; Karlene Kent, review of *Roving Through Southern China*, in the *New York Herald-Tribune*, December 20, 1925, 14.

3.  Harry A. Franck, *A Vagabond Journey Around the World: A Narrative of Personal Experience* (New York: The Century Co., 1911), 457–60.

4.  Harry A. Franck, *Wandering in Northern China* (New York: The Century Co., 1923); *Roving Through Southern China* (New York: The Century Co., 1925); *Glimpses of Japan*

*and Formosa* (New York: D. Appleton-Century Company, 1924); *East of Siam: Ramblings in the Five Divisions of French Indo-China* (New York: The Century Company, 1926).

5. Harry Franck's papers have recently been deposited in the University of Michigan library where, however, they still await organization and indexing.

6. Barry Curtis and Claire Pajaczkowska, " 'Getting There': Travel, Time and Narrative," in *Travellers' Tales: Narratives of Home and Displacement*, eds., George Robertson et al. (London and New York: Routledge 1994), 201.

7. Franck, *Glimpses of Japan and Formosa*, 11, 159–60.

8. R. L. Franck, *I Married a Vagabond: The Story of the Family of the Writing Vagabond* (New York: D. Appleton-Century Co., 1939).

9. Stephen Clark, *Travel Writing and Empire: Postcolonial Theory in Transit* (London: Zed Books, 1999), 20.

10. Franck, *Northern China*, ix, 9.

11. Franck, *Northern China*, 360; *Southern China*, 5.

12. Franck, *Northern China*, vii–viii.

13. Franck, *Southern China*, vii.

14. Sara Mills, *Discourses of Difference: An Analysis of Women's Travel Writing and Colonialism* (London and New York: Routledge, 1991), 69–70.

15. Franck, *Northern China*, 82*ff*; 222; *Southern China*, 14.

16. Franck, *Northern China*, 95–7; *Southern China*, 274; Agnes Smedley, *Battle Hymn of China* (New York: Alfred A. Knopf, 1943), 59.

17. Franck, *Northern China*, 95–7; *Southern China*, 274, 285.

18. Nicholas Clifford, *"A Truthful Impression of the Country": British and American Travel Writing in China, 1880–1949* (Ann Arbor: University of Michigan Press, 2001), Chapter IV.

19. James Buzard, *The Beaten Track: European Tourism, Literature, and the Ways to Culture, 1800–1918* (London: Oxford University Press, 1993), *passim*; John Pemble, *The Mediterranean Passion: Victorians and Edwardians in the South* (Oxford and New York: Oxford University Press, 1998), 69–71, 260.

20. Bertrand Russell, *The Problem of China* (London: G. Allen Unwin, 1922), 75.

21. Franck, *Northern China*, 105–6; *Southern China*, 1.

22. Isabella L. Bird, *The Golden Chersonese And the Way Thither* [1883] (Reprint, Kuala Lumpur: Oxford University Press, 1967), 30, 92; Elizabeth Kendall, *A Wayfarer in China: Impressions of a Trip across West China and Mongolia* (Boston and New York: Houghton Mifflin, 1913), viii.

23. Helen Carr, "Modernism and Travel," in *The Cambridge Companion to Travel Writing*, eds. Peter Hulme and Tim Youngs (Cambridge: Cambridge University Press, 2002), 70–86.

24. See, for example, Roderick Nash, *The Nervous Generation: American Thought, 1970–1930* (Chicago: Rand McNally and Co., 1970); David J. Goldberg, *Discontented America: the United States in the 1920s* (Baltimore: Johns Hopkins University Press, 1999); Lynn Dumenil, *The Modern Temper: American Culture and Society in the 1920s* (New York: Hill and Wang, 1995).

25. Franck, *Northern China*, 82*ff*, 164, 398–9; *Southern China*, 169, 591.

26. Franck, *Southern China*, ix, 146, 382; *Northern China*, 449.

27. Mary Louise Pratt, *Imperial Eyes: Travel Writing and Transculturation* (London and New York: Routledge, 1992), 64, 75; Mills, *Discourses*, 73–5.

28. Peter Fleming, *One's Company: a Journey to China* (New York: Charles Scribners' Sons, 1934); Harold Speakman, *Beyond Shanghai* (New York: Abingdon Press, 1922); Edgar Snow, *Red Star Over China* (New York: Random House, 1938); Graham Peck, *Two Kinds of Time* (Boston: Houghton Mifflin, 1950). For a treatment of Snow as travel writer, see *"Truthful Impression"*, 133–42; Clifford, "White China, Red China: Lighting out for the Territory with Edgar Snow, *New England Review*, xviii, no. 2 (Spring, 1997), 103–11.

29. Franck, *Northern China*, 244.

30. Franck, *Northern China*, 235, 165; *Southern China*, 31–2, 279; John Dewey and Alice Chipman Dewey, ed. Evelyn Dewey, *Letters from China and Japan* (New York: E. P. Dutton, 1920), 183.

31. Franck, *Northern China*, 286, 401.

32. Franck, *Southern China*, 30, 129; *Northern China*, 141.

33. Clifford, *"Truthful Impression"*, 73–5; Russell, *Problem of China*, 167.

34. Franck, *Southern China*, 623–4; *Northern China*, 372.

35. J. R. Wallace, review of *Southern China*, *The Independent* (Boston, October 31, 1925), 507, 512. "Carping Through Southern China" is the title of the review.

36. Japanese Government Railways, *Guide to China With Land and Sea Routes Between the American and European Continents*, 2nd ed. (Tokyo: n.p., 1924).

37. *Saturday Review of Literature* (January 16, 1926), 501.

38. Franck, *Northern China*, 201.

39. Franck, *Vagabond Journey*, 457.

40. Franck, *Southern China*, 292.

41. Franck, *Northern China*, 261.

42. Franck, *Southern China*, 266–8, 274, 294.

43. "East and West Clash Anew at Shanghai," *New York Times,* June 14, 1925, sec. xx, p. 5; "Harry A. Franck: Wandering in China and Japan" (publicity brochure).

44. Franck, *Southern China*, 51.

45. Pemble, *Mediterranean Passion*, 274.

46. Joseph Warren Beach, "The Naive Style," *American Speech* I (August 1926): 576–83.

47. Harry A. Franck, *East of Siam: Ramblings in the Five Divisions of French Indo-China* (New York: The Century Company, 1926), viii.

CHAPTER **11**

1. W. H. Auden and Christopher Isherwood, *Journey to a War* (London: Faber and Faber, 1939), 20. Subsequent references to *Journey* are in parenthesis in the text.

2. Valentine Cunningham, *British Writers of the Thirties* (Oxford: Oxford University Press, 1988), 349.

3. Samuel Hynes, *The Auden Generation: Literature and Politics in England in the 1930s* (London: Faber and Faber, 1976), 229.

4. Martha Gellhorn, *The Face of War* (London: Granta Books, 1988), 15.

5. Hynes, 341.

6. Evelyn Waugh, "Spectator," March 24, 1939, in *W. H. Auden: The Critical Heritage,* ed. John Haffenden (New York and London: Routledge and Kegan Paul, 1983), 289–91.

7. Randall Swingler, "Daily Worker," March 29, 1939, in *W. H. Auden: The Critical Heritage,* 291.

8.  Paul Fussell, *Abroad* (New York and Oxford: Oxford University Press, 1980), 219–20.
9.  Cunningham, 391.
10. See Douglas Kerr, "*Journey to a War*: 'A Test for Men from Europe'," in *W. H. Auden: A Legacy*, ed. David Garrett Izzo (West Cornwall, CT: Locust Hill Press, 2002), 275–96; Tim Youngs, "Auden's Travel Writings," in *The Cambridge Companion to W. H. Auden,* ed. Stan Smith (Cambridge: Cambridge University Press, 2004), 68–81; Maureen Moynagh, "Revolutionary Drag in Auden and Isherwood's *Journey to a War*," *Studies in Travel Literature* 8 (2004): 125–48.
11. "Evelyn Waugh on a Pantomime Appearance, Mr. Isherwood and Friend," March 24, 1939, in *W. H. Auden: The Critical Heritage*, 289.
12. Youngs, 71.
13. Christopher Isherwood, *Christopher and His Kind* (London: Methuen, 1976), 289.
14. In his diary for August 31, 1939, he wrote: "Nearly every day I force myself to get on with the writing of my part of our book about the trip to China," Christopher Isherwood, *Down There on a Visit* (London: New Signet Modern Classics, 1974), 133.
15. Joanna Bourke, *The Second World War: A People's History* (Oxford: Oxford University Press, 2001), 3–4.
16. John K. Fairbank and Albert Feuerwerker, eds., *The Cambridge History of China, Volume 13: Republican China 1912–1949, Part 2* (Cambridge: Cambridge University Press, 1986), 547.
17. I quote from the original 1939 text on the grounds that the heavily revised 1973 edition of *Journey to a War* offers a re-ordered text that diminishes and dilutes the power of the original.
18. W. H. Auden and Louis MacNeice, *Letters from Iceland* (London: Faber and Faber, 1937), 227.
19. Kerr, 278.
20. John Fuller, *W. H. Auden: A Commentary* (London: Faber and Faber, 1998), 235.
21. See Moynagh, 125–48.
22. Kerr emphasizes the importance of "the distinction of the medium, between poetry and prose" rather than the authors, arguing that "Isherwood drew on Auden's (prose) travel notes as well as his own, to write up the 'Travel Diary,' and Auden for his part was famously ready to incorporate his friends' ideas and even phrases into his verse," 292.
23. W. H. Auden and Christopher Isherwood, *Journey to a War* (London: Faber and Faber, rev. ed., 1973), 8.
24. William Empson to John Hayward, May 23, 1938, *William Empson: Volume One: Among the Mandarins,* ed. John Haffenden (Oxford: Oxford University Press, 2005), 483.
25. In his introductory "Second Thoughts" to the revised edition Auden records being "shocked to discover how carelessly" he had written the sonnets originally, and that he had "never revised earlier work quite so extensively as I have revised these poems," *Journey to a War* (rev. ed., 1973), 7.
26. This makes a striking contrast to Robert Capa's heroic photo (taken from below) of the "Chinese Defender" that appeared on the cover of *Life* in May 1938.
27. Geoffrey Grigson reviewing it, thought Isherwood's prose "rather small beside the moral weight and tenderness" of Auden's poems, but thought "it is a good thing that the poems have come out in this way with photographs, a map and a war story," since it would be "read by people who might not have bought them in a separate book," in *W. H. Auden: The Critical Heritage* (1983), 296.

28. *The Cambridge History of China, Volume 13: Republican China 1912–1949, Part 2,* 552.
29. Kerr, 294.
30. Empson to John Hayward, May 23, 1939, *William Empson: Volume 1: Among the Mandarins,* ed. John Haffenden (Oxford: Oxford University Press, 2005), 483.
31. William Empson, *The Complete Poems,* ed. John Haffenden (London: Penguin, 2000), 91–8.
32. See Edward Mendelson, *Early Auden* (London: Faber and Faber, 1981), 360–1.
33. Christopher Isherwood, *Diaries: Volume One: 1939–1960,* ed. Katherine Bucknell (London: Methuen, 1996), 6.
34. Ibid.

CHAPTER **12**

1. Janice R. MacKinnon and Stephen R. MacKinnon, *Agnes Smedley: The Life and Times of an American Radical* (Berkeley: University of California Press, 1988), 338.
2. Ruth Price, *The Lives of Agnes Smedley* (Oxford: Oxford University Press, 2005). The German connection arises from Smedley's alignment with Indian nationalists in the U. S. A. receiving money from the German government to foment revolution in British India.
3. Agnes Smedley, *Daughter of Earth,* 1929, Afterword by Paul Lauter (New York: Feminist Press, 1973). Hereafter *DE*, with reference to page number in the text.
4. Wilfred Owen, *The Complete Poems and Fragments*, ed. Jon Stallworthy (London: Chatto and Windus, Hogarth Press, and Oxford University Press, 1983), 535.
5. T. S. Eliot, *The Complete Poems and Plays of T. S. Eliot* (London: Faber, 1969), 125.
6. Agnes Smedley, *Battle Hymn of China* (London: Gollancz, 1944), 10. Hereafter *BHC*.
7. "And maybe the fever shall have a cure, the true journey an end / Where hearts meet and are really true . . ." Auden wrote the poem on his own journey to China in 1938. W. H. Auden and Christopher Isherwood, *Journey to a War* (London: Faber and Faber, 1939), 17–8.
8. Linked to the moral rectitude of the revolution was the sexual restraint of the Red Army, which she was to describe as "largely an army of sexual ascetics." Agnes Smedley, *China Fights Back: An American Woman with the Eighth Route Army*, Left Book Club Edition (London: Gollancz, 1938), 34. Hereafter *CFB*.
9. Earlier in the year her friend Edgar Snow had visited the revolutionary base in northern Shaanxi where the Red Army regrouped after the Long March. His extensive interviews with Mao Zedong form the core of his remarkable *Red Star over China* (London: Gollancz, 1937), the first book to introduce the Chinese Communists to a Western readership. It was reissued by Gollancz the following year as a Left Book Club edition.
10. Auden and Isherwood, 50. Auden and Isherwood met Smedley in Hankou. "It is impossible not to like and respect her, so grim and sour and passionate," Isherwood reported. "[S]he sits before the fire, huddled together, as if all the suffering, all the injustice of the world were torturing her bones like rheumatism" (60).
11. Letter quoted in MacKinnon, 209. The house in Shaw comes under aerial bombardment in the last act of the play. "Did you hear the explosions?" says one character. "And the sound in the sky: it's splendid: it's like an orchestra: it's like Beethoven." George Bernard Shaw, *Heartbreak House*, 1919 (Harmondsworth: Penguin, 2000), 158. Smedley may not have seen a performance of *Heartbreak House* but she was aware of Shaw as a socialist writer.
12. MacKinnon, 212.

13. "The Battle Hymn of the Republic" is quoted in *BHC*, 143.
14. Though she was uncomfortable in the role of foreign expert thrust upon her, on an earlier occasion Smedley found herself explaining that the earth was round, what a piano was, and why the American workers did not have a Red Army (*BHC*, 232–3). Visitors were expected to perform as well as to gather information. Edgar Snow recalled entertaining the troops in a place called Pao An with a rendering of the vaudeville song "The Man on the Flying Trapeze" (*Red Star over China*, 117).
15. "Looking Back on the Spanish War" in *The Complete Works of George Orwell*, ed. Peter Davison (London: Secker and Warburg, 1998), Vol. 13, 497–511. Orwell records saying to Arthur Koestler, "History stopped in 1936" (503). He details the fantastically differing "facts" reported as true by adherents of both sides, and concludes: "This kind of thing is frightening to me, because it often gives me the feeling that the very concept of objective truth is fading out of the world" (504). The essay, probably written in 1942, is of the greatest importance to students of the historiography of ideological wars.
16. Smedley's account is more partisan than that of Edgar Snow in his highly influential *Red Star over China* (1937). It would be equally interesting to investigate the rhetoric of negative accounts of the revolution and its leadership, such as in the unremittingly hostile narrative of Jung Chang and Jon Halliday, *Mao: The Untold Story* (London: Cape, 2005).
17. On this journey she was accompanied by five bearers, two bodyguards and a boy, a translator, and a spare horse.
18. In Hong Kong, "Ernest Hemingway blew in, offering to stand everybody to drinks with the lucre won in his last literary victory, and entertaining us with tales of far-off places" (*CFB*, 361). Smedley's scorn for literary travel writers appears to outflank the usual scorn of the literary travel writer for tourists. See Helen Carr, "Modernism and Travel (1880–1940)," in *The Cambridge Companion to Travel Writing*, eds. Peter Hulme and Tim Youngs (Cambridge: Cambridge University Press, 2002), 70–86.
19. Agnes Smedley, *Chinese Destinies: Sketches of Present-Day China* (London: Hurst and Blackett, 1934), 121. Hereafter *CD*. Those executed had been identified as police officers, police spies, and officers and members of the Kuomintang. The executioners had no rifles so the condemned men were killed with long knives. "They should die like dogs, for they had betrayed the workers" (*CD*, 121).
20. There is a similar theme, but a quite different politics of form, in Brecht's *The Measures Taken*, written in 1929/1930. There, the sacrifice of an individual to the cause of the revolution in China is presented in Brecht's version of epic theatre, a form that foregrounds its own artifice and is supposed to invite the audience to study and debate the action. Bertolt Brecht, *The Measures Taken and Other Lehrstücke* (London: Eyre Methuen, 1977), 7–34.
21. Agnes Smedley, *China's Red Army Marches* (London: Lawrence and Wishart, 1936), 91–2.
22. It is not too anachronistic to trace this formula back as far as Bunyan's *Grace Abounding* and the Puritan seedbed of English realism.
23. See Roland Barthes, *Mythologies*, 1957, trans. Annette Lavers (London: Paladin, 1973), 117–74. It may seem perverse to suggest that Smedley's representation of the Red Army is a Barthesian myth, when Barthes defined myth as "depoliticized speech" (155), and wanted to exempt revolutionary language from it: "revolutionary language proper cannot be mythical" (159). But her naturalization of the revolution does depoliticize it insofar as it is represented as organic, inevitable, and unarguable.

24.  Smedley several times writes ruefully of a Chinese subjectivity which must remain hidden to her. "I can never know fully the meaning, the essence of the Chinese struggle for liberation which lies embedded in the hearts of these workers and peasants . . . And I hungered for the spark of vision that would enable me to see into their minds and hearts and picture their convictions about the great struggle for which they give more than their lives" (*CFB*, 123).

# Bibliography

## China Travel Writings

Auden, W. H. and Christopher Isherwood. *Journey to a War*. London: Faber, 1939. Rev. ed. 1973.

Ball, James Dyer. *Things Chinese: Being Notes on Various Subjects Connected with China*. London: Sampson Low, Marston, 1892.

"Bird's Nest Soup." *The Cornhill Magazine* 8 (January 1887): 80.

Bishop, Isabella Bird. *Chinese Pictures: Notes on Photographs Made in China*. London: Cassell, 1900. Also published in New York: Bowman, 1900.

——. *Collected Travel Writings*. 12 vols. Bristol: Ganesha, 1997.

——. *The Golden Chersonese and the Way Thither*. N.p. [1883.] Reprint, Kuala Lumpur: Oxford University Press, 1967.

——. "A Journey in Western Sze-Chuan." *The Geographical Journal* 10, no. 1 (July 1897): 19–50.

——. *The Yangtze Valley and Beyond: An Account of Journeys in China, Chiefly in the Province of Sze Chuan and among the Man-Tze of the Somo Territory*. London: John Murray, 1899. Reprint, under the title *The Yangtze Valley and Beyond: An Account of China, Chiefly in the Province of Sze Chuan and among the Man-Tze of the Somo Territory*. Boston: Beacon Press, 1987.

Bowring, John. *The Political and Commercial Importance of Peace: A Lecture Delivered in the Hall of Commerce London*. London: Peace Society, n.y. [1846?].

——. "Sir John Bowring and the Arrow War in China." In *Bulletin of the John Rylands Library* 32, no. 2 (March 1961): 299.

"Chinese Cookery." Reprinted from *The Pall Mall Gazette* in *Littells Living Age*, 5th ser. 144.1857 (January 17, 1880): 190.

"Chinese Cookery." *Temple Bar* 93 (1891): 112.

Colquhoun, Archibald R. *Overland to China*. London: Harper, 1900.

Cooke, George Wingrove. *China and Lower Bengal: Being "The Times" Correspondence from China in the Years 1857–58*. London: Routledge, Warne, and Routledge, 1861.

Crow, Carl. *The Travelers' Handbook for China*. Shanghai: Hwa-Mei Book Concern, 1913.

Cumming, Constance Frederica Gordon. *Wanderings in China*. 2 vols. Edinburgh and London: Blackwood, 1886.

Davis, John Francis. *The Chinese: A General Description of the Empire and its Inhabitants: With the History of Foreign Intercourse Down to the Events which Produced the Dissolution of 1857*. London: Murray, 1857.

——. *Sketches of China: Partly During an Inland Journey of Four Months, Between Peking, Nanking, and Canton; With Notices and Observations Relative to the Present War*. Vol. 1. N.p.: Knight, 1841.

De Burgh, Daly [Mrs. Emily Lucy French]. *An Irishwoman in China*. London: Laurie, n.y. [1915].

Denby, Jay. *Letters of a Shanghai Griffin to His Father and Other Exaggerations*. Shanghai: The China Printing Company, 1910.

Dewey, John and Alice Chipman Dewey. *Letters from China and Japan*. Edited by Evelyn Dewey. New York: Dutton, 1920.

Distant, W. L. "Eastern Coolie Labour." *Journal of the Anthropological Institute* 3 (1874): 139–44.

Dudgeon, John. "Diet, Dress, and Dwellings of the Chinese in Relation to Health." In *The Health Exhibition Literature*. London: Executive Council of the International Health Exhibition, and for the Council of the Society of Arts/William Clowes and Sons, 1884.

——. *Notes by the Way: Taken during a Journey by the So-called Overland Route to China*. London: Williams and Strahan, 1866.

"East and West Clash Anew at Shanghai," *New York Times,* June 14, 1925.

"The Edible Birds' Nests of the Eastern Islands." *The Penny Magazine of the Society for the Diffusion of Useful Knowledge* 10 (1841): 368.

Edkins, Jane R. *Chinese Scenes and People*. London: Nisbet, 1863.

Elgin, Earl. *Letters and Journals of James, Eighth Earl of Elgin*. Edited by Theodore Walrond. London: Murray, 1872.

Eliot, Charles. *Letters from the Far East*. London: Arnold, 1907.

Empson, William. *The Complete Poems*. Edited by John Haffenden. London: Penguin, 2000.

Enders, Elizabeth Crump. *Swinging Lanterns*. New York and London: Appleton, 1923.

Fleming, Peter. *One's Company: A Journey to China*. New York: Scribner, 1934.

Fortune, Robert. *Three Years' Wandering in the Northern Provinces of China, Including a Visit to the Tea, Silk and Cotton Countries*. London: Murray, 1847.

Franck, Harry A. *East of Siam: Ramblings in the Five Divisions of French Indo-China.* New York: Century, 1926.

——. *Glimpses of Japan and Formosa.* New York: Appleton-Century, 1924.

——. *Roving Through Southern China.* New York: Century, 1925.

——. *A Vagabond Journey Around the World: A Narrative of Personal Experience.* New York: Century, 1911.

——. *Wandering in Northern China.* New York: Century, 1923.

Gamewell, May. Edited by A. H. Tuttle. *Mary Porter Gamewell and Her Story of the Siege of Peking.* New York: Eaton and Mains, 1907.

Gaunt, Mary. *A Broken Journey: Wanderings from the Hoang-Ho to the Island of Saghalien and the Upper Reaches of the Amur River.* London: Laurie, n.y. [1919?].

——. *A Woman in China.* London: Laurie, 1914.

Gützlaff, Karl. *Journal of Three Voyages Along the Coast of China in 1831, 1832, and 1833.* London: Westley and Davis, 1834.

"Hong Kong's New Governor: Scenes of his arrival." *The Hong Kong Telegraph*, July 29, 1907.

Huc, Evariste Regis. *Travels in Tartary, Thibet, and China in the Years 1844, 1845, and 1846.* Translated by William Hazlitt. London: Nelson, 1856.

Japanese Government Railways. *Guide to China With Land and Sea Routes Between the American and European Continents.* 2nd ed. Tokyo: n.p., 1924.

Kemp, Elizabeth Georgina. *Chinese Mettle.* London: Hodder and Stoughton, 1921.

——. *The Face of China: Travels in East, North, Central and Western China. With some Account of the New Schools, Universities, Missions, and the Old Religious Sacred Places of Confucianism, Buddhism, and Taoism.* London: Chatto and Windus, 1909.

Kendall, Elizabeth. *A Wayfarer in China: Impressions of a Trip Across West China and Mongolia.* London: Constable, 1913. Also published in Boston: Houghton Mifflin, 1913.

LaMotte, Ellen Newbold. *Peking Dust.* New York: Century, 1919.

Little, Archibald John. *Mount Omi and Beyond.* London: Heinemann, 1901.

——. *Through the Yang-tse Gorges or, Trade and Travel in Western China.* London: Sampson, Low, Marston, Searle and Rivington, 1888. Reprint, London: Sampson Low, Marston, 1898.

Little, Mrs Archibald [Alicia]. *Guide to Peking.* Tientsin: Tientsin, 1904.

——. "In the Wild West of China." *The Nineteenth Century* 39 (January/June 1896): 58–64.

——. *Intimate China: The Chinese As I Have Seen Them.* London: Hutchinson, 1899.

——. *The Land of the Blue Gown.* London: Fisher Unwin, 1902.

——. *Round About My Peking Garden.* London: Fisher Unwin, 1905.

Lugard, Frederick. *Lugard Papers.* MSS. Brit. Emp. S.66.

Macartney, George Earl. *An Embassy to China: Lord Macartney's Journal 1793–1794.* Edited by J. L. Cranmer-Byng. London: Longmans, 1962.

Medhurst, W. H. *China Its State and Prospects, with especial reference to the spread of the gospel; containing allusions to the antiquity, extent, population, civilization, literature and religion of the Chinese*. London: Snow, 1838.

——. *Chinese Dialogues*. Shanghai: n.p., 1861.

——. *A Glance at the Interior of China Obtained During a Journey to the Silk and Green Tea Countries*. London: Snow, 1850.

——. Letter to LMS Directors. June 30, 1832. In *Oriental and Indian Collections*. British Library.

——. Letter to [recipient unknown]. September 6, 1855. In *CWM-LMS Archives, School of Oriental and African Studies*. Central China Correspondence.

——. Letter to Rev. Dr. Tidman. October 11, 1854. In *CWM-LMS Archives, School of Oriental and African Studies*. Central China Correspondence.

Milne, William C. *Life in China*. London: Routledge, 1858.

Peck, Graham. *Two Kinds of Time*. Boston: Houghton Mifflin, 1950.

Russell, Bertrand. *The Problem of China*. London: Allen Unwin, 1922.

Seton, Grace Thompson. *Chinese Lanterns*. New York: Dodd, Mead, 1924.

Smedley, Agnes. *Battle Hymn of China*. New York: Alfred A. Knopf, 1943. Also published in London: Gollancz, 1944.

——. *China Fights Back: An American Woman with the Eighth Route Army*. Left Book Club Edition. London: Gollancz, 1938.

——. *China's Red Army Marches*. London: Lawrence and Wishart, 1936.

——. *Chinese Destinies: Sketches of Present-Day China*. London: Hurst and Blackett, 1934.

Smith, Arthur H. *Chinese Characteristics*. London: Kegan Paul, Trench, Trübner, 1892.

Snow, Edgar. *Red Star over China*. London: Gollancz, 1937. Also published in New York: Random, 1938.

Speakman, Harold. *Beyond Shanghai*. New York: Abingdon Press, 1922.

Thomson, G. [*sic*]. "Notes of Cambodia and Its Races." *Transactions of the Ethnological Society of London*. N.s. 6. N.p., 1869.

Thomson, John. *Illustrations of China and Its People, A Series of Two Hundred Photographs with Letterpress Descriptive of the Places and People Represented*. 4 vols. Reprint, under the title *China and its People in Early Photographs*, Chicago: University of Chicago Press, 1997. Also published in London: Sampson Low, Marston, Low and Searle, 1973, and (edited by Janet Lehr) New York: Dover Publications, 1982.

——. "Notes of a Journey to Southern Formosa." *Journal of the Royal Geographical Society* 43 (1873): 97.

——. *Straits of Malacca, Indo-China, and China, or, Ten Years' Travels, Adventures, and Residence Abroad*. New York: Harper, 1875.

——. *Thomson's China: Travels and Adventures of a Nineteenth Century Photographer*. Edited by Judith Balmer. Hong Kong: Oxford University Press, 1993.

——. *Through China with a Camera*. Westminster: Constable, 1898.

[Webb, Beatrice and Sidney Webb.] *The Webbs in Asia: The 1911–1912 Travel Diary*. Edited by George Feaver. London: Macmillan, 1992.

Williamson, Alexander. *Journeys in North China, Manchuria, and Eastern Mongolia, with some account of Corea*. London: Smith, Elder, 1870.

Williamson, Isabelle. *Old Highways in China*. London: The Religious Tract Society, 1884.


## Other Works Discussed


Allen, Alexandra. *Traveling Ladies*. London: Jupiter, 1980.

Anonymous. "Miscegenation." *Anthropological Review* 2 (1864): 116–21.

Arendt, Hannah. *The Origins of Totalitarianism*. San Diego, New York, London: Harcourt Brace Jovanovich, 1973.

Armstrong, Nancy. *Fiction in the Age of Photography: The Legacy of British Realism*. Cambridge, MA: Harvard University Press, 1999.

Ashbee, Henry Spencer. *The Metropolis of the Manchus*. London: n.p., 1882.

Auden, W. H. *The Dyer's Hand and Other Essays*. London: Faber, 1962.

Auden, W. H. and Louis MacNeice. *Letters from Iceland*. London: Faber, 1937.

Auerbach, Nina. *Woman and the Demon: The Life of a Victorian Myth.* Cambridge, MA: Harvard University Press, 1982.

Austen, Jane. *The Complete Novels*. Oxford: Oxford University Press, 1994.

Bach, Evelyn. "A Traveller in Skirts: Quest and Conquest in the Travel Narratives of Isabella Bird Bishop." *Canadian Review of Comparative Literature* 22, no. 3–4 (September/December 1995): 587–600.

Balfour, Henry. "Presidential Address." *Journal of the Anthropological Institute* 34 (1908): 13.

Barr, Pat. *A Curious Life for a Lady: The Story of Isabella Bird, A Remarkable Victorian Traveller*. Garden City, NY: Doubleday, 1970.

Barthes, Roland. *Mythologies*, 1957. Translated by Annette Lavers. London: Paladin, 1973.

Beach, Joseph Warren. "The Naive Style." *American Speech* I (August 1926): 576–83.

Bell, Gertrude. "To her Father." *Letters*, May 5, 1903. http://www.gerty.ncl.ac.uk/letters/1610.htm

Bell, Morag and Cheryl McEwan. "The Admission of Women Fellows to the Royal Geographic Society, 1892–1914; The Controversy and the Outcome." *The Geographical Journal* 62, no. 3 (November 1996): 295–312.

Bishop, Peter. *The Myth of Shangri-la: Tibet, Travel Writing and the Western Creation of Sacred Landscape*. Berkeley: University of California Press, 1989.

Bivona, David. *British Imperial Literature 1870–1940: Writing and the Administration of Empire*. Cambridge: Cambridge University Press, 1998.

Blake, Andrew. "Foreign Devils and Moral Panics: Britain, Asia and the Opium Trade." In *The Expansion of England: Race, Ethnicity and Cultural History*. Edited by Bill Schwarz. London: Routledge, 1996.

Bourke, Joanna. *The Second World War: A People's History*. Oxford: Oxford University Press, 2001.

Bowring, John. *The Influence of Knowledge on Domestic and Social Happiness*. London: Chapman, n.y. [1840?].

Bridges, Roy. "Exploration and travel outside Europe (1720–1914)." In *The Cambridge Companion to Travel Writing*. Edited by Peter Hulme and Tim Youngs. Cambridge: Cambridge University Press, 2002.

Broomhall, A. J. *Hudson Taylor and China's Open Century*. 7 vols. Sevenoaks, Kent: Hodder and Stoughton and the Overseas Missionary Fellowship, 1981.

Burton, David. *The Raj at Table: A Culinary History of the British in India*. London: Faber, 1993.

Buruma, Ian and Avishai Margalit. *Occidentalism: The West in the Eyes of its Enemies*. New York: Penguin, 2004.

Butor, Michel. "Travel and Writing." In *Temperamental Journeys: Essays on the Modern Literature of Travel*. Edited by Michael Kowalewski. Athens, GA: University of Georgia Press, 1992.

Buzard, James. *The Beaten Track: European Tourism, Literature, and the Ways to Culture, 1800–1918*. Oxford and London: Oxford University Press, 1993.

———. "The Grand Tour and after (1660–1840)." In *The Cambridge Companion to Travel Writing*. Edited by Peter Hulme and Tim Youngs. Cambridge: Cambridge University Press, 2002: 37–52.

Byron, George Gordon. "The Curse of Minerva." *Poetical Works*. Edited by Frederick Page, new edition corrected by John Jump. London: Oxford University Press, 1970: 142–5.

Cain, P. J. and A. G. Hopkins. *British Imperialism, 1688–2000* (1993). 2nd ed. London: Longman, 2002.

Calder, Jenni. *Women and Marriage in Victorian Fiction*. London: Thames and Hudson, 1976.

Cameron, Nigel. *Barbarians and Mandarins: Thirteen Centuries of Western Travellers in China*. New York: Walker/Weatherhill, 1970.

Campbell, Mary Baine. "Travel Writing and Its Theory." In *The Cambridge Companion to Travel Writing*. Edited by Peter Hulme and Tim Youngs. Cambridge: Cambridge University Press, 2002: 261–78.

Carr, Helen. "Modernism and Travel (1880–1940)." In *The Cambridge Companion to Travel Writing*. Edited by Peter Hulme and Tim Youngs. Cambridge: Cambridge University Press, 2002.

Chang, Elizabeth H. " 'Eyes of the Proper Almond Shape': Blue and White China in the British Imaginary 1823–1883." *19th-Century Studies* 19 (2005): 17–34.

Chang, Jung and Jon Halliday. *Mao: The Untold Story*. London: Cape, 2005.

Checkland, Sydney. *The Elgins, 1766–1917: A Tale of Aristocrats, Proconsuls and Their Wives*. Aberdeen: Aberdeen University Press, 1988.

Chen, Xiaomei. *Occidentalism: A Theory of Counter-Discourse in Post-Mao China*. Oxford: Oxford University Press, 1995.

Chen, Yueh-Hung. "Anglo-American Policy toward China." M.A. thesis. Kent State University, 1958.

Clark, Stephen. *Travel Writing and Empire: Postcolonial Theory in Transit*. London: Zed, 1999.

Clifford, Nicholas. *"A Truthful Impression of the Country": British and American Travel Writing in China, 1880–1949*. Ann Arbor: University of Michigan Press, 2001.

———. "White China, Red China: Lighting Out for the Territory with Edgar Snow." *New England Review* xviii, no. 2 (Spring, 1997): 103–11.

Cobden, Richard. "Letter to John Bowring." August 28, 1859. Special Collections, the University of Hong Kong Library.

Cooper, Michael. "Unbeaten Tracks in Japan." *Monumenta Nipponica* 28, no. 2 (Summer, 1973): 246–8.

Cowling, Maurice. *Mill and Liberalism*. Cambridge: Cambridge University Press, 1990.

Crawfurd, John. *History of the Indian Archipelago: Containing an Account of the Manners, Arts, Languages, Religions, Institutions, and Commerce of Its Inhabitants*. Edinburgh: Constable, 1820.

Crew, Ernest. "The Golden Chersonese and the Way Thither; The Soul of Malaya; The Making of Modern Malaysia." *Modern Asia Studies* 4, no. 1 (1970): 93–4.

Cunningham, Gail. *The New Woman and the Victorian Novel*. London: Macmillan, 1978.

Cunningham, Valentine. *British Writers of the Thirties*. Oxford: Oxford University Press 1988.

Curtis, Barry and Claire Pajaczkowska. " 'Getting There': Travel, Time and Narrative." In *Travellers' Tales: Narratives of Home and Displacement*. Edited by George Robertson et al. London and New York: Routledge, 1994.

Cutler, John. "Review of *Wandering in Northern China* by Harry A. Frank." *Boston Evening Transcript*, November 3, 1923.

Dai, Yifeng. "Food Culture and Overseas Trade: The Trepang Trade between China and Southeast Asia during the Qing Dynasty." In *The Globalization of Chinese Food*. Edited by David Y. H. Wu and Sidney C. H. Cheung. London: Curzon, 2002.

Dawson, W. H. *Richard Cobden and Foreign Policy: A Critical Exposition, with Special Reference to Our Day and Its Problems*. New York: Frank-Maurice, 1927.

Dickens, Charles. *Little Dorrit*. Oxford: Oxford University Press, 1989.

Domosh, Mona. "Toward a Feminist Historiography of Geography." *Transactions of the Institute of British Geographers,* New ser. 16, no. 1 (1991): 95–104.

Dumenil, Lynn. *The Modern Temper: American Culture and Society in the 1920s*. New York: Hill and Wang, 1995.

Duncan, James and Derek Gregory. Introduction to *Writes of Passage: Reading Travel Writing*. Edited by James Duncan and Derek Gregory. London: Routledge, 1999: 1–13.

Dunch, Ryan. "Beyond Cultural Imperialism: Cultural Theory, Christian Missions, and Global Modernity." *History and Theory* 41 (October 2002): 301–25.

"Editorials." *The Hongkong Telegraph*, February 17–July 3, 1909.

Edwards, E. W. *British Diplomacy and Finance in China, 1895–1914*. Oxford: Clarendon, 1987.

Edwards, Elizabeth. "Photographic 'Types': The Pursuit of a Method." *Visual Anthropology* 3, no. 2–3 (1990): 241–7.

Eliot, Charles. *The East Africa Protectorate*. London: Arnold, 1905.

Eliot, T. S. *The Complete Poems and Plays of T. S. Eliot*. London: Faber, 1969.

Emerson, P. H. *Naturalistic Photography for Students of the Art*. London: Sampson Low, Marston, Searle and Rivington, 1889.

Fabian, Johannes. *Time and the Other: How Anthropology Makes Its Object*. New York: Columbia University Press, 1983.

Fairbank, John King. *Trade and Diplomacy on the China Coast: The Opening of the Treaty Ports 1842–1854*. 2nd ed. Stanford: Stanford University Press, 1969.

Fairbank, John K. and Albert Feuerwerker, eds. *The Cambridge History of China, Volume 13: Republican China 1912–1949*. Cambridge: Cambridge University Press, 1986.

Fang, Karen. "Empire, Coleridge, and Charles Lamb's Consumer Imagination." *SEL: Studies in English Literature, 1500–1900*. 43, no. 4 (2003): 824.

Fergus, Walter and G. F. Radwell. Presented by Francis Galton. "On a Series of Measurements for Statistical Purposes recently made at Marlborough College." *Journal of the Anthropological Institute* 4 (1875): 126–30.

Foster, Shirley. *Victorian Women's Fiction: Marriage, Freedom, and the Individual*. London: Croom Helm, 1985.

Foucault, Michel. *The Archaeology of Knowledge*. London: Tavistock, 1974.

——. *The Order of Things: An Archaeology of the Human Sciences*. New York: Vintage, 1994.

Fox, Colonel A. Lane [Pitt-Rivers]. "Principles of Classification." *Journal of the Anthropological Institute* 4 (1875): 293–308.

Fraiman, Susan. "Jane Austen and Edward Said: Gender, Culture, and Imperialism." *Critical Inquiry* 21, no. 4 (1995): 805–21.

Franck, R. L. *I Married a Vagabond: The Story of the Family of the Writing Vagabond*. New York: Appleton-Century, 1939.

Froger, François. *A Journal of the First French Embassy to China, 1698–1700*. London: Newby, 1859.

Fuller, John. *W. H. Auden: A Commentary*. London: Faber, 1998.

Fussell, Paul. *Abroad*. New York and Oxford: Oxford University Press, 1980.

Gadamer, Hans-Georg. *Truth and Method*. Translated by Joel Weinsheimer and Donald G. Marshall. 2nd rev. ed. New York: Continuum, 1997.

Galton, Francis. "Notes on the Marlborough School Statistics." *Journal of the Anthropological Institute* 4 (1875): 130–5.

Gardella, Robert. *Harvesting Mountains: Fujian and the China Tea Trade, 1737–1935.* Berkeley, CA: University of California Press, 1994.

Gelber, Harry G. *Opium, Soldiers and Evangelicals: Britain's 1840–42 War with China and Its Aftermath.* New York: Palgrave Macmillan, 2004.

Gellhorn, Martha. *The Face of War.* London: Granta, 1988.

Ghose, Indira and Manfred Pfister. "Still Going Strong: The Loneliness of the Long-Distance Traveller in Victorian and Modern Travel Writing." *Journal for the Study of British Cultures* 3, no. 2 (1996): 149–64.

Ginsberg, Elaine K., ed. *Passing and the Fictions of Identity.* Durham, NC: Duke University Press, 1996.

Giradot, Norman J. *The Victorian Translation of China: James Legge's Oriental Pilgrimage.* Berkeley, CA: University of California Press, 2002.

Goldberg, David J. *Discontented America: The United States in the 1920s.* Baltimore: Johns Hopkins University Press, 1999.

Griffin, John Howard. *Black Like Me.* Boston: Houghton Mifflin, 1961.

Haffenden, John. *W. H. Auden: The Critical Heritage.* London: Routledge and Kegan Paul, 1983.

——. *William Empson: Among the Mandarins.* Oxford: Oxford University Press, 2005.

Haggard, Robert F. *The Persistence of Victorian Liberalism: The Politics of Social Reform in Britain, 1870–1900.* Westport, CT: Greenwood, 2001.

Halévy, Elie. *The Growth of Philosophic Radicalism.* Translated by Mary Morris. London: Faber, 1949.

*Handbook to the Ethnographic Collections.* London: British Museum, 1910.

Hanne, Michael. Introduction to *Literature and Travel.* Edited by Michael Hanne. *Rodopi Perspectives on Modern Literature Series* 11. Amsterdam: Rodopi, 1993: 3–7.

Harper, Lila Marz. *Solitary Travelers: Nineteenth-Century Women's Travel Narratives and the Scientific Vocation.* Cranbury, NJ: Associated University Presses, 2001.

"Harry A. Franck: Wandering in China and Japan" http://sdrcdata.lib.uiowa.edu/libsdrc/details.jsp?id=/franck/2. (Accessed March 23, 2005.)

Havely, Cicely Palser. "Bird, Isabella (1831–1904)." In *Literature of Travel and Exploration: An Encyclopedia.* 3 vols. Edited by Jennifer Speake. New York and London: Fitzroy Dearborn, 2003.

Hayford, Charles W. "Chinese and American Characteristics: Arthur H. Smith and His China Book." In *Christianity in China: Early Protestant Missionary Writings.* Edited by Suzanne Wilson Barnett and John King Fairbank. Cambridge, MA: Harvard University Press, 1985.

Hernon, Ian. *The Savage Empire: Forgotten Wars of the 19th Century.* Thrupp, Gloucestershire: Sutton, 2000.

Hevia, James L. *English Lessons: The Pedagogy of Imperialism in Nineteenth-Century China.* Durham, NC: Duke University Press, 2003.

UNIVERSITY OF WINCHESTER
LIBRARY

Ho, Elaine Yee Lin. "Imperial Globalization and Colonial Transactions: 'African Lugard' and the University of Hong Kong." In *Critical Zone 2*. Hong Kong and Nanjing: Hong Kong University Press and Nanjing University Press, 2006.

Holland, Patrick and Graham Huggan. *Tourists with Typewriters: Critical Reflections on Contemporary Travel Writing*. Ann Arbor: University of Michigan Press, 1998.

Hong, Fan. *Footbinding, Feminism and Freedom: The Liberation of Women's Bodies in Modern China*. London: Frank Cass, 1997.

Hulme, Peter. "Introduction", *Studies in Travel Writing* 1 (1997): 1–8.

Hulme, Peter and Tim Youngs. Introduction to *The Cambridge Companion to Travel Writing*. Cambridge: Cambridge University Press, 2002: 1–13.

Hunt, James. "On the Negro's Place in Nature." *Journal of the Anthropological Society of London* 2 (1864): xviii.

Huxley, T. H. "On the Methods and Results of Ethnology." In *Man's Place in Nature and Other Anthropological Essays*. New York: Greenwood, 1968.

Hynes, Samuel. *The Auden Generation: Literature and Politics in England in the 1930s*. London: Faber, 1976.

Im Thurn, E. F. "Anthropological Uses of the Camera," *Journal of the Anthropological Institute* 22 (1893): 191–4.

Isherwood, Christopher. *Christopher and His Kind*. London: Methuen, 1976.

——. *Diaries: Volume One: 1939–1960*. Edited by Katherine Bucknell. London: Methuen, 1996.

——. *Down There on a Visit*. London: Nel Signet Modern Classics, 1974.

Johnson, James Weldon. *Autobiography of an Ex-Coloured Man*. New York: Vintage, 1989.

Johnston, Anna. *Missionary Writing and Empire, 1800–1860*. Cambridge: Cambridge University Press, 2003.

Kant, Immanuel. *The Critique of Judgement*. Translated by James Creed Meredith. Oxford: Clarendon, 1952.

Kaplan, Caren. *Questions of Travel: Postmodern Discourse of Displacement*. Durham and London: Duke University Press, 1996.

Kennedy, W. P. M. *Lord Elgin*. London and Toronto: Oxford University Press, 1926.

Kent, Karlene. "Review of *Roving Through Southern China* by Harry A. Frank." *New York Herald-Tribune*, December 20, 1925.

Kerr, Douglas. "Journey to a War: 'A Test for Men from Europe'." In *W. H. Auden: A Legacy*. Edited by David Garrett Izzo. West Cornwall, CT: Locust Hill, 2002.

Kowalewski, Michael. "Introduction: The Modern Literature of Travel." In *Temperamental Journeys: Essays on the Modern Literature of Travel*. Edited by Michael Kowalewski. Athens, GA: University of Georgia Press, 1992: 1–16.

Lane-Poole, Stanley. *The Life of Sir Harry Parkes, Sometime Her Majesty's Minister to China and Japan vol. 1*. Wilmington: Scholarly Resources, 1973.

Larsen, Nella. *Quicksand: and, Passing*. Edited with an introduction by Deborah E. McDowall. New Brunswick, NJ: Rutgers University Press, 1986.

Leask, Nigel. *British Romantic Writers and the East*. Cambridge: Cambridge University Press, 1992.

———. *Curiosity and the Aesthetics of Travel-Writing, 1770–1840: "From an Antique Land."* Oxford: Oxford University Press, 2004.

Leitner, G. W. "The Siah Posh Kafirs." *Journal of the Anthropological Institute* 3 (1874): 341–60.

Leonard, Jane Kate. "W. H. Medhurst: Rewriting the Missionary Message." In *Christianity in China: Early Protestant Missionary Writings*. Edited by Suzanne Barnett and John Fairbank. Cambridge, MA: Harvard University Press, 1985: 47–59.

Liao, Kuang-sheng. *Anti-foreignism and Modernization in China 1860–1980*. Hong Kong: Chinese University Press and New York: St. Martin's, 1984.

Liao, Tim Futing. "Women in the Taiping Movement in Nineteenth-Century China." In *Women and Social Protest*. Edited by Guida West and Rhoda Lois Blumberg. New York and Oxford: Oxford University Press, 1990.

Liu, Lydia H. Introduction to Arthur H. Smith. *Chinese Characteristics*. Norwalk, CT: EastBridge, 2003.

Lloyd, Valerie. *The Camera and Dr. Barnardo*. Hartford: Barnardo School of Printing, 1974.

Lodwick, Kathleen L. Smith, "Arthur Henderson." In *American National Biography Online* database. (Accessed April 3, 2006.)

Lorimer, Douglas. *Colour, Class and the Victorians: English Attitudes to the Negro in the Mid-Nineteenth Century*. New York: Leicester University Press, 1978.

———. "Theoretical Racism in Late-Victorian Anthropology, 1870–1900." *Victorian Studies* 31, no. 3 (1988): 421–5.

Lovett, Richard. *The History of the London Missionary Society 1795–1895*. London: Frowd, 1899.

Low, Gail Ching-Liang. *White Skins Black Masks: Representation and Colonialism*. London: Routledge, 1996.

Lueck, Beth Lynne. *American Writers and the Picturesque Tour: The Search for National Identity*. New York: Garland, 1997.

Lugard, Frederick. *The Dual Mandate in British Tropical Africa*. London: Frank Cass, 1965.

———. *Political Memoranda*. London: Cass, 1970.

Mackerras, Colin. *Western Images of China*. Hong Kong: Oxford University Press, 1989.

MacKethan, Lucinda H. "The Setons at Home: Organizing a Family Biography." http://www.nhc.rtp.nc.us:8080/biography/mackethan.htm. (Accessed March 21, 2005.)

MacKinnon, Janice R. and Stephen R. MacKinnon. *Agnes Smedley: The Life and Times of an American Radical*. Berkeley: University of California Press, 1988.

Mallon, Ron. "Passing, Traveling, and Reality: Social Constructionism and the Metaphysics of Race." *Noûs* 38, no. 4 (2004): 644–73.

Martineau, Harriet. *A British Friendship and Memoir of the Earl of Elgin and Kincardine*. Windermere: Garnett, 1866.

Marx, Karl. "Parliamentary Debates on the Chinese Hostilities." In *Karl Marx and Frederick Engels, Collected Works*. Vol. 15. London: Lawrence and Wishart, 1986.

Marx, Karl and Frederick Engels. "Manifesto of the Communist Party." In *Collected Works* 6. New York: International Publishers, 1976: 476–519.

McClintock, Anne. *Imperial Leather: Race, Gender, and Sexuality in the Colonial Conquest*. New York: Routledge, 1995.

Mehta, Uday Singh. *Liberalism and Empire: A Study in Nineteenth-Century British Liberal Thought*. Chicago: University of Chicago Press, 1999.

Melancon, Glenn. *Britain's China Policy and the Opium Crisis: Balancing Drugs, Violence and National Honour, 1833–1840*. Aldershot, Hampshire: Ashgate, 2003.

Mendelson, Edward. *Early Auden*. London: Faber, 1981.

Michaels, Walter Benn. "The No-Drop Rule." *Critical Inquiry* 20 (Summer 1994): 758–69.

Middleton, Dorothy. "Some Victorian Lady Travellers." *The Geographical Journal* 139, no. 1 (Feburary 1973): 65–75.

——. *Victorian Lady Travelers*. Chicago: Academy Chicago Publishers, 1982 [1965]. Reprint, 1993.

Mill, John Stuart. *On Liberty*. Edited by David Spitz. New York: Norton, 1975.

Mills, Sara. *Discourses of Difference: An Analysis of Women's Travel Writing and Colonialism*. London and New York: Routledge, 1991.

[Montagu, Mary Wortley.] *The Selected Letters of Lady Mary Wortley Montagu*. Edited by Robert Halsband. Harmondsworth: Penguin, 1970.

Moretti, Franco. *Atlas of the European Novel*. London: Verso, 1999.

Morgan, David. *The Sacred Gaze: Religious Visual Culture in Theory and Practice*. Berkeley, CA: University of California Press, 2005.

Morgan, Susan. *Place Matters: Gendered Geography in Victorian Women's Travel Writings about Southeast Asia*. New Brunswick, NJ: Rutgers University Press, 1996.

Morison, J. L. *British Supremacy and Canadian Self-Government, 1839–1854*. Glasgow: James MacLehose, 1919.

——. *The Eighth Earl of Elgin: A Chapter in Nineteenth-Century Imperial History*. London: Hodder and Stoughton, 1928.

Moynagh, Maureen. "Revolutionary Drag in Auden and Isherwood's *Journey to a War*." *Studies in Travel Literature* 8 (2004): 125–48.

Mungello, David. *Curious Land: Jesuit Accommodation and the Origins of Sinology*. Honolulu: University of Hawaii Press, 1989.

Nash, Roderick. *The Nervous Generation: American Thought, 1970–1930*. Chicago: Rand McNally, 1970.

Nelson, Robert S., ed. *Visuality Before and Beyond the Renaissance: Seeing as Others Saw*. Cambridge: Cambridge University Press, 2000.

Newhall, Beaumont. *History of Photography*. New York: MOMA, 1982.

Newsinger, John. "Elgin in China." *New Left Review* 15 (May–June 2002): 139.

Ng, Maria Noelle. *Three Exotic Views of Southeast Asia: The Travel Narratives of Isabella Bird, Max Dauthendey and Ai Wu, 1850–1930.* White Plains, NY: EastBridge, 2002.

Nichols, Shaun. *Sentimental Rules.* Oxford: Oxford University Press, 2004.

Ogden, C. K. "Jeremy Bentham, 1832–2032." Paper delivered as Bentham Centenary Lecture, University College, London, June 6, 1932. Bristol: Thoemmes, 1993.

Orwell, George. "Looking Back on the Spanish War." In *The Complete Works of George Orwell.* Vol. 13. Edited by Peter Davison. London: Secker and Warburg, 1998: 497–511.

Owen, Wilfred. *The Complete Poems and Fragments.* Edited by Jon Stallworthy. London: Chatto and Windus, Hogarth Press, and Oxford University Press, 1983.

Ozinga, James R. *Altruism.* Westport, CT and London: Praeger, 1999.

Pemble, John. *The Mediterranean Passion: Victorians and Edwardians in the South.* Oxford and New York: Oxford University Press, 1998.

Perham, Margery. *The Life of Frederick Dealtry Lugard Later Lord Lugard of Abinger.* 2 vols. London: Collins, 1960.

Pfister, Lauren F. *Striving for "the Whole Duty of Man": James Legge and the Scottish Protestant Encounter with China.* Frankfurt: Lang, 2004.

Porter, Andrew. *Religion versus Empire? British Protestant Missionaries and Overseas Expansion, 1700–1914.* Manchester: Manchester University Press, 2004.

Prasch, Thomas. *Fixed Positions: Working-Class Subjects and Photographic Hegemony in Victorian Britain.* Ph.D. dissertation, Indiana University, 1994.

——. "Photography and the Image of the London Poor." *Victorian Urban Settings: Essays on the Nineteenth-Century City and Its Contexts.* Edited by Debra N. Mancoff and D. J. Trela. New York: Garland, 1996.

Pratt, Mary Louise. *Imperial Eyes: Travel Writing and Transculturation.* London and New York: Routledge, 1992.

Price, Ruth. *The Lives of Agnes Smedley.* Oxford: Oxford University Press, 2005.

Radler, F. W. "Report on Anthropology at the Meeting of the British Association." *Journal of the Anthropological Institute* 3 (1874): 333.

Read, C. H. Preface to *Notes and Queries on Anthropology.* Edited by C. H. Read and John George Garson. 3rd ed. London: Anthropological Institute, 1899.

Reade, Winwood. *Savage Africa: Being the Narrative of a Tour in Equatorial, Southwestern, and Northwestern Africa.* London: Smith, Elder, 1863.

Reinders, Eric. *Borrowed Gods and Foreign Bodies.* Berkeley: University of California Press, 2004.

"Rev. of *China: the Long-Lived Empire*, by Eliza Ruhamah Scidmore." *The Literary World* 10 (August 1, 1900): 147–8.

"Rev. of *China: the Long-Lived Empire*, by Eliza Ruhamah Scidmore." *The Academy* 59 (July–December 1900): 68–70.

"Rev. of *Wandering in Northern China*, by Harry Franck." *Saturday Review of Literature,* January 16, 1926. N.p.

Richards, Thomas. *The Imperial Archive: Knowledge and the Fantasy of Empire*. London: Verso, 1993.

Ride, Lindsay. *Robert Morrison: The Scholar and the Man*. Hong Kong: Hong Kong University Press, 1957.

Rinaker, Clarissa. "Review of *Wandering in Northern China* by Harry A. Franck." *Nation*, December 26, 1923.

Robinson, Amy. "It Takes One to Know One: Passing and Communities of Common Interest." *Critical Inquiry* 20 (Summer 1994): 715–36.

Robinson, H. P. *Pictorial Effect in Photography*. Piper and Carter, 1869.

Robinson, Jane. Introduction to *Unsuitable for Ladies: An Anthology of Women Travellers*. Oxford: Oxford University Press, 1994.

Russell, Alison. *Crossing Boundaries: Postmodern Travel Literature*. New York: Palgrave, 2000.

Ryan, James R. *Picturing Empire: Photography and the Visualization of the British Empire*. Chicago: University of Chicago Press, 1997.

Said, Edward. *Culture and Imperialism*. London: Chatto and Windus, 1993.

Schmeller, Erik. *Perceptions of Race and Nation in English and American Travel Writers, 1833–1914*. New York: Lang, 2004.

Schriber, Mary Suzanne. *Writing Home: American Women Abroad, 1830–1920*. Charlottesville: University Press of Virginia, 1997.

Seeley, J. R. *The Expansion of England*. Edited by John Gross. Chicago: The University of Chicago Press, 1971.

Semmel, Bernard. *The Rise of Free Trade Imperialism: Classical Political Economy, the Empire of Free Trade and Imperialism, 1750–1850*. Cambridge: Cambridge University Press, 1970.

Shaw, George Bernard. *Heartbreak House*, 1919. Harmondsworth: Penguin, 2000.

Shih, Shu-mei. *The Lure of the Modern: Writing Modernism in Semicolonial China, 1917–1937*. Berkeley: University of California Press, 2001.

Siegel, Kristi. "Introduction: Travel Writing and Travel Theory." In *Issues in Travel Writing: Empire, Spectacle, and Displacement*. Edited by Kristi Siegel. New York: Lang, 2002: 1–9.

Slung, Michele. *Living with Cannibals and Other Women's Adventures*. Washington, DC: National Geographic, 2000.

Smedley, Agnes. *Daughter of Earth*, 1929. New York: Feminist Press, 1973.

Snodgrass, Judith. *Orientalism, Occidentalism, and the Columbian Exposition: Presenting Japanese Buddhism to the West*. Chapel Hill: University of North Carolina Press, 2003.

Sontag, Susan. "Homage to Halliburton." In *Where the Stress Falls: Essays*. New York: Farrar, Straus and Giroux, 2001.

Spence, Jonathan D. *The Memory Palace of Matteo Ricci*. New York: Penguin, 1985.

———. *The Search for Modern China*. 2nd ed. New York: Norton, 1999.

Steele, E. D. *Palmerston and Liberalism: 1855–1865*. Cambridge: Cambridge University Press, 1991.

Stefoff, Rebecca. *Women of the World: Women Travelers and Explorers*. New York: Oxford University Press, 1992.

Stocking, George. *Victorian Anthropology*. New York: Free Press, 1987.

Stubbs, Patricia. *Women and Fiction: Feminism and the Novel, 1880–1920*. London: Methuen, 1981.

Suleri, Sara. *The Rhetoric of English India*. Chicago: The University of Chicago Press, 1992.

Swingler, Randall. "Daily Worker, March 29, 1939." In *W. H. Auden: The Critical Heritage*. Edited by John Haffenden. New York and London: Routledge and Kegan Paul, 1983.

Talib, Ismail. "After the (Unwritten) 'Postcolonial' in Southeast Asia: What Happens Next?" In *The Silent Word: Textual Meaning and the Unwritten*. Edited by Robert Young, et al. Singapore: Singapore University Press, 1998.

Tambling, Jeremy. "Opium, Wholesale, Resale, and for Export: On Dickens and China, Part I." *Dickens Quarterly* 21, no. 1 (2004): 28–43.

Taylor, Mark. *Disfiguring: Art, Architecture, Religion*. Chicago: University of Chicago Press, 1992.

Teng, Ssu-Yu and John K. Fairbank. *China's Response to the West: A Documentary Survey 1839–1923*. New York: Atheneum, 1970.

Thomson, John. "Geographical Photography." *Scottish Geographical Magazine* 23, no. 1 (1907): 14.

Thurin, Susan Schoenbauer, ed. *The Far East, Nineteenth-Century Travels, Explorations and Empires: Writing from the Era of Imperial Consolidation 1835–1910*. Vol. 4. London: Pickering and Chatto, 2003.

——. *Victorian Travelers and the Opening of China, 1842–1907*. Athens: Ohio University Press, 1999.

Tinling, Marion. *Women into the Unknown: A Sourcebook on Women Explorers and Travelers*. New York: Greenwood, 1989.

Tong, Q. S. "The Aesthetic of Imperial Ruins: The Elgins and John Bowring." *boundary 2: an international journal of literature and culture* 33, no. 1 (Spring 2006): 124–50.

Trollope, Anthony. *The Way We Live Now*. New York: Modern Library, 2000.

Tylor, E. B. "Dammann's Race-Photographs." *Nature* 15 (January 6, 1876): 185–6.

Van Keuren, David K. "Museums and Ideology: Augustus Pitt-Rivers, Anthropological Museums and Social Change in Victorian Britain." *Victorian Studies* 28, no. 1 (1984): 171–89.

Venn, Couze. *Occidentalism: Modernity and Subjectivity*. London: Sage, 2000.

Verne, Jules. "The Troubles of a Chinaman." In *The Leisure Hour*. N.p., 1880: 55–8.

Vicinus, Martha. "Introduction: The Perfect Victorian Lady." In *Suffer and Be Still: Women in the Victorian Age*. Edited by Martha Vicinus. Bloomington: Indiana University Press, 1972.

Vohra, Ranbir. *China's Path to Modernization: A Historical Review from 1800 to the Present*. Upper Saddle River, NJ: Prentice Hall, 2000.

Von Martels, Zweder. "Introduction: The Eye and the Mind's Eye." In *Travel Fact and Travel Fiction: Studies on Fiction, Literary Tradition, Scholarly Discovery and Observation in Travel Writing*. Edited by Zweder Von Martels. Leiden: Brill, 1994: xi–xviii.

Wagner, Tamara S. *Longing: Narratives of Nostalgia in the British Novel, 1740–1890*. Lewisburg: Bucknell University Press, 2004.

——. *Occidentalism in Novels of Malaysia and Singapore, 1819–2004: Colonial and Postcolonial Financial Straits*. Lewiston: Mellen, 2005.

Wald, Gayle. *Crossing the Line: Racial Passing in Twentieth-Century U. S. Literature and Culture*. Durham, NC: Duke University Press, 2000.

Wallace, Alfred Russel. "On the Varieties of Men in the Malay Archipelago." *Transactions of the Ethnological Society of London* 3 (1865): 196–215.

——. *Studies in Science and Society*. 2 vols. London: Macmillan, 1900.

——. *The Malay Archipelago: The Land of the Orang-Utan, and the Bird of Paradise: A Narrative of Travel, with Studies of Man and Nature*. New York: Harper, 1869.

Wallace, J. R. "Carping Through Southern China." Review of *Roving Through Southern China* by Harry A. Franck. *The Independent* (Boston), October 31, 1925.

Walls, Andrew. *The Cross-Cultural Process in Christian History: Studies in the Transmission and Appropriation of Faith*. Maryknoll, NY: Orbis Books; Edinburgh: Clark, 2002.

——. *The Missionary Movement in Christian History: Studies in the Transmission of Faith*. Maryknoll, NY: Orbis Books; Edinburgh: Clark, 1996.

Walrond, Theodore. "Memoir of James, Eighth Earl of Elgin." In *Letters and Journals of James, Eighth Earl of Elgin*. Edited by Theodore Walrond. London: Murray, 1872.

Wang, Gungwu. *Anglo-Chinese Encounters Since 1800: War, Trade, Science and Governance*. Cambridge: Cambridge University Press, 2003.

Waugh, Evelyn. "Evelyn Waugh on a Pantomime Appearance, Mr. Isherwood and Friend. *Spectator*, March 24, 1939." In *W. H. Auden: The Critical Heritage*. Edited by John Haffenden. London: Routledge and Kegan Paul, 1983.

——. Preface to *When the Going was Good*. Boston: Little, Brown and Company, 1947.

Webb, Sidney. *Soviet Communism: A New Civilization*. London: Gollancz, 1937.

White, Stephen. *John Thomson: A Window to the Orient*. London: Thames and Hudson, 1985.

Wilgus, Mary H. *Sir Claude MacDonald, the Open Door, and British Informal Empire in China, 1895–1900*. New York: Garland, 1987.

Wilkins, W. H., ed. *The Jew, the Gypsy, and El Islam*. London: Hutchinson, 1898.

Windschuttle, Keith. "Liberalism and Imperialism." In *The Betrayal of Liberalism: How the Disciples of Freedom and Equality Helped Foster the Illiberal Politics of Coercion and Control*. Edited by H. Kramer and R. Kimball. Chicago: Dee, 1999.

Wong, J. Y. *Deadly Dreams: Opium, Imperialism and the Arrow War (1856–1860) in China*. Cambridge: Cambridge University Press, 1998.

Woodhouse, Eiko. *The Chinese Hsinhai Revolution: G. E. Morrison and Anglo-Japanese Relations, 1897–1920*. London: Routledge, 2004.

Xu, Wenying. "The Opium Trade and *Little Dorrit*: A Case of Reading Silences." *Victorian Literature and Culture* 25, no. 1 (1997): 53–6.

Young, L. K. *British Policy in China, 1895–1902*. Oxford: Clarendon Press, 1970.

Youngs, Tim. "Auden's Travel Writings." In *The Cambridge Companion to W. H. Auden*. Edited by Stan Smith. Cambridge: Cambridge University Press, 2004.

Zhang, Longxi. "The Myth of the Other: China in the Eyes of the West." *Critical Enquiry* 15 (Autumn 1988): 108–31.

Ziff, Larzer. *Return Passage: Great American Travel Writing, 1780–1920*. New Haven: Yale University Press, 2001.

# Index

UNIVERSITY OF WINCHESTER
LIBRARY